MANAGERS IN THE CONGLOMERATE ERA

MANAGERS IN THE CONGLOMERATE ERA

STANLEY C. VANCE

H. T. Miner Professor of Business Administration

Graduate School of Management and Business

University of Oregon, Eugene

WILEY-INTERSCIENCE

a Division of John Wiley & Sons, Inc.

New York · London · Sydney · Toronto

10 9 8 7 6 5 4 3 2 1
Library of Congress Catalogue Card Number: 78-137112

ISBN 0-471-90273-X

Printed in the United States of America

With sincere appreciation for the financial assistance given me over a period of more than ten years by the H. T. Miner family through their generous gift of the H. T. Miner endowed chair at the University of Oregon, I wish to dedicate this book to the memory of Mrs. Virgie Miner who died November 13, 1970. This support of research and the advancement of knowledge is gratefully appreciated.

PREFACE

To merge or not to merge is the big question plaguing at least half of America's corporations. The magnitude of this question is obvious in the fact that this year between 6000 and 6500 American firms will actually yield to merger. In the process they will relinquish their sovereignty and autonomy and many will even lose their identities. In addition to the accomplished mergers, three or four times as many attempts at merging are unsuccessful. Some of these would-be combinations are prevented by legal means; some are resisted and fought off by reluctant managements; some merger proposals are never intended seriously, and a large number turn sour when the participants get to know each other better.

In addition to the 20,000 or more corporations that this year will be directly affected by merger overtures, at least another 40,000 to 50,000 are unobtrusively being watched with ultimate merger in mind. Peter C. R. Huang "figures that he has considered about 1000 companies—and acquired ten—since joining City Investing in 1966. John Rollins, Jr., and Charles Dey together screened 500 companies for Rollins Leasing last year. After spending anywhere from 'five minutes to five weeks' considering each of them about thirty-five were selected as possibilities." [1]

In many cases the merger quarry is not even aware that it is being watched and studied for acquisition purposes. Over a 10-year span it seems safe to assume that at least one-half and perhaps closer to two-thirds of all incorporated American business will be a subject in or the object of acquisition. With such universal coverage it is logical to expect strong feelings, pro and con, regarding the value of merger.

The pluses and minuses of merger and particularly of conglomeration are of such high public interest that scarcely an issue of any business-oriented publication appears without substantial conglomerate commentary. Much of the debate suffers from the relative newness of this phenomenon, with consequent conjecture, speculation, and emotional outburst. Then, too, there are so many ramifications, touching nearly all sectors of American life, such as legal, political, social, financial, international, and managerial, that a simplistic analysis is impossible.

[1] *Dun's Review*, 27 (December, 1968).

The following presentation attempts to provide a slightly clearer focus on merger-conglomeration by concentrating largely on a single aspect—the impact of managers on mergers and, in turn, the impact of mergers on tomorrow's managers. It seems reasonable to assume that since all mergers are man-made certain types of men, the merger-initiators, and other types of men, the merger-implementors, would have an important influence on the incidence and character of mergers. But merging does not end with acquisition. The integrative process, over the long run, demands other kinds of talent. In today's complex economy the entrepreneurial drive that initiates and consummates mergers is the spark that kindles or rekindles. Yet a spark is not enough; enterprise needs a flame that is intense and consummates in its burning. In prosaic terms the entrepreneur responsible for merger needs managers who will stoke and not bank this corporate combustion.

What kind of managers will tomorrow's large-scale, conglomerated, multiactivity, and multinational firms need to perform this function? Even more significant, in the hierarchical progression what kinds of executives and corporate directors will the new megocorporations seek? Will the meshing of many heterogeneous firms result in the evolution of new models of organization structure? Perhaps the rather symmetrical and hierarchical structure, held together with strong authoritarian controls typifying the twentieth century corporation, must give way to a new more advanced organizational form. If so, will the new form be equivalent to a confederation rather than a corporation? Would it then be more appropriate to view the new large-scale, superdiversified business entity as a confederation of corporate states rather than just a conglomerate, a corporation, or even a megocorporation?

Confederation, versus conventional incorporation, will definitely create demands for directors, executives, managers, and even rank-and-file workers with specific attributes. In particular, the dynamic and competitive spirit must be maintained, yet at the same time the conglomerated confederates must work in consort with an increased number of colleagues from unrelated and even unfamiliar lines of enterprise. Then, too, the evolutionary process will be affected by current constraints, managerial, legal, and many others. Inevitably new parameters will be set within which the megocorporation, or the confederation of corporate states, will be permitted to function. Out of all this great change hopefully we will develop a higher order of managers: the macromanagers.

The purpose of this study is to look at the intriguing phenomenon of merger-conglomeration and in the context of pertinent case illustrations (a) study the role of today's professional manager in merger-conglomeration and (b) speculate on the role of tomorrow's macromanager in the megacorporation.

STANLEY C. VANCE

Eugene, Oregon
January 1971

CONTENTS

MANAGERS IN THE
CONGLOMERATE ERA

1

INTRODUCTION

Everybody loves a winner. Nothing succeeds like success. These and similar adages describe fittingly the merger-conglomerate story during the 1960's. Scores of midtwentieth century Horatio Algers were prominent on the success scene proving that the route to the top was still open to those possessing the proper attributes. James Joseph Ling, at the age of 14 a dropout from school in Hugo, Oklahoma, is a prime example. His $3000 investment in 1946 in an electrician's shop expanded through merger-conglomeration into a $3 billion dollar asset empire in slightly over a 20 year period.

There are numerous equally fascinating success stories. In 1964 Cortes Wesley Randell, then only 28 years of age, started his National Student Marketing Corporation which was first limited to publishing a summer employment guide for students. The instantaneous success of this venture led to National Student Marketing (N.S.M.) going public in 1968 at $6 a share. Within two years of hectic stock swapping and cash deals the new conglomerate acquired 27 companies and annual sales hit $68 million. N.S.M. stock sold at $72 per share in late December 1969 and was acquired in large blocs by prestigious firms such as "Morgan Guaranty, Continental Illinois National Bank, and the endowment funds of Harvard and Cornell." [1]

Another classic climb-to-the-top is H. Ross Perot's sudden catapulting into the billionaire's club. At 31 he founded his Electronic Data Systems Corporation on a $1000 investment. He retained 9,400,000 shares in Electronic Data Systems (EDS) and when it climbed to a 1970 high of 161, H. Ross Perot was a paper billionaire worth more than $1,-500,000,000. At one point EDS stock sold at the fantastic ratio of 342

---

[1] *Time*, 94 (April 13, 1970).

times current earnings, and even in 1970 it was selling at an extraordinary 215 times that year's expected earnings. The soundest of blue chip
stocks were then available at P/E ratios between 10 and 12.

Bernard Cornfeld, a former social worker turned securities salesman,
incorporated his Investors Overseas Services in 1960. This and related
mutual funds subsequently set up developed within the decade into a
$2.3 billion-asset enterprise catering to foreign investors abroad. None of
the issues were registered with our Securities and Exchange Commission
and none could be sold in the United States or to Americans overseas.
Bernard Cornfeld was referred to as "the Midas of mutual funds" perhaps with double meaning, since he was invariably in the company of
beautiful women and seemed to live the life of an Eastern potentate.

Millionaire Kirk Kerkorian, builder of the 1519-bedroom International
Hotel in Las Vegas and architect of International Leisure Corporation,
saw his $4-per-share investment in 5.4 million shares of International
Leisure stock soar to $64 per share. Together with his other holdings,
principally in Western Air Lines and MGM, Kerkorian's worth was estimated at more than two-thirds of a billion dollars.

During this era of seemingly unlimited quick-money horizons, millions
of investors flocked after the conglomerating conquerors. For the most
part these conglomerators were brash young men, many in their 20's or
early 30's. Few had any significant industrial or business experience.
These were new people with new ideas, using new weapons and building new empires. Even in their personal lives, they displayed a flamboy-
ance that shocked their elders but thrilled their followers. As hundreds
of establishment managements were ousted it seemed for a period that,
like Alexander the Great's dilemma in victory, there would soon be no
new corporate worlds to conquer.

However, then came the day of reckoning, as the shepherd David
sings in an Old Testament psalm, "HE put down the mighty from their
seats, and He exalted those of low degree." Unfortunately, "those of low
degree" once they are exalted too become the mighty, vulnerable to
overthrow. The scene and time for the fulfillment of shepherd David's
admonition were set by the 1969–1970 bear market.

Jim Ling saw his parent firm Ling-Temco-Vought (LTV) grow in 10
years from a sales volume of $150 million to sales in excess of $4 billion.
Its stock rose to $136 per share and then came the decline. In less than a
half year, LTV's stock slipped to a low of 8, representing over a half-bil-
lion dollar devaluation. In the exalting-of-the-humble phase, Ling's prospects were so great that he was able to borrow over $1500 million in
order to finance his conglomerate blitzkrieging. This leverage tactic, or
trading-on-the-equity, is a wonderful device during boom times, but as

Ling came to realize, paying more than $1,000,000 per week in interest charges for even a conglomerate giant such as LTV could be a guarantee of ultimate insolvency. Thus, Ling turned to demerging. In mid-1970 he proposed a massive turnabout, seeking to sell three of his major acquisitions, Braniff Airways, Okonite Company, and Wilson Sporting Goods Company, for a total of $633 million. He had previously disposed of a number of other acquisitions including Allied Radio Corporation and National Car Rental System.

In mid-May 1970 James J. Ling was forced to step down as chairman and chief executive of LTV under pressure from his creditors. Although Ling was named president, the head of First National Bank in Dallas, Robert H. Stewart, became chairman sharing top management responsibilities with Ling. The creditors among whom Bank of America had the biggest commitments also asserted their prerogatives in the LTV board of directors which was pared from 20 to 14 members.

Cortes Wesley Randell's precipitous rise to power and his almost equally precipitous decline have significant managerial connotations which are explored in subsequent chapters. Randell, throughout National Student Marketing's rapid growth, kept a very tight grip on his organization. Even after his board of directors gave him a mandate to delegate more authority to other officers and after a subsequent study by Peat, Marwick recommended reorganization with decentralization, Randell continued to run the show. His downfall came after he made public pronouncements that NSM would have 1970 sales of $150 million and earnings of $2 per share. This boast was made despite vehement objections from his staff that these figures included the hoped-for but unsubstantiated performance of several acquisitions that NSM had not even begun to make.

Following this bravado, NSM's stock predictably spurted until the financial community realized the implications. Even then Randell continued his confident sales pitch. "He acted like Cort Randell, the Messiah," stated one of his financial friends, quoting Randell, "Who do they look up to? Who do they respect? . . . As long as I do a good job, I'll continue. If I don't do a good job, I don't deserve to be president." [2]

A little more than a week after making this prophetic statement, Randell was eased out of his job. The slump in NSM's market price from a high of $72 per share to a post-split low of 2⅝, certainly contributed to his fall. Perhaps less recognizable but even more important was this conglomerator's inability to build an organization that could adapt to

[2] *Fortune,* "How Cortes Randell Drained the Fountain of Youth," by Rush Loving, Jr., 168 (April, 1970).

success. Commenting on his Wall Street roller coaster ride, Randell stated, "You can't take anything for granted, even success." [3]

H. Ross Perot the third conglomerate Horatio Alger, saw himself in a two-day period demoted from billionaire to merely multimillionaire. In the unbelievable two-day debacle (April 21–23, 1970), Electronic Data System's stock slumped from $150 to $90 bid on the over-the-counter market. H. Ross Perot who still owns 81% of EDS stock thus lost nearly $550 million on paper. In the following month Electronic Data stock slumped to 50 bid, and Ross Perot's investment shriveled by another $400 million.

Bernard Cornfeld's rags-to-riches-to-blue-jeans saga is somewhat similar. By May 1970 his I.O.S. Ltd. stock fell from a peak of $19 to a low of $5. Pressures, presumably from large lenders, soon led to Cornfeld's exile from the empire he had pasted together. His all-vital sales force which was essential to his mutual fund hard sell was supposed to rise to 20,000 but was cut to 14,000. Most significantly, the high-living, high-flying I.O.S. executives who emulated their flamboyant leader were "ordered to go tourist instead of first class, or phone or write if these will do." [4]

Kirk Kerkorian likewise saw his stockholdings shrivel over 80% from about $650 million to about $120 million and he was forced to sell a controlling interest in his International and Flamingo hotels to Hilton Hotels Inc. Some of this can be attributed to a run of bad luck in gambling stocks, which together with a generally depressed market and rumors of underworld links and Government investigations have tarnished the investment luster of the gambling industry.[5]

The five illustrations of conglomerate architects who had sudden success followed by almost equally sudden defeat point to a fundamental flaw in human nature. Heroes are loved only as long as they remain heroes but in their ignominy they are pariahs. Cortes Randell after his ouster retreated to his $600,000 Virginia castle, complete with mock dungeon. "In the investment world, of course, his name is all but unmentionable." [6] Not only were the investors in these five specified instances hurt financially and immensely angered, but millions more were bilked, so they felt, in the slump of several hundred other once fast-paced conglomerates.

The relative degree of financially burnt fingers is shown in Figure 1. Here we have a visual comparison between the Dow Jones' 30 blue chip industrial stocks' composite performance and that of 32 representative

[3] *Time*, 94 (April 13, 1970).
[4] *The Wall Street Journal*, 28 (April 30, 1970).
[5] *Time*, "A Run of Bad Luck in Gambling Stocks," 81 (April 20, 1970).
[6] *Fortune, op. cit.*, p. 169.

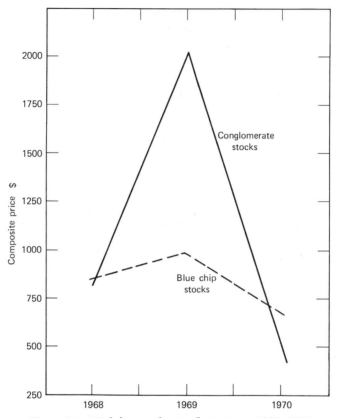

Figure 1-1   High-low stock price fluctuations, 1968–1970.

conglomerates. These are listed in Table 1-1. In vivid contrast to the tried-and-true, staid blue chip Dow Jones (DJ) industrial averages we have here what, for want of a better term, can be termed a conglomerate Go-Go Gyration Gauge (GGGG). Both the DJ averages and the GGGG when measured by their 1967 lows had approximately the same levels: 810 for DJ and 820 for GGGG. In 1968 the Dow Jones industrial averages climbed to a high of nearly 1000, a gain of about 25%. But in vivid contrast the GGGG skyrocketed to more than 2000, an almost vertical takeoff with a gain of 150%. Subsequently, in about the same time span, while the Dow Jones averages tumbled to below the 630 level, or a loss of 37%, the conglomerate Go-Go Gyration Gauge stocks plummeted from their 2000-plus high to the 387 level, or a drop of nearly 81%.

The inference should be obvious. Virtually the entire investing com-

munity welcomed the conquering conglomerate heroes. They were idol-
ized and canonized and it seemed for a while that we were to have a
new management mythology replete with new dieties.

If a conclusion can be drawn from Figure 1, it would seem that few if

Table 1-1   Go-Go Gyration Gauge

	1967 Low	1968 High	1969–1970 Low	Percent Drop 1968–1970
AMK Corp.	13	105	12	87
ATO	26	74	6	90
AVCO	15	65	9	86
AVNET, Inc.	12	51	6	88
Bangor Punta	24	61	6	89
City Investing	22	69	11	82
Colt Industries	19	66	13	81
Dresser Industries	28	43	22	49
General Host	16	39	7	82
Gulf and Western	30	66	10	83
Indian Head	19	46	14	70
International Tel & Tel	36	60	31	49
Kidde (Walter)	46	87	15	83
Kinney National	26	65	21	68
LEASCO Data	12	54	7	87
LTV	49	132	8	93
Litton	80	105	16	85
Loew's	11	63	16	75
Maremont	18	29	7	76
National General	9	46	9	80
National Industries	3	25	4	84
Ogden	16	52	7	87
Penn Central	52	72	6	92
Rapid American	9	46	7	85
Republic Corp.	5	76	8	90
Studebaker Worth	35	61	35	43
Teledyne, Inc.	40	72	13	82
Textron, Inc.	25	45	15	67
Transamerica	29	58	12	80
U. S. Smelting	45	99	21	79
White Consolidated	36	36	8	78
Whittaker Corp.	14	47	5	90
	820	2015	387	81

any of the current conglomerators will ever be re-elevated into the ranks of the management mythology. Rather the prospects are that most of these neoentrepreneurs will qualify better for a management martyrology. Regardless of personal sentiments, the conglomerate phenomenon and particularly the people sparking these exciting business ventures should be looked at in a more dispassionate fashion.

The following pages are such an attempt. If there is a single conclusion to be drawn it is that the conglomerators, despite their frailties and fiascos, have made some positive and lasting contributions to our enterprise system, giving it a new vigor, a new structure, and a new outlook.

2

MERGER—BACKGROUND

There seems to be ample precedent for merger in all spheres of human activity. In the political sphere, for instance, the history of nations, from the clan to the confederation of empires, is a rather monotonous sequence of attempts by aggressors to absorb one's neighbors. Much of this national expansionism was, and still is, achieved through brute force. World history over the past millennium records a minimum of a hundred major wars, together with thousands of minor fracases, ranging from forays into neighboring fiefdoms to our own 300 year undeclared war against the American aborigines. What prompts this violence among nations? Although there are as many conjectures as there are wars, the single most probable cause is the desire to grow and to dominate. In a sense this is the pressure of national territorial imperative.

Similarly, in the business sphere, there seems to be an insatiable urge to grow and to become superior. History corroborates this inference. In the last century we have witnessed the transformation in the dominant form of enterprise from the individual, through the partnership, into the corporation. In the United States it was the post-Civil War period, from 1865 through 1890, with its relative prosperity which gestated the first wave of meaningful mergers. Prosperity was the *sine qua non,* the all-vital prerequisite. During this period savings banks' assets alone rose from $243 million to about $2 billion, and new firms increased twice as fast as did the nation's population. Between 1880 and 1890 the number of business firms increased from 750,000 to 1,100,000. In such an environment it was natural to expect growth by acquisition.

This phenomenon can be best comprehended if the analysis is focused on a single industry; for instance, let us consider the steel industry. For more than two centuries, from the building of its first iron-making facility at Saugus, Massachusetts in 1644, the iron and steel industry was

8

characterized by small-scale, independent operations. However, in the post-Civil War era, considerable impetus was toward consolidation and larger-scale operations. In the Chicago area Judge Elbert H. Gary used his legal expertise to put little steel companies together into larger scale firms. Gary, together with John W. "Bet-a-Million" Gates, created the American Steel and Wire Company—the "wire trust." [1] Other major combinations in the steel industry which in themselves were comparable trusts soon followed, including National Tube Company, American Tin Plate Company, American Bridge Company, and Federal Steel Company.

In 1901, under the guidance of J. P. Morgan, these trusts were further trustified through their juncture into U. S. Steel Corporation. In addition to Morgan there were about 300 participants in the syndicate which produced the greatest merger of its kind. With capitalization of nearly $1.5 billion, it far surpassed the other trusts of its day, such as American Smelting and Refining Company, American Sugar Refining Company, American Woolen Company, American Hide and Leather Company, American Tobacco Company, and a dozen other amalgamations, consolidations, and mergers.

In the steel industry J. P. Morgan succeeded in convincing five frequently antagonistic groups (Morgan-Moore-Carnegie-Rockefeller-Gates) to pool their resources and, as a result, 10 companies, with a valuation of approximately $940 million, formed the new supertrust, United States Steel. The inducement was a 40% markup in the value of the new securities given the amalgamators, and as a consequence the new United States Steel Corporation began its new career with a capitalization of approximately $1320 million consisting of the following:

$303 million collateral trust 5's 1951
$510 million preferred 7% stock
$509 million common stock

It must be stressed that just before the legal existence of the new U. S. Steel "trust," these same 10 firms which joined to form U. S. Steel had stock and long-term borrowings totaling only about $940 million. From this example it can be readily seen that the same inducement—the enhancement of one's investment through inflation by board-room fiat—which prompts firms to merge today was equally effective at the turn of the century. Subsequent commentators called this technique, in U. S. Steel's case, "watered stock." In today's comparable situations financial analysts refer to the same generous practice of inflating the merger partners' stock values as leverage.

[1] *Fortune*, "History of American Business," 118 (January 1962).

At its formation this giant among huge trusts, U. S. Steel, accounted for nearly two-thirds of the iron and steel industry's output. It was viewed with extreme perturbation, ". . . the impact on public opinion was swift and almost physically tangible. Expressing the prevalent consensus of horror, President Arthur Twining Hadley of Yale remarked that if public sentiment would not regulate such monster businesses, there would be an 'emperor' in Washington within twenty-five years." [2] The architect of this supertrust, John Pierpont Morgan, was nicknamed Jupiter and also was referred to as Pierpontifex Maximus.

Because of a variety of constraints, legal pronouncements, technological advancements, population growth, and market expansion, these fears of trust domination have not materialized. In fact, most of yesterday's giants have shrunk in relative size and some have even withered away and been interred; for example, American Woolen Company, originally put together at the turn of the century as an amalgamation of 56 mills, was then referred to as the $65 million wool trust. By 1953 its equipment had dwindled from 11,000 looms to 1600 looms and the firm succumbed to a merger maneuver by Textron. Ten years later the once-powerful wool trust, American Woolen Company, ceased to exist even as a Textron subsidiary.

Similarly, almost from its inception U. S. Steel began to lose its relative dominance. Its capital structure in 1901 included slightly more than $1 billion in common and preferred stock plus $300 million in long term debt. Twenty years later the capital stock had increased, largely resulting from the World War I boom era, to about $1.5 billion. By 1945, however, book value of both categories of stock was still at the $1.5 billion level, indicating almost a half century of very slow growth.

At present U. S. Steel has an owners' equity of approximately $3.4 billion. In other words, the increase has been from $1.0 billion to $3.4 billion or about 240%. In the same interval inflationary forces have so affected dollar values that a dollar today is worth only $0.206 in terms of 1901 purchasing power. In other words, if U. S. Steel's initial investment were adjusted to reflect current prices, then the $1 billion equity (in 1902) would be equal to approximately 4.8 billion in current dollars. Since owners' equity is presently $3.4 billion, it would thus appear that the giant "steel trust" has scarcely made any progress; in fact, it has retrogressed.

At its inception U. S. Steel had no peers; today eight American manufacturing corporations are bigger in terms of invested capital. Standard Oil Company (New Jersey) and General Motors each has three times

[2] *Ibid.*, p. 107.

that of U. S. Steel's equity. On the basis of net assets 27 American corporations, including banks and insurance companies, are bigger than U. S. Steel. In terms of volume of output U. S. Steel had a commanding two-thirds of the steel industry's sales in 1901; today it has slightly more than one-fifth of total industry sales. In addition to the astounding growth of big steel's domestic competitors such as Bethlehem, Republic, National, Inland, and Armco, the rapid expansion of foreign steel imports now accounts for nearly 16% of domestic sales.

The saga of trust-busting through growth of competitors can be extended to most industries. Standard Oil could not inhibit the growth of firms such as Texaco, Gulf, Shell, Continental, or Phillips. Aluminum Company of America just a quarter of a century ago had a virtual monopoly in its field but today produces only about one-third of that industry's output. American Can Company, *the* dominant force in the container field for many years, has had to make room for Continental Can, National Can, and numerous package users who make their own containers not only out of steel but also from aluminum, glass, paper, and plastic. The Ford Motor Company, in the mid-1920's, appeared to be on the verge of transforming the automobile industry into a one-company domain, but by the 1940's was itself engaged in a serious fight for survival.

It can be estimated conservatively that of the 1000 largest industrial corporations which existed at the turn of the century there are probably less than 250 in recognizable form today. Of the 500 largest corporations on *Fortune*'s 1956 listing only 291 remain on the comparable 1970 listing. This represents an annual attrition of 3% from the ranks of our very largest industrial corporations. These are but a few obvious examples showing that corporate growth, internal or by merger, cannot be guaranteed. Nevertheless the corporate "territorial imperative" which might be paraphrased as the corporate "market imperative" or the corporate "profit imperative" seems to exert a compulsive force.

Before the Civil War and for perhaps a decade or so after company growth was almost entirely from within. Even in the growing number of instances where a firm expanded its horizons by adding new product lines, the new venture was usually generated internally. However, in the quarter century of post-Civil War prosperity (despite temporary setbacks such as the Panic of 1873), the urgency to grow at better than the normal "internal" rate resulted in the first real merger movement and the era of trusts. Invariably, these mergers were single-industry-concentrated and could readily be identified as steel-, tobacco-, sugar-, cement-, or wool-oriented; for example, between 1908–1910, the then newly created (by merger) General Motors Corporation acquired about

25 companies. These merged firms included 11 automobile companies and the remainder were auto parts and accessories suppliers. The propensity to concentrate a very large percentage of an industry into a single corporation inevitably led to much needed legal constraints.

Implementation of the Sherman Antitrust Act and the Clayton Antitrust Act slowed this monopolistic, or at least oligopolistic, growth momentum. This led to the second merger phase in which, although still expanding vertically and horizontally, stress was also put on moving into new product lines. Generally, these added products had some manufacturing or marketing relationship to the firm's main product line; for example, U. S. Steel acquired Universal Portland Cement in 1906, presumably because both products have a relationship in certain sectors of the construction industry. Tremendous progress in technology facilitated this urge to merge. In some instances, as new products gained in acceptance, the firm's original product line was subordinated or even abandoned. Armstrong Cork is now only an incidental user of cork. Du Pont's black powder output is today a minimal contributor to that firm's sales. National Distillers' liquor sales are outpaced by sales of its other products. Only about 30% of Corn Products' sales are of corn-based items.

In some instances, this technological impetus resulted in growth from within. In many other instances the growth was accomplished by acquiring a dynamic smaller firm which had already demonstrated its competency in making and selling the new products. Consequently, this second phase in the merger movement seems to have been prompted by innovation or technological necessity. Development of new products, expansion of previously limited product lines, by-product utilization, and fuller use of plant capacity to make complementary products characterize this second merger phase. It can properly be called diversification although the moves invariably were into related products or into related technologies.

By contrast the first merger surge was prompted by efficiencies resulting from large-scale manufacturing of a relatively limited product line. Profit maximization was consequently associated with monopolistic control. Although phase two of the merger movement cannot be pegged precisely on a chronological basis, it did have considerable impact in the post World War I period.

Interestingly enough, the third and current merger phase is likewise associated with an era of strife and upheaval. The first symptoms of the incipient trend became noticeable about six or seven years after the end of World War II and almost concurrently with the end of the Korean War. This was the takeoff on an unprecedented business boom. Although a few daring enterprisers, such as Royal Little and Textron, ventured into the new conglomerate or nonrelated type of diversification in the early 1950's, the manifestation became paroxysmal only in the mid-1960's. There seems to be minimal need to describe the character of this third-phase merger movement since it is so much in the headlines. Even as thousands of American firms, small and large alike, exhibit a lemming-like compulsion (perhaps into a turbulent economic sea), countervailing forces seem to be slowly generating new rules for the business game.

THE CENTRIPETAL CRUSH

The great fear is that if the current merging trend continues all our economic power within 10 to 20 years will be concentrated in a relatively few massive corporations. Nicholas Salgo, the entrepreneur who junctured a very tiny Hooterville Hollow railroad (Bangor and Maine) and a sugar firm that had lost its financial sweetness (Punta Allegre) and in sorcerer fashion transformed these "nothings" into a multimillion "something" (Bangor Punta), has publicly stated that within 10 years there will be only 200 corporations in the United States, all conglomerates. Although this strong statement might be attacked both factually and semantically, there is an element of reality in the contention. One might argue negatively that even if we have 5000 or more mergers annually, new corporations are being formed at an annual rate of about 240,000. Failures, at about 800 per month, decrease the net addition of corporations, before merger, by about 10,000. Thus, even with 10,000 failures and 5000 mergers and perhaps another 50,000 gentle and unnoticed corporate evaporations, our corporate count increases by about 175,000 each year. These statistics refute the corporate "numbers" concentration argument.

Another set of data sheds a different cast. In 1955 only 70 American corporations in all phases of business activity had assets, individually, of more than $1 billion. Twenty-two of them were in manufacturing industry. The last *Fortune* count showed that in 1969 there were 229 such billion-dollar-or-more-asset corporations (92 in manufacturing industry). Projecting growth trend expectations up to 1979, just 10 years from now, show about 380 of these corporate mammoths. In 1955 the $70 billion companies had a combined asset valuation of $210 billion, that is, about one-third the assets of all American business. In 1969 the 229 biggest corporate giants had total assets of about $826 billion which was over one-half of American business assets. On this basis in 10 years, the expected 380 firms with billion dollar assets will have a total valuation of over $3 trillion, accounting for at least two-thirds and perhaps even three-fourths of American enterprise assets. This astronomical figure is probably greater than today's value of the corporate assets owned by all companies throughout the world.

When tossed about in the aggregate such multitrillion-dollar statistics do arouse fears of giantism and a centralization in Big Business akin to the centralization associated with Big Government. We have visions of a Japanese-style Zaibatsu, or a Mussolini-version corporate state, or of a Russian-model of State-run enterprise. These public fears of a centripetal corporate crush, reflected in our congressmen and senators, will almost certainly lead to controls over conglomeration, merger, acquisition, takeovers, and perhaps even over diversification through internal expansion. Before such repressive measures can be advocated, it is only fair and reasonable that we consider a few positive features, even of conglomeration.

3

MERGER—INCIDENCE

Mergers are big news. Within the past several years the news media, and particularly the printed page, has given merging and conglomeration a coverage almost equal to that given to our most pressing social and political problems. During the last two or three years it is reasonable to estimate that almost every issue of our leading periodicals— *Business Week, Fortune, The New York Times, Barron's, Forbes, Dun's Review,* and *The Wall Street Journal*—had at least one major reference to mergers. In 1970 during a typical early week in spring a check on merger-mention in *The Wall Street Jounrnal* showed an average per issue of 21 merger news items, ranging in length from 1 to 23 inches each. On the average about 134 column inches out of a total of approximately 600 column inches pertained directly or indirectly to merger and conglomeration. This constituted more than one-fifth of each issue during this test period and indicates the newsworthiness of the merger topic.

Despite the intensive coverage in the news media, at business conferences, in academic circles, and in conversations between businessmen at lunch, on the golf course or in cocktail circuits, there is considerable confusion on this theme. Although the pro- and the antigroups have some immutable convictions, the mass of people do not comprehend either the merits or evils of mergers. This nonpartisan public is subjected either to the old, hackneyed antitrust "damn monopoly" arguments that have been gathering moss since the 1880's or, similarly, they are sweet-talked by glib merchants of the fast buck into believing that through merger two slowpoke firms are instantaneously transformed into an economic decathlon champion. The public, and particularly the rapidly growing segment of investing public, must have facts—easily digestible —in order to judge the issue rationally and equitably.

Probably the most publicized tabulation on the incidence of mergers is that compiled periodically by W. T. Grimm and Company, a consulting firm specializing in mergers. The Grimm tabulation shows a 350% increase in merger incidence in the last six years. There was a total of 1361 mergers in 1963, and in 1969 6132 mergers. These W. T. Grimm data are somewhat limited insofar as they are composite figures including all types, sizes, and degrees of merger.

Another reliable source is the magazine, *Mergers and Acquisitions*, which reported that 1968 mergers were taking place at the rate of 1600 per year, a 22.5% increase over 1967. However, in this tabulation only those mergers are counted in which the value of cash or securities involved was in excess of $700,000.

The Federal Trade Commission also publishes data on corporate acquisitions but limits its count to manufacturing and mining firms. These FTC data show about a tenfold gain since 1950, increasing to 2268 mergers in 1968. One of the more interesting aspects of the FTC analyses is the concern shown over gigantism in mergers; for example, FTC data show that in 1950, in considering only firms which had assets in excess of $10 million, there were a scant half dozen of them which yielded to merger. Their combined total assets were slightly more than $100 million.

In extremely sharp contrast there were 192 such large-scale takeovers in 1968 and their total assets reached $12.6 billion. (The total assets of all 2268 mining and manufacturing firms gobbled up by the 200 largest United States corporations in 1968 were estimated by the FTC to have exceeded $40 billion.) This is more than a 100-fold increase over 20 years. Even more significantly these data show the susceptibility to merger takeover of even the largest corporations. As recently as 1962 more than 90% of these large (with assets exceeding $10 million) mining and manufacturing firms capitulating to merger individually had assets under $100 million. In 1968 nearly two-thirds of these large-scale merger-capitulating firms had assets ranging above $100 million. Figure 3-1 graphically shows this phenomenon. Note in particular the precipitous climb, beginning in 1966, of supersize corporations, those with assets above $100 million that yielded to merger. This susceptibility to merger of once-assumed impregnable corporations has caused anxiety not only in corporate headquarters but also in our legislative chambers.

Another excellent and pertinent statistical source is *Moody's Industrials*. This compendium contains the basic business data on approximately 15,000 corporations. The total, however, must be adjusted downward to less than 6000 companies since the remainder are subsidiaries of larger firms. These data on the total of *Moody*-listed corporations and the net

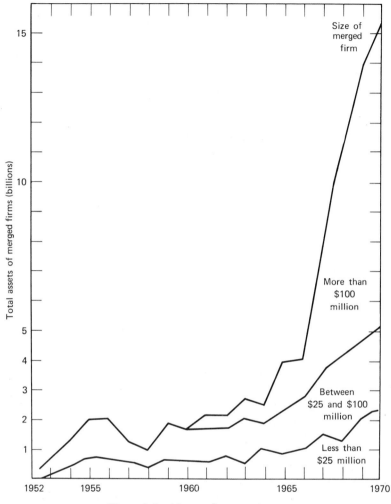

Figure 3-1   Mergers by asset size.

figure after subsidiaries are subtracted have varied over the past half century. There is, however, an obvious decline in the number of independent companies. In the 1920's the ratio of "sovereign" corporations to subsidiaries was about 5:2. In the 1930's this ratio had declined to about 8:5. The severe economic shakeout following the Great Depression reversed this ratio to about 1:2 during the 1940's and 1950's. There has been in this decade a slight increase to a current ratio of about 3:5. However, this change could be due entirely to the increase in total listings from a previous average of about 12,000 to a present figure of slightly over 15,000.

The pertinent data compressed in Table 3-1 show the following:

1. A steady rise in total *Moody* listings after a significant shakeout in the 1935–1955 period.

2. A fairly stable 3:5 ratio over the last 20 years in the ratio of autonomous firms to large-scale subsidiaries.

Table 3-1 *Comparison of Autonomous and Subsidiary Firms as Listed in* Moody's *1921–1969*

Year	(1) Total Listings	(2) Subsidiaries	(3) Autonomous Firms	(4) Ratio Columns 3:2
1969	15,100	9500	4500	3:5
1959	13,200	8800	4400	1:2
1949	12,200	8000	4200	1:2
1939	13,100	4700	8400	9:5
1929	14,800	5700	9100	8:5
1921	7,600	2200	5400	5:2

These data, in gross form, certainly indicate that there is a long-term trend toward amalgamation, consolidation, conglomeration, synthesis, and merger—whatever the term may be. It must also be emphasized that *Moody's Industrials* does not even approach listing every subsidiary of every major firm. Actually, for every *Moody* listing of a subsidiary firm, at least 12 and probably closer to 20 of important subsidiaries of major companies are not detailed in this compilation. For example, Standard Oil Company (New Jersey), a classic example of a nonconglomerate, has several dozen subsidiaries, but only four are *Moody* listings. Similarly, Textron, a pioneer conglomerate, with a rather volatile subsidiary membership, had only one subsidiary *Moody* listing in 1969 but actually encompassed 31 divisions, the successors to more than 60 merged firms.

Other *Moody* data provide an even more meaningful index of corporate turnover. Despite textbook allusions to the attribute of infinite life which corporations are supposed to possess, we have ample evidence of their mortality. Strewn across the business horizon are the bleached bones of defunct corporations—stark mementos of hapless ventures. A compendium to the annual *Moody* listings sets forth those firms which were dropped from listing during the past 10 years. The reasons for disappearance are many; for example, the latest tabulation involving the 1959–1968 attritions shows the following:

Table 3-2   Corporate Attritions, 1959–1968 *

		Total
Acquisitions		1392
Acquired by	320	
Merged with	267	
Merged into	241	
Merged by	47	
Assets acquired by	158	
Control acquired by	143	
Sold to	30	
Subsidiary of	20	
Consolidated with	26	
Amalgamated	8	
No public interest	125	
Nationalized	7	
Liquidations		206
Succeeded by	7	
Reorganized	13	
Dissolved	20	
Liquidated	102	
No recent information	64	
Name change		872
		2470

* Source: *Moody's Industrials*, 1969.

These data take on more meaning when compared with corporate turnover in previous periods. Figure 3-2 is a graphic and summary portrayal of the changes that have taken place during the last 50 years in the attrition rates and causes affecting the top 12,000 to 16,000 major American corporations. There is a very obvious decline in loss-of-face delistings, categorized here as *liquidations*. The other two major classifications, *acquisitions* and *name changes*, have increased significantly. The total attritions, after dropping perceptibly during the 1930's, have turned markedly upward in the 1950's and especially in the 1960's. Barring any unforeseen economic or political interferences, it can be safely

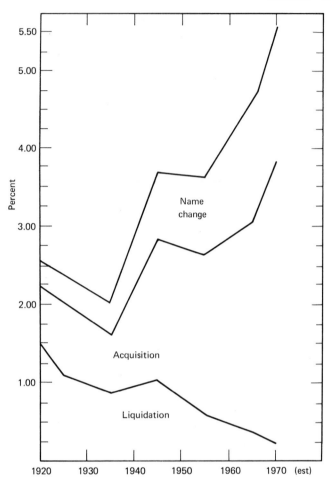

Figure 3-2   Relative annual attrition of company listings in
Moody's Industrials, 1920–1970.

estimated that by 1970 the annual turnover rate for the top 6000 American corporations will be approximately 5.5%. In this composite rate the
incidence of liquidations will reach an abysmally low figure of one-
fourth of 1%. This compares with an approximately 1.5% liquidation
rate in the early 1920's and a 1% rate in the 1930's.

By contrast the broad category of acquisitions will increase to an annual rate of about 3.5%. This figure compares with a rate of approximately 1% 50 years ago. Similarly, name changing by major corporations should continue at a rather high annual rate of 1.7%, whereas 50

years ago name changes accounted for only about 0.2% of attritions.

As a caution the obvious must be pointed out, namely, that a company is not strictly an attrition just because it changes its name. If, however, name changing is symptomatic of firms trying to improve their image, it could be a mild measure of face saving. A large portion of name-changing firms have had relatively poor performance records. Another big group are firms that have done well in the past but seek a new name because they have drastically changed their structure and objectives and a new name implies a new look and a new vigor. The name

Table 3-3   Relative Annual Attrition of Companies Listed in Moody's Industrials, 1920–1970

	(1) Liquidation	(2) Acquisition	(1) + (2)	(3) Name Change	(1) + (2) + (3)
1920	1.48	0.78	2.26	0.28	2.54
1920–1929	1.11	1.07	2.18	0.25	2.43
1930–1939	0.86	0.83	1.69	0.37	2.06
1940–1949	1.04	1.80	2.84	0.86	3.70
1950–1959	0.61	2.08	2.69	0.98	3.67
1960–1969	0.39	2.68	3.07	1.68	4.75
1970 (est)	0.27	3.53	3.80	1.77	5.57

change category has been included in this analysis to emphasize that in a dynamic economy forward-looking firms seek to adapt to their environment, and name changing is indicative of adaptation. This theme is developed further in Chapter 16, *The Corporate Name Game*.

If only acquisitions and liquidations are considered as actual attritions, then the average annual losses have tended to range between 2 and 3%. The very noticeable steady decline in liquidations, which has been more than balanced by an equally noticeable upward progression in mergers, has some social as well as economic implications. Liquidation, in addition to severe money losses, also carries a stigma implying culpable incompetency, defeat, and desertion. At current bankruptcy and liquidation rates, it almost seems impossible for a major firm to suffer this ignominy. In 1931 *Moody's Industrials* listed by name 93 companies which were then going through the legal process of bankruptcy. In 1935 the number in this category had increased to 126, but by 1945 there were only nine such casualties, seven in 1950 and four in 1955. No bankruptcy, receivership, liquidation, or dissolution listing is currently included in *Moody's Industrials*, attesting to the disuse of these embarrassing procedures which are economically and socially quite costly, and extremely demoralizing from a psychological point of view.

Although the disappearance of bankruptcies from big business could be interpreted as a compliment to our prosperity, it can also mean that companies in relative difficulty prefer to merge rather than undergo dissolution. If so, this could have positive connotations; the defeated firms are not destroyed through dissolution, rather they are absorbed and rebuilt by more aggressive and successful firms. This theme will be developed further in the subsequent sections describing the regression syndrome and catharsis through merger.

One final source of data on merger incidence must be noted, namely, *Fortune's* annual ranking of our top 500 industrial corporations. The particular significance in using this source is the size of these listed firms. (The 1970 listing showed total sales for the 500 companies at approximately $445 billion.) Over the 16-year period since *Fortune* instituted this ranking, less than 12 of these industrial giants have not engaged in some type of merger activity. More than 209 companies currently or previously listed disappeared from this honor roll— virtually all through merger. On the basis of these data it is reasonable to estimate an average annual merger rate between 1.9 and 2.2%. The exact rate is difficult to determine because over the 16-year period *Fortune's* 500 came closer to a total of 750, counting mergers and delistings. The significant trends come more into focus when the rates are compared on a time basis.

Years	Approximate Annual Merger Rates (%)
1967–1969	4.7
1964–1966	2.9
1959–1963	1.8
1954–1958	1.6

These fairly reasonable estimates for loss of corporate autonomy through merger support the contention that mergers are increasing even at the top of the industrial pyramid. As previously stated only 291 of *Fortune's* 1956 top industrial ranking firms were still on *Fortune's* 1970 listing.

Corporate turnover in the manufacturing sector is paralleled in other sectors of our economy. In the 16-year interval covered by *Fortune's* major firm ranking, there has been an attrition of at least 20 from the list of our 50 largest mercantile firms. In considering that about 75 firms were included at one time or other in *Fortune*'s 50 top merchants, this is equivalent to nearly a 2.1% annual loss. Nearly all of this loss is due to mergers—there have been no liquidations and name changes have not been considered in this particular tabulation.

The decline and disappearance of individual corporations is certainly not a phenomenon found exclusively in American business. In Great Britain, during 1875–1960, approximately 22,500 firms once listed on the London Stock Exchange disappeared from the business scene. "The majority of these are defunct companies removed owing to liquidation, dissolution, etc. . . ." [1] These historical records indicate an attrition rate in middle-size and large-scale enterprise in Great Britain of about one company per (working) day.

This last item has been mentioned to stress that until very recently mergers and especially conglomerates have been almost exclusively an American phenomenon. Britain and the rest of the world still let many business casualties and corporate weaklings be tossed to the eagles and vultures in Spartan-like style, but, even abroad, particularly in Japan, West Germany, and Great Britain, there seems to be a growing awareness of the economic and social values accompanying both large-scale enterprise and multiline endeavor accomplished through merger.

In Japan there were 440 mergers in 1960, but the 1969 incidence was about 1200. More significant than this 170% increase is the trend toward amalgamation of big firms rather than very small firms. Before 1960 not a single Japanese merging firm had a capitalization over 10 billion yen (about $28 million in United States dollars). In 1960 one merging firm came from this major industry category, whereas in 1963 there were 13 such large-sized firms involved in merging.[2] This trend in Japanese industries to get bigger through merger has had noticeable impact on that country's industrial concentration. Currently 1% of Japan's manufacturers employ over 40% of the labor force and produce half the nation's industrial products. The stress on bigness, through mergers when feasible, has resulted in a concentration so that "in each of 37 major industries the top five companies' share of total output varies from 50 per cent to 100 per cent. . . . The pattern very closely resembles a postwar version of the zaibatsu." [3]

Actually, a large portion of the recent Japanese mergers follows from

---

[1] *Register of Defunct and Other Companies Removed from the Stock Exchange Official Yearbook, 1960*, Thomas Skinner and Co., Ltd., Gresham House, London, p. 1.
[2] Gen Numaguchi "Trend toward Merger and Reorganization in Japanese Industry," *Management Japan.* 2 No. 1, 16 (1968).
[3] *U. S. News and World Report*, 89. (May 27, 1968).

a resurgence of the zaibatsu; for example, the 1968 merger of three lead-ing paper companies (Oji Paper, Jujo Paper Mfg., and Houshu Paper Mfg.) reunites three former members of the Oji group. Similarly, three former components of the Kawasaki group were reunited as were the Nippon Seitetsu interest's Yawata Iron and Steel Works and the Fuji Iron and Steel Company. Even more recently two important former members of the Mitsui interest, Toyo Koatsu Industries and Mitsui Chemical Industries, were reunited.

This resurgence of the pre-World War II zaibatsu gives the current Japanese merger movement distinctively vertical integration and hori-zontal integration characteristics. There is also a noticeable move by ag-gressive firms into acquisitions of related process and related product fa-cilities. Conglomeration, or the juncture of nonrelated firms, is a just-beginning phenomenon.

Great Britain also has its new empire builders who use every trick in the merger bag. Leonard Matcham, chairman and president of Cope All-man International, is one of the better known of the new breed entrepre-neurs. Over a 10-year period he put together a conglomerate with sales approaching the $200 million level. On a much grander scale, English Electric Company and General Electric Company, Ltd. (no connection with the American General Electric) late in 1968 agreed in principle to a merger. Sales of these two giants would have a combined value of about $2.2 billion. It is interesting to note that in 1958 English Electric was the 36th largest corporation outside the United States, but by 1967 it had dropped to the 71st position. Similarly, General Electric Com-pany, Ltd., had been 71st largest and had declined to the 100th rank by 1966 but moved upward in rank by acquiring the huge Associate Elec-trical Industries, Ltd. (1966 *Fortune* rank, 56 and sales, $750 million). This would seem to indicate that there is an identity in the reasons for mergers here and abroad. This item will be discussed subsequently.

The British, far more than the Americans or the Japanese, seem to be committed to a gentlemen's code, a Queensberry Rules decorum, which inhibits the superaggressiveness so frequently found in American busi-ness merger maneuvers. In addition to this straightlaced moral code, there are professional and legal constraints: there is a British Board of Trade Monopolies Commission and London's financial community's (re-ferred to as "the City") self-policing Panel on Takeovers and Mergers. However, in recent test cases (American Tobacco's takeover of Gallaher, Ltd.) these quasi-regulatory bodies proved to be surface controls lacking enforcement power.

In summary, there is no question as to the growing incidence of merg-ers, here and abroad. Both the first merger peak which occurred in 1899 when 1208 mergers took place and the second peak in 1929 with 1245 mergers caused considerable apprehension in government and financial circles. With an increase from 1321 mergers in 1963 to a current peak of 6132 in 1969, the tempo is accelerating from andante through allegro into a wild scherzo. Hypothetically, at current merger rates, nearly half of our largest corporations (those on *Fortune*'s "Honor Roll") could disappear during the next decade. If the 1967–1969 merger rate of nearly 5% continues unchecked, then in just 10 years *Fortune*'s 500 should list 250 new names as replacements for an equal number that have capitulated to merger. This intensified activity must inevitably invite controls—even now countervailing Federal forces are grouping and preparing for the onslaught.

4

MERGER—CONGLOMERATION

Although it is universally agreed that mergers are on the upswing, there is considerable controversy as to the character, structure, objectives, and consequences of this corporate synthesis. We do know that by definition a merger is a consolidation of one firm or trading company with another. More specifically, it is a fusion of two or more corporations by the transfer of all property and authority to a single corporation. The term has semantic nuances; for example, a merger differs from a consolidation since a consolidation assumes that all the merging parties terminate their existence and simply become parties to and components of the new firm. The British generally refer to such unions as amalgamations, a combining into the one uniform whole. The terminological problem is presented in Table 3-2 where *Moody's Industrials* shows that even when the term merger is used, it can be interpreted as merger *with*, merger *into*, or merger *by*. The first connotes a union of equals, the second a somewhat less voluntary action, and the third a mandated act. The term "acquired by" likewise implies merger by or a union of a superior with an inferior.

The semantics confusion has been heightened by the recent increased use of the terms conglomerate and conglomeration. The relative newness of this term in its business context is matched by the equally undefinable character, structure, objectives, and consequences of conglomeration. Many of the conglomerate firms and their spokesmen object to the term —they seem to sense a derogatory connotation. Originally the word conglomerate had a geological meaning—it was a rock composed of fragments of preexisting rocks. The glacial periods, for example, produced a wide variety of rock boulders fused from glacial scrappings, water-worn pebbles, shells and mud, cemented into a heterogeneous whole. This unsystematic origin and hodgepodge constituency of geological conglomerates is probably not conducive to good image building for corporate conglomerates. George T. Sharffenberger, Jr., president of City Investing Company, has long complained that the word reminds him of "cold congealed oatmeal." "David N. Judelson, president of Gulf and Western Industries, Inc., says the word 'is commonly used to imply that those who run these newfangled kind of corporation don't know what they're doing and are going madly about gathering up companies in a haphazard way.'"[1] Rupert C. Thompson "bristles at the word 'conglomerate,' which, he says, his first and only association is 'mess.' (He suggests 'nonrelated diversification.')"[2] Tenneco purchased space in *The Wall Street Journal* to proclaim that "diversification—not conglomeration is our business."[3] Similarly, Combustion Engineering has advertised extensively that it is not a conglomerate. Judging from these and kindred statements it is obvious that many conglomerates dislike the term.

Among suggested synonyms are terms such as multiindustry or multimarket. In at least one instance (GAF Corporation) the preference is for "congeneric" which implies that the joining units are allied in origin, nature, or action. Terms such as concentric and circular integration have likewise been suggested but have not gained any appreciable acceptance. CNA Financial Corporation invented the term "synerance," which according to the firm's president indicates first, an insurance company and second, an insurance company that for synergistic reasons is acquiring other but closely allied companies that will make it a stronger insurance company. In his best selling *Up the Organization,* Robert Townsend is caustic of what he labels "conglobulations." Another candidate could be the tongue-twister tangential integration. Tangential implies moving at an angle quite different from the conventional up or down of vertical integration or of the single-level horizontal integration. Although the tangentially integrated firm can differ in structure and objectives from the parent firm it is nevertheless in constant touch with the corporate arc.

By analogy it provides a very high degree of flexibility because even a slight twist in the radius can give the tangent quite a new angle of direction. Yet, despite such sudden shifts, the tangent is geometrically an integral part of the corporate circle.

Diagrammatically, tangential integration would differ from the conventional and better known vertical and horizontal integration as follows:

[1] *The Wall Street Journal,* 12 (July 25, 1968).
[2] *Fortune,* 155 (April, 1964).
[3] *The Wall Street Journal,* 6 (October 3, 1968).

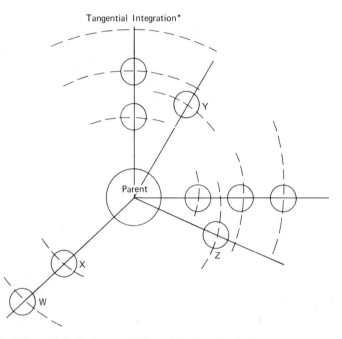

Tangential Integration*

Parent

Y

X

W

Z

* Firms W, X, Y, Z are vertically and horizontally nonrelated
to parent's original endeavor.

Note that there is no beautiful vertical or horizontal symmetry which
might imply product, process, or market relationship. Yet the satellites
are controlled by the parent. If these satellites are visualized as orbiting
in separate paths around the focal point, then perhaps another term, or-
bital integration, might be ventured.

Although these and other names for the current merging phenomenon
could be used, it does seem that the term conglomerate will continue to
be used at least colloquially and even legally. This is rather significant
since it is variously estimated that current mergers are between 80 and
90% conglomerate in character.

What, then, are a conglomerate's characteristics? The American Institute of Certified Public Accountants has set forth the following:

1. The acquisition of businesses in many widely divergent industries.
2. The operation of these businesses on a highly decentralized basis,
with decentralized management and accounting information.
3. The possession of few common manufacturing or distribution facilities and the infrequent transfer of products between divisions.
4. The existence of limited joint costs, except for financing and central
administration.[4]

[4] *Business Week,* 69 (August 10, 1968).

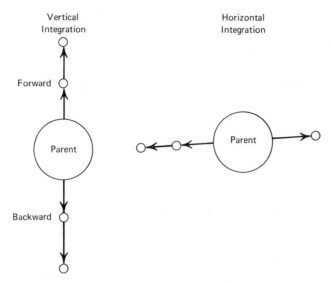

The stress, then, seems to be on diversification and decentralization. On decentralization, Signal Companies recently advertised nationally by headlining: "We told our companies to mind their own business."[5] Then follows the explanation:

And they smiled. Because our corporate philosophy is like a declaration of independence for every one of the Signal Companies. It means Garrett can concentrate on aerospace. Mack thinks about trucks. Signal Oil and Gas Company pushes ahead in petroleum. Signal Equities Company (formerly Arizona Bancorporation) watches its many interests like banking, steel, and insurance. And Dunham-Bush sticks to air conditioning.[6]

After this statement of "states rights" this particular Signal Companies' advertisement reiterates the principles of confederation stating: "But the big corporate-type problems, like long-range financing, acquisitions and capitalization, are handled by our strong corporate management team. Strong and versatile, because we bring executive talent up from each of the companies, rather than just impose authority down from above."[7]

This statement of the Signal Companies' philosophy of conglomerate confederation does not necessarily hold for other such firms. Consequently, the confusion. Prompted by the urgency of the situation, the Federal Trade Commission and the Justice Department are striving to establish definitions and guidelines. Likewise, the American Bar Asso-

[5] *Fortune*, 161 (September, 1968).
[6] *Ibid.*, p. 161.
[7] *Ibid.*, p. 161.

ciation and leading business groups such as the National Industrial Conference Board, the American Management Association, and various accounting and financial groups are trying to get some order out of the confusion.

Perhaps the principal reason for this chaotic state is the very slowness with which big government adjusts to change. A lag factor is inherent in every large organism's response mechanism and the bigger the beast the slower it responds to stimuli or to irritants. The dinosaur's pea-sized brain, far removed from its body extremities, was slow to sense and slow to respond, resulting in a consequent extinction of these outsized saurian reptiles. By analogy big government, with its multiplicity of bureaucratic nerve centers, has not as yet fathomed the significance of conglomerates. Hopefully, with today's fantastically efficient communications media, the Federal Saurians will in the near future take studied action.

In the summer of 1968 the Justice Department's Antitrust Division set down some pertinent guidelines based on market structure. The objective of these guidelines (Figure 4-1) was to tell prospective merging partners what sort of unions the Justice Department would not tolerate.

It should be noted in this guideline summary that the Justice Department still seems to be focusing on vertical and horizontal mergers. It was the overincidence of the backward and forward vertical moves into additional manufacturing stages, together with horizontal integration into wider marketing areas, which prompted the Sherman Antitrust and the Clayton Antitrust Acts.

The present guidelines are in some respects quite anachronistic because they are concerned primarily with Section 7 of the Clayton Act which charges the government to challenge any merger that tends to substantially lessen competition. However, the concept of competition which prevailed until recently has now undergone drastic modification. It was a rather simple task to determine a company's competitive position in a given industry when most firms concentrated their efforts on a single easily discernible line of endeavor. We can readily digest, for example, a breakdown of the automobile makers' market share as G. M., 50%; Ford, 30%; Chrysler, 15%; others, 5%. This is a neat and meaningful categorization. As vertical and horizontal integration (mergers) give way to diversification and other forms of circular integration (conglomerates), the precise market share allocations lose their meaning. Five years ago it was fairly simple to determine the economic impact of almost any firm in its industry. In meat packing there was no argument over the relative ranking and economic importance of the big three, Swift, Armour, and Wilson on a 3:2:1 sales volume basis. The other meat

If four top companies control 75% or more of a market and . . .

. . . the acquiring company holds	. . . the acquired company holds at least
Market share in percent	
4%	4%
10	2
15	1

If four top companies control less than 75% of a market and . . .

. . . the acquiring company holds	. . . the acquired company holds at least
Market share in percent	
5%	5%
10	4
15	3
20	2
25	1

If a supplier has at least 10% of its market—and the customer takes at least 6% of that total market. But such mergers are O.K. if they won't keep newcomers out of the customer's market

If a supplier has about 20% of its market, if its product is essential to a customer's business, and if the customer has 10% of its own market

If a company with 25% of a market acquires a company with potential to enter that market

If one of four largest companies in a market where top eight control 75% or more acquires a company with potential to enter that market

If the companies involved could make reciprocal buying agreements

Source: Business Week, 32 (June 8, 1968).

Figure 4-1 [8]

packers could also be fitted very neatly into this ranking scheme. But with Wilson's capitulation to Ling-Temco-Vought and an active soliciting for almost every other meat packer by acquisitive-minded conglomerates, the market-share comparison is now meaningless. Even before the conglomerate confusion, diversification by the leading meat packers into areas such as chemicals tended to cloud economic comparisons, but these few exceptions could be identified and seemingly be justified.

Interestingly enough, the Justice Department's merger guidelines touch gingerly on the new conglomerates. Prohibitions on conglomerating are quite vaguely stated with antitrust action threatened only if the

[8] *Business Week*, 32 (June 8, 1968).

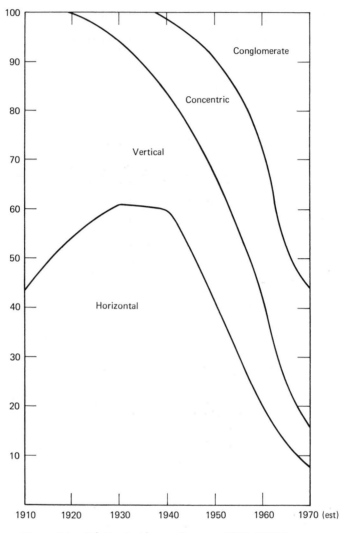

Figure 4-2   Relative incidence of merger, 1910–1970, by type.

companies involved engaged in reciprocity or if the acquired firms had a potential to enter a market already substantially served by the conglomerate. Yet it is the conglomerate which is gaining in acceptance. In Figure 4-2 is an estimate of the relative incidence of four basic forms of corporate union. In the nineteenth century vertical merger was the fastest and surest way to success in the manufacturing phase. It was, and still is, quite logical for an aggressive and successful manufacturing firm to integrate both forward and backward in order to maximize manufacturing potential. Similarly, around the turn of the century, horizontal merger was accelerated by widening market endeavor. However, market saturation in some industries and the boom-or-bust character of other industries, together with the threat of antitrust action, has now pushed many growth-minded entrepreneurs out of the manufacturing and marketing expansion routes and forced them to move into a new superform of "management" merger—conglomeration.

Admitting the semantics dispute over the term, conglomeration, Figure 4-2 attempts to differentiate between the congeneric or concentric types of merger and the pure conglomerates. As previously stated the congeneric or concentric mergers involve companies which have some product, process, or market relationship. Pure conglomerates are those whose products, processes, and markets are almost completely unrelated. Despite this semantics distinction both categories, concentric merger and pure conglomerate merger, are most frequently lumped indiscriminately.

For all practical purposes, even though there are many kinds of conglomerates, the salient feature of each seems to be a vesting of control in a new breed of manager. He is neither the sole owner of the conglomerate nor does he supply mechanical or marketing innovations as did the classic entrepreneur of past generations. Rather he is a professional supermanager who welds a hodgepodge of components into a harmonious entity. His genius lies in his ability to get the divisional heads to operate their components to the maximum potential. This function of the conglomerate's chief executive is not exactly new. In some respects it is a modification of the holding-company concept; a technique that has quite successfully been used at Standard Oil Company (New Jersey) but with at least one major difference—Standard Oil concentrated its major endeavors on a single product line. Similarly, General Motors Corporation, with its stress on centralized staff activities but with decentralized operations, anticipated the conglomerate corporate control philosophy by almost half a century.

SUMMARY

Table 4-1 is an attempt at contrasting the five major merger manifestations. United States Steel Corporation, put together more than two-thirds of a century ago as an amalgam of five groups of steel-making corporations encompassing several score companies, is probably the best example in our business history of merger in all shapes, sizes, colors, and functions. The listings in the five merger categories are simply examples and do not show all the merger components. Note that the first of America's supermergers included most of the nation's then major iron and steel-making companies such as Carnegie, Federal, National, and a dozen others. These were peer-firms, engaged in the same basic activity —making iron and steel. This is the horizontal merger phase, a union of firms with similar functions.

In the second column vertical backward integration includes the coke, coal, limestone, and iron-ore producing components. These are secondary activities essential to U. S. Steel's prime purpose. In this classic merger, the reverse movement, vertical forward integration, included another 12 or so fabrication facilities, companies such as American Bridge and American Steel and Wire.

The preceding illustrates the typical mergers of the past, horizontal and vertical. The two illustrations in the concentric merger column, B. &L.E.R.R. and Pittsburgh Steamship Lines, were companies ancillary to the basic purpose yet related to steelmaking, in this case for transport purposes. Perhaps these are not the best examples of concentric merger, which generally assumes related products, markets, processes, by-product utilization, and so on.

In the last column are two examples from this turn-of-the-century merger which approximate true conglomeration, but even here the Universal Portland Cement Company acquisition (in 1906) might be questioned as a pure-conglomerate example, since cement and steel are first cousins related through the construction function.

The subsequent illustrations are quite fragmentary when compared with the maximerger, U. S. Steel. Pittsburgh Steel's absorption of Wheeling Steel illustrates horizontal merger—an extension of the same activity geographically by the swallowing of a potential competitor.

Weyerhaeuser is presented as an example of horizontal merger in its acquisition of Dierks Forest, and as a blend of concentric and conglomerate merger in its incorporation of Par-West Financial which is definitely removed from the forest products industry. However, with Weyerhaeuser's entrance into a new and more sophisticated business endeavor, now called the Shelter Industry, Par-West Financial in its financing and mortgaging of homes does seem to be more concentric than conglomerate in its relationship to Weyerhaeuser's prime business purpose.

Boise Cascade provides still another merger-mix. Union Lumber's acquisition is basically horizontal merging. Yet the huge tracts of land involved in this and related mergers give Boise Cascade much needed raw materials sources and thus could be viewed as vertical backward

Table 4-1

Acquiring Company \ Kind of Merger →	Horizontal	Vertical Backward	Vertical Forward	Concentric	Conglomerate
United States Steel Corp. (1901)	Carnegie Co. Federal Steel National Steel	Lake Superior Iron Mines Frick Coke Co.	American Bridge American Steel & Wire	B & L.E. R.R. Pittsburgh Steamship	Universal Portland Cement Gary Heat, Light and Power Co.
	Basic Steel Producers	Raw Materials	Steel Fabrication	Related Activities	Nonrelated Activities
Pittsburgh Steel Weyerhaeuser Co.	Wheeling Steel Dierks Forests, Inc.				
Boise Cascade	Union Lumber Co. and several sand companies		Kingsbury Homes	Par-West Financial (Mortgage Banking and Homebuilding) Divco-Wayne Corp. (Mobile Homes)	Ebasco Industries
Armstrong Cork				Thomasville Furniture E&B Carpet Mills	Princess Lines
Ling-Temco-Vought					Jones and Laughlin, Wilson, Braniff, Greatamerica. Continental Baking, Sheraton Corp., Levitt and Sons, Avis, Canteen Corp., Hartford Fire Insurance, Grinnel Corp. (Fire protection)
International Telephone & Telegraph					

integration. Kingsbury Homes' addition is an example of the opposite vertical integration, a forward movement. Divco-Wayne's merger into Boise Cascade should be classified as concentric merger, since this important maker of mobile homes, although consuming only a limited quantity of Boise Cascade's plywood (and hence not vertical forward integration), is nevertheless part of the Shelter Industry in which Boise Cascade is primarily active. The last column includes two Boise Cascade acquisitions that must be categorized as real conglomerates. Neither Ebasco Industries, dealing with engineering, financial, and other services, or Princess Lines, providing luxury cruises for travelers, can be pegged to Boise Cascade's presumed basic activities.

Armstrong Cork is presented as an example of a company with considerably narrower merger aspirations than Boise Cascade's. Both the acquisitions listed, Thomasville Furniture and E & B Carpet Mills, are related intimately to Armstrong Cork's prime business purpose— homebuilding and home furnishing. These mergers have a logical relationship to the company's business function and yet they show a revamping and perhaps an expansion of the company's horizons through diversification. What does not appear on the chart but strengthens this inference is Armstrong's recent divestiture and spin-off through sale of activities unrelated to home furnishing. For example, the company's long-time components making glass containers and closures were sold off at about the same time that Armstrong Cork moved into the new concentric lines through merger. The making of glass bottles and bottle closures had been an unrelated line of endeavor and could be attributed to a much earlier conglomeration attempt. Now, however, Armstrong Cork seems to be moving, through merger and divestiture, into a narrower but more purposeful concentric diversification.

The last two examples, Ling-Temco-Vought and International Telephone and Telegraph, show nothing in any of the first four columns but make up for this deficiency by an overabundance of the "real-thing," conglomerate mergers. In LTV's case it is evident there is no relationship, horizontal, vertical, or concentric, in the four merged firms selected from LTV's multiacquisitions. It would take a superimagination to tie steel, meatpacking (sporting goods and chemicals), an airline, and a finance firm into a homogeneous firm.

The International Telephone and Telegraph example is even more extreme. The seven acquisitions (the last three still in abeyance because of governmental objections) typify the nonrelated merger integral to conglomeration. Baking, hotel keeping, home building, car rentals, food services, insurance, and fire protection have only the most ephemeral threads tying these disparate activities together.

This summary illustrative of five basic kinds of merger is just that—it is a summary—it does not attempt to pigeonhole the many variations, modifications, mutations, or permutations, each of which is properly called a merger. It is important to realize there is simply no homogeneous kind of merger. Consequently, it is impossible to provide a single and simple definitive description of *the* merger, its characteristics, contributions, frailties, or accomplishments.

5

MERGER—SYMPTOMS

REGRESSION SYNDROME

The regression syndrome, borrowing from the medical field, is a fairly good index of impending merger, name change, or at worst dissolution. By definition a syndrome is a concurrence of several symptoms as in a disease. In this analogy the affliction is evidenced by the economic deterioration of a business enterprise. Among the more obvious of the syndrome's symptoms is the relative decline in sales, a deteriorating profit pattern, a shrinking labor force, and slow or no growth in owners' equity. The following example based on data from *Fortune*'s annual ranking of the top 500 American industrial firms provides some rather obvious illustrations of the regression syndrome.

	Relative *Fortune* Sales Ranking		
	1954	At Merger	Decline
Baldwin-Lima-Hamilton	199	381	182
Blaw-Knox	233	363	130
Wilson	37	81	44

Note, for instance, that Baldwin-Lima-Hamilton, itself the product of merger, became the subject of acquisition by Armour in 1965. In the 10-year interval of 1954–1965, Baldwin-Lima-Hamilton slumped in *Fortune*'s listing from a rank of 199 to 381. This is a loss of 182 in the relative sales ranking over a decade or an average annual decline of about 18 positions. The other firms in this three-company example show similar sizable declines.

Although the preceding data reflect only relative sales declines, the regression syndrome invariably shows equally serious slumps in all performance norms. The three-firm illustration, viewed as to asset, net income, and number of employees relative rankings, shows the following premerger changes:

	Assets		Net Income		Employees	
	1954	At Merger	1954	At Merger	1954	At Merger
Baldwin-Lima-Hamilton	172	312	302	480	144	349
Blaw-Knox	256	395	255	403	174	323
Wilson	168	294	332	298	66	172

The regression syndrome, illustrated numerically in the three-company sample, is certainly not confined to a few highly publicized examples. It is an almost universal manifestation as can be shown by an analysis of the entire 209 firms which have disappeared by merger from *Fortune*'s 500 in the past 16 years. In this larger sample measurable sales performance ranges from a gain of 83 positions to a loss of 408. The ratio of losers to gainers is 10:1. In approximately 11% of the cases the precise decline cannot be measured because the firm's slumping sales volume fails to qualify it for subsequent inclusion on *Fortune*'s list. The median decline for the 209 companies is 62 ranks over an average eight-year period before merger. On a simple arithmetical basis this would indicate that the merger-prone companies retreat saleswise about eight positions annually. However, remember that this is a minimal figure because many of the merging firms (11%) have had such significantly poor performances that before merger they no longer qualified for listing on *Fortune*'s 500.

These relative changes in ranking, although significant, do not adequately reveal the extent to which these companies have stood still or declined on a dollar and manpower basis. During the approximately 16-year period, the companies in question compare as follows with industry in general:

	Regression Syndrome Companies (%)	Large-Scale Nonmerging Industry (%)
Sales	+17	+ 87
Assets	+29	+138
Net income	+16	+ 35
Employees	-33	+ 38

It becomes somewhat more evident from this generalized comparison that the regression syndrome-type companies grow in sales and assets at only one-fifth the rate of growth for large-scale nonmerging firms. Net income for the large-scale nonmerging firms increased at double the rate recorded by regression-syndrome firms. However, the most obvious index of decline is in the manpower category. Although the large non-merging firms have boosted employment by about 3% annually, the merger-prone regression syndrome firms actually *declined* by almost 3% each year, which is a most significant contrast. The ailing firms are not only failing to meet their obligation to our society by creating new jobs for a national work force expanding at an annual rate of about 1½%, but they are actually decreasing their labor force and are adding to the nation's unemployment roles. These statistics are probably less significant for their arithmetical accuracy than for their very definite confirmation of the regression syndrome. On the basis of these data it seems legitimate to infer that *a firm in a chronic slump is a highly likely prospect for merger.*

The regression syndrome is probably only half the answer as to why certain fairly large firms are agreeable to merger and conglomeration. Other reasons include the recognition that the merging company has a serious need for the following:

1. Capital funds
2. Material resources
3. More complete product lines
4. Technical talent
5. Qualified managers
6. National advertising
7. More effective collective bargaining
8. Tax amelioration in closely held firms
9. Centralized research and development

An even more pressing argument is quite evident in a growing number of cases, that of the hefty dollar differential between the current market price of the courted firm's common stock and the acquisition package deal or tender offer. During 1968–1969 this "money motivation margin," discussed more fully in Chapter 6, averaged between 25 and 50%. This bonus, dangled as an inducement to merge, can be a powerful factor in the final decision. It is difficult to imagine any prudent investor arbitrarily rejecting a price for his stock which is so high that the chances are that it will be years before "normal" market forces push the stock price into this bonus range.

CATHARSIS

Although the regression syndrome does indicate a declining firm, it does not necessarily indicate a dying firm. In fact, in most cases in which the merger tender offer seems to be very generous, the probabilities are that the ailing firm, despite its progressive decline, still has reasonable prospects for recovery. The implication is that a drastic catharsis is needed and that the acquiring firm has the necessary medications and can apply the requisite treatment.

In the "good old days," at the height of individual entrepreneurship, lagging corporate performance was almost generally sensed by the interested owner and it was he who had to take therapeutic action. With diffused ownership and professional managers, the needed drastic action is not always forthcoming. In other words, what today may frequently pass for professional management turns out to be procrastinating management, and in such instances a merger threat can serve the very excellent purpose of jolting a moribund firm into action.

There was much fuss in the early 1950's concerning "raiding," the sudden, and by implication unethical, acquisition of a "tired-blood" company by an aggressive investor. Among the better known "raiders" were Louis E. Wolfson, Edward Lamb, and Patrick Lannan. It was alleged, and sometimes with justification, that these "raiders" captured control merely to sell off the captives' assets with no regard for rejuvenation. It can be argued, to the contrary, that in this liquidation or sell-off process the nonsalvagable components are mercilessly disposed of, frequently by closure and dissolution, giving the less afflicted segments of the raided firm much improved prospects for survival or even for successful performance.

The pros and cons of the raiding function will be discussed at greater length in a subsequent chapter, but it is important at this point to stress that the old-fashioned catharsis of insolvency, bankruptcy, and dissolution does not seem to be appropriate for twentieth and twenty-first century enterprise. Although this competitive cleansing is still an integral part of our business system, bankruptcy is today reserved solely for the relatively small-scale unsuccessful firm. In the present merger-fevered environment, statistics show that an amazingly few large-scale companies, even when they have deplorable performance records, are forced into involuntary dissolution. Instead, they are invariably absorbed by a more aggressive firm. In a sense this is both a charitable act and one that generally has sound economic motivation. Historically, bankruptcies tend to net perhaps 10 cents per dollar on the disintegrating firm's fixed investments. This low return results from the fact that the insolvent firm's assets are generally sold as scrap or, at best, are functionally degraded into lower yield activities. The same is true of the bankrupt firm's personnel—many are laid off permanently. Even those who eventually find other employment do so in lower level jobs. Thus the dissolved firm becomes a net producer of scrapped machinery and scrapped men, resulting in a functional degradation for both.

By contrast the incidence of scrappage and functional degradation is considerably smaller when a troubled firm is absorbed by another going concern. Much of the equipment can be used for continued productive endeavor. Similarly, a far greater proportion of the manpower at all levels of skill is kept at work doing the job it has been trained to do. As a consequence, not only is there less shock and loss to the individuals involved, there is also less loss to society, not only economically but also socially and psychologically.

Corroboration of this point is rather difficult because of the way statistics are compiled. Probably the most detailed information on business failures is that presented monthly in *Dun's Review*. These data show that throughout the country there is an annual attrition of approximately 13,000 to 14,000 enterprises. As is evident the vast majority of these failures are in small and relatively new firms. Then, too, the incidence is considerably higher in the trade and service ventures than in manufacturing industry. *Dun's Review*, unfortunately, does not differentiate between the firms that fail, scrap their facilities, and cease to exist and those which fail but have their assets acquired by a more successful firm. But *Dun's Review* is not alone in this limitation. Consequently, the real losses to society because of corporate disintegration can only be guessed at. (On the average the failing firm, in all industry, has liabilities of about $90,000. On the other hand, the average liabilities of the approximately 2000 mining and manufacturing firms that fail annually are about $170,000.)

The cathartic value of merger deserves more attention. Whereas our business system can easily withstand the bankruptcy of a hundred or more firms with million-dollar-a-year-sales, it might not react so placidly to the dissolution of even one or two members of the billion-dollar-a-year Sales Club firms. In the latter half of the last century, even one outstanding business failure was sometimes sufficient to induce a panic. Today, with all sectors of our society far more inextricably meshed into the business sector and with instant public communication, there is an even stronger probability that outright failure by one or two of our biggest corporations could result in a late-twentieth panic. Merger, then, might be viewed as the modern and more merciful way to (a) inter a de-

funct firm quietly, without all the fuss and embarrassment of bankruptcy; (b) deftly cut away from an otherwise healthy organism, a component that is pathologically beyond recovery; (c) administer a bitter
purgative to a sluggish yet curable firm and jolt it into rejuvenation.

THE HUDSON'S BAY COMPANY

The Hudson's Bay Company chartered in 1670 illustrates this point.
After an initial period of aggressive exploration and development, "The
Great Company" lapsed into somnolence and was stirred out of its leth-
argy only after the appearance of a very vigorous competitor, the North
West Company. A period of intensive and often bloody rivalry ended in
the amalgamation of the two giants in 1821. This amalgamation or
merger was a prototype of the trust—in this instance, a merger of like
and competing firms—a horizontal integration.

Elimination of competition and the subsequent monopolistic dominance of the merged Hudson's Bay Company resulted in another period
of prosperity which reached its peak in the mid-1800's. Prosperity, however, once again seemed to soften the giant, which showed acute symptoms of the regression syndrome and became the subject of several par-
liamentary investigations. In 1863 the company's stock was bought up
by the International Finance Society. This financial coup was almost
identical in pattern to so many of today's corporate takeovers. The
closely held stock of The Great Company was reissued so that the ownership base became widespread. The new management also broadened
the company's endeavors to include a great variety of activities. This
was probably the earliest prototype of the conglomerate. As in so many
of our own established firms that turn conglomerate, the conglomerating
Hudson's Bay Company seemed to develop almost a disdain for the line
of endeavor that had produced the company's previous prosperity; in
this instance, the fur business that was now drastically deemphasized.

Since statistical data for the earlier periods of the Hudson's Bay Company are not comparable with current data, it is impossible to show the
regression syndrome symptoms arithmetically. Nevertheless this illustration does make inferences that even 150 years ago, at the very onset of
the modern corporation, a very logical and effective antidote to the regression syndrome causes was *merger*. On at least two occasions, in the
1821 horizontal integration and also in the 1863 diversification, the Hudson's Bay Company was rejuvenated through the merger technique.

The sequel to this success-through-merger illustration occurred two-
thirds of a century after the company's venture into diversification. In
1930, as a consequence of the economic depression, the board of gover-

nors made a momentous decision to split the company into smaller units. This, the reverse of merger, was resolutely opposed by the company's governor who consequently resigned. The fragmented firm then went into relative decline and oblivion. What was once the biggest corporation in the world is today not even qualified for *Fortune*'s listing of the 200 largest foreign firms.

BALDWIN-LIMA-HAMILTON CORPORATION

The 1965 juncture of Baldwin-Lima-Hamilton Corporation into Armour and Company provides a good illustration of the regression syndrome. Before and even during World War II Baldwin Locomotive Works, with extensive facilities originally in midtown Philadelphia and later in a 5 million square foot plant at Eddystone, Pennsylvania, was a leading railroad equipment producer. Unfortunately, it missed the signal of the coming of the diesel engine and made a series of other injudicious decisions.

By 1950 Baldwin had so deteriorated that it sought refuge in a merger with Lima-Hamilton, itself a merger of two railroad equipment manufacturers. During the following decade Baldwin-Lima-Hamilton struggled unsuccessfully and actually abandoned its locomotive business completely in 1956. With the abandonment of its once major product, B-L-H attempted a measure of diversification but without seeming success. In 1965 the company capitulated, conglomerating with Armour and Company.

It is interesting to note that in the absorption process only two B-L-H directors were moved to the parent company's board of directors and that only two of the B-L-H subsidiary's board members were B-L-H representatives. The subsidiary board, in the transition period, consisted of two B-L-H spokesmen and four Armour and Company representatives. This directorate balance is just one example of the tendency for the acquiring firm to depose the former directors of the acquired firm. This inference is discussed more fully in a subsequent chapter.

Focusing on the regression syndrome, it is easy to see why B-L-H was amenable to merger. The following figures show in percentages how B-L-H compared with approximate averages for large-scale industry in the decade before 1965:

	Sales	Assets	Net Income	Employees
B-L-H	− 15	− 9	− 30	− 48
Industry average	+ 73	+ 115	+ 30	+ 32

There can be no argument that B-L-H was retrogressing while industry in general was making very significant gains. These poor performance symptoms, taken as a whole, constitute the regression syndrome. In this as in most similar instances, the regression syndrome is an almost infallible sign of impending merger.

ARMOUR AND COMPANY

It is probably somewhat premature to judge the effectiveness of B-L-H's merger into Armour and Company. What data are available, however, indicate a continued second-rate performance. The following comparison combines B-L-H and Armour performance data (sales, assets, and net income are in million dollars) and shows:

	Sales	Assets	Net Income	Employees
1954	$2129	$616	$14.6	74,224
1964	2024	638	26.0	40,503
1968	2096	560	12.0	32,800
13-year change	−1%	−10%	−18%	−56%

This unimpressive record would qualify Armour and Company for ranking, performance-wise, in the bottom 10% of the billion dollar sales club. In this instance, as with B-L-H, the regression syndrome seems to be functioning. In the last two years three major financial maneuvers have been made to capture control of Armour. The first of these, Gulf and Western's acquisition of 750,000 Armour shares and subsequent pressure for merger, came to an end when the Justice Department let it be known that it was investigating the proposal for possible antitrust violations. Gulf and Western then profitably disposed of its massive block of stock by selling it at approximately $60 per share to General Host Corporation. (The open market price for Armour common stock was currently about $46, indicating a $10 million premium paid by General Host to Gulf and Western.)

This sudden shift in merger pressure, despite disclaimers by Richard C. Pistell, General Host's chairman, that this was simply an investment, prompted immediate Armour action. The company sold its fertilizer facilities to U. S. Steel for $130 million cash. In addition, it partially spun-off its Armour-Dial division, giving the stockholders the right to buy one Armour-Dial share for each four Armour shares held. This partial spin-off (up to 18% of Armour's total holding) raised $33 million and set a market price for its subsidiary's stock. In addition to the more than $160 million raised from the Armour-Dial partial spin-off and from the proceeds of its fertilizer plant sale, Armour sought additional liquidity by proposing a tender offer for nearly 20% of its outstanding stock. Eventually about 1.5 million shares were purchased at $50 per share. This substantial reduction in outstanding stock had a positive effect in reducing General Host's opportunities for purchasing Armour stock on the open market and, more significantly, in increasing Armour's per share earnings. This latter consideration was very important since the higher per share earnings would invariably lead to a higher market quotation and, consequently, more difficulty for any merger-minded conglomerate in a large-scale acquisition of Armour stock.

However, this financial maneuvering was in vain. General Host continued the battle and another contestant, Greyhound, entered the fray. Eventually, the price for Armour stock tenders rose to $72 per share. General Host claimed a 57% stock interest, whereas Greyhound said it had acquired 32% of Armour's stock. If these assertions were true, then this is a unique case where a large, publicly owned firm with 43,827 stockholders as recently as 1967 saw its public ownership become rather private as a result of merger maneuvers.

Late in 1969 General Host Corporation, suffering from the protracted "tight-money" squeeze, sold its 3,650,000-share equivalent in Armour to the Greyhound Corporation for a $220-million package in cash, preferred stock, Greyhound warrants, and Greyhound notes. With its previous 32% interest together with the 54% share acquired from General Host, Greyhound's 86% stake in Armour virtually guaranteed an imminent merger. However, the Justice Department almost immediately threatened action, contending that the sale to Greyhound violated the 1920 meat packers' consent decree. Under the 50-year-old consent decree, certain meat packers, including Armour, were enjoined from directly or indirectly dealing in certain listed commodities. Greyhound, because it has restaurant and food-catering operations, is engaged in lines of business that Armour cannot enter under the 1920 decree.

The battle for control of Armour had some very interesting organization-practice sidelights. At the May 1970 meeting of the 17-man board of directors, two of the directors failed to attend. This reversed the 9 to 8 balance of power in which the Greyhound group had control. Both absentee directors were members of the Greyhound faction and consequently the balance of power was 8 to 7, pro-General Host. Seizing this unusual opportunity the General Host faction succeeded in having the Armour board increased from 17 to 21 members with all four new positions being filled with General Host representatives. In addition, General Host's chairman, Harris J. Ashton, was designated chairman and chief executive of Armour. This episode brings into sharp focus the dangers inherent in a too-tight split-boardroom seat allocation between contending parties. Yet this practice is very common, particularly when two big corporations decide to merge (U. S. Plywood-Champion Papers; Montgomery Ward and Container Corporation).

A few days later in an equally surprising move the Interstate Commerce Commission approved the Greyhound plan to purchase a controlling interest in Armour. Although this ICC clearance was not the final step in the fight for control of Armour, it was a significant move. Meanwhile the Justice Department which had declared the purchase illegal made no comment.

As a sidelight General Host reported a $67.3 million loss for 1969, of which $58.3 was attributed to an extraordinary loss from sale of the company's investment in Armour.

ALLIS-CHALMERS MANUFACTURING COMPANY

In the last two years Allis-Chalmers, a firm with a very pronounced regression syndrome, has been considered for merger by aggressive conglomerators such as Ling-Temco-Vought, General Dynamics Corporation, Signal Companies, City Investing Company, Gulf and Western Industries, and White Consolidated Industries. The big, still unanswered question was aptly put by *Fortune* in a commentary on the first of these attempts. "The news that Ling was making a bid for Allis-Chalmers came as a stunning surprise to the business community. When the news broke it baffled a lot of people. First, why would Jimmy Ling—or anyone for that matter—*want* Allis-Chalmers?" [1]

Analysis of Allis-Chalmers' performance record further underscores this question. Since 1954 Allis-Chalmers has given more than adequate evidence that it suffers acutely from the regression syndrome. The data are summarized as follows:

Relative *Fortune* 500 Ranking

	1954	1968	Drop in Rank
Sales	54	130	76
Assets	59	121	62
Net income	64	499	435
Employees	43	110	67

[1] *Fortune*, "The Hidden Appeal of Allis-Chalmers," by Stanley H. Brown, 155 (November 1967).

This summary is a negative record not matched by many other large-scale corporations. Despite this long-run period of doldrums, James Ling offered as much as $55 per share of Allis-Chalmers' stock which up to that point had been selling at about $25 per share, reflecting a premium of about 100%. Allis-Chalmers' board rejected this bountiful offer stating it was holding merger talks with General Dynamics. This second proposal did not materialize and shortly after Signal Companies made its bid. Despite the apparent favorable inclination of both boards, stock-holders of both companies reacted negatively and the plans were called off reluctantly.

Within several months an attempt was made by City Investing Company to gain control through a stock exchange. When this failed, Gulf and Western Industries offered a package deal valued at about $120 million for three million shares of Allis-Chalmers' stock. The tender offer was successful and Gulf and Western acquired a 33% interest in Allis-Chalmers. The presumed merger, however, did not materialize. In a very short time White Consolidated Industries announced that it had agreed to purchase the 3,240,000 shares acquired by Gulf and Western for approximately $122 million.

The point to this narrative is that Allis-Chalmers continues to be a highly likely merger prospect as long as it manifests very obvious symptoms of the regression syndrome. (Its 1968 pretax *loss* was almost $55 million.) Ironically, Allis-Chalmers itself "became a conglomerate long before the sophisticated techniques for managing such diverse and far-flung enterprises evolved." [2] At present the firm's multiproduct manufacturing could be divided as follows:

33% :   Farm, industrial tractor, and outdoor power equipment
27% :   Industrial equipment
24% :   Construction, earth-moving, and processing equipment
16% :   Electrical equipment

In many respects this pristine conglomerate makes sense—its endeavors, although quite diverse, have logical production and marketing relationships. It could be that Allis-Chalmers, with its many complex problems, provides us with a preview of things to come for many a current-glowing conglomerate. The crux of this dilemma is the centralization-decentralization dichotomy. At Allis-Chalmers experience mandated a large measure of centralization with consequent imbalance between production and nonproduction employees. Late in 1968, with its 32,000 employees including 14,000 production workers and 18,000 nonproduc-

[2] *Ibid.*, p. 157.

tion employees, the firm's newly designated president, David C. Scott, embarked on an economy move. Three major production facilities were closed and consolidated with other more efficient plants. About 5000 nonproduction workers were to be dropped. The corporate staff was reduced sharply from 1500 to 100, with many functions moved from headquarters in an attempt to decentralize. These and similar steps taken to obtain greater efficiency seem to be the result of the six nonconsummated merger-marriage proposals. If this is so, then even the threat or imminence of merger can have therapeutic consequences. In this instance Allis-Chalmers' top decision makers, reacting to the chronic imminence of conglomeration, have hopefully been jolted out of their too-long complacency.

As a sequel Allis-Chalmers did seem to rebound, reversing its 1968 loss of $54.3 million into a 1969 profit of $18.4 million. Further encouragement was given management in its battle to retain sovereignty and identity by the early 1970 Supreme Court decision declining to review a lower court ruling that granted a preliminary injunction barring the takeover of Allis-Chalmers by White Consolidated Industries. This classic decision, a single typewritten line on a case to which the Government is not a party, might even be a turning point in future Government antitrust actions against large conglomerate mergers.

SUMMARY

Chronic, below-par corporate performance is the most obvious manifestation of what has been termed the regression syndrome. Merger and particularly conglomeration is, in a number of instances, suggested as a most effective catharsis for the causes that produce the corporate regression syndrome. In other words, merger, and even the threat of merger, can serve to jolt the somnolent into action. In such cases mergers provide a real therapy and valuable service to our society.

Considered from another angle, mergers provide the firm manifesting serious regression syndrome symptoms an opportunity to avoid the ordeal and embarrassment of bankruptcy. In this process, not only is there much "face-saving" but there also is a minimal wasting of the afflicted firm's resources in the scrappage of insolvency. Merger, then, is the enlightened method for bringing a sluggish but potentially productive firm back into the economic mainstream.

6

MERGER—MOTIVATION

Although there seems to be ample justification for a company, characterized by regression syndrome symptoms, to seek a union with a more dynamic firm, what about the firm making the merger offer? Why would any successful firm be prompted to acquire a chronic poor performer? Any attempt at establishing merger motivation from this direction must take into consideration at least these four broad causal categories:

1. Altruistic do-goodism, the urge to help the underdog to get back on his feet;
2. Recognition of hyperdepressed investment opportunities.
3. Money manipulation;
4. Managerial megalomania.

The mention of altruism—a sort of "help the underprivileged firm" attitude—should probably be set aside as a facetious comment. Nevertheless it is interesting to note that the current merger movement toward conglomeration coincides perfectly with the stress on ecumenism and do-goodism in virtually every other sector of society. Churches, universities, political parties, social clubs, and practically every type of American organization has accepted the "come-one, come-all" and "I am my brother's keeper" philosophies. Despite the lack of definitive evidence most Americans assume that the current ecumenism flows from an inherent humanitarianism. Perhaps a measure of this salvation mentality has seeped into the hearts and minds of what are generally assumed to be crass, cold, calculating captains of business.

On the other hand, it could be that the ecumenical mentality is strictly coincidental since industry has for a very long time pursued kindred mixing practices—blending in liquor and cigarettes, homogenation in milk and margarine, synthesis in rubber, chemicals and petroleum, and standardization in practically every stage in the industrial process. Although it would be difficult to prove that conglomeration in industry is affected by ecumenism in society, the two trends seem to move in parallel fashion. Perhaps, at least subconsciously, the social-ecumenical conditioning of the investing public has resulted in its viewing of conglomerates as ecumenical economic umbrellas.

More logic and evidence can be given to support the second causal factor: the recognition of hyperdepressed investment opportunities. In by far the great majority of acquisitions there is solid evidence to show that the merger-prone company is valued inadequately by the investing public. This stock market neglect is manifested in the following:

1. A price to earnings ratio (P/E) significantly lower than the average prevailing in the current market.

2. A book value in excess of the prevailing market price for the company's stock.

3. Closely correlated to the preceding condition is the company's excess liquidity. This characteristic can be measured in a higher-than-average ratio of cash and equivalent to productively used resources.

4. An inability by the general public to appraise properly a company's undervalued assets. This is a bookkeeping gimmick which frequently gives the "insider" and the shrewd analyst an inordinate advantage.

There is ample evidence to support all these contentions; for example, in checking the 40 major companies which were merged, or almost merged, into other leading corporations in 1967 and 1968 only eight had P/E ratios of 15 or higher. Conversely, of the 40 aggressor firms, 25 had P/E ratios of 15 or higher. The median P/E ratios for these 40 mergers was 16 for the dominant firms and 11 for the acquired firms. This is indicative of the overall investment psychology; the investing public seems to have ignored, avoided, or forgotten the great majority of firms that ultimately capitulated to merger offers.

Yet it is intriguing to note the disparity in investment yields between these two categories—the aggressor and the acquired firms. The 40 aggressors had yields averaging 1.3% as contrasted with an average yield of 3.4 for the 40 acquired firms. Table 6-1 provides six examples of this disparity in both yields and price to earnings ratios between aggressor and acquiescing partners in some fairly recent mergers.

Among the 73 corporations which, during 1967–1968, could be called institutional favorites, the P/E ratio averaged 17 (with a range from 9 to 67) and yields averaged 3.5 (with a range from 0.4 to 5.9). These institutional favorites, including a very large proportion of blue chip stocks,

Table 6-1   Some Examples of P/E and Yield Variance Between Merging Companies

	Yield	P/E Ratio
LTV	1.3	14
Wilson	5.0	10
Jones and Laughlin	5.8	11
ITT	1.8	21
Rayonier	4.4	8
Canteen	3.5	18
FMC	2.3	17
Link Belt	5.9	9
RCA	2.2	20
St. Regis Paper	4.6	13
Illinois Central	2.7	17
ABEX	5.6	9
American Standard	3.1	26
WABCO	4.3	16

Note. Indentation indicates merged firm.

might be considered as the epitome of investor acceptance. It should be noted that the 40 companies which capitulated to merger during the test period had yields quite comparable to those of the typical institutional favorite. By contrast the aggressor firms in these mergers had significantly lower yields. On the other hand, the 40 acquired firms had considerably lower P/E ratios than the institutional favorites, whereas the merger-aggressor firms approximated the institutional favorites' P/E ratios. If the 73 institutional favorites can be visualized as being in "balance" (as shown in Figure 6-1), the acquired firms can be assumed to be strong on yield but rather weak on P/E ratios. Conversely, the firms aggressively seeking merger are strong on P/E ratios but weak on yields. As a related item it should be pointed out that during this test period not a single one of the 73 institutional favorites capitulated to merger and only 11 of these 73 leading firms made merger proposals of any consequence to other companies.

The investing public's lack of faith in the 40 companies recently acquired by other corporations, as evidenced in the low P/E ratios, has a logical basis. During the period 1956–1966 these firms had a considerably below par performance as measured by earnings per share. *Fortune's* total listing of 500 top industrial corporations during this period had an average earnings per share growth rate of 5.83%. The 40 acquired com-

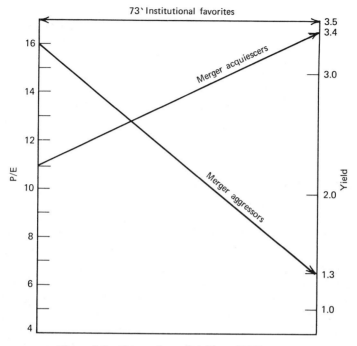

Figure 6-1 Comparison of yields and PIE ratios.

panies averaged only 2.57% and 11 of this group (or 28%) actually had declined in the earnings per share norm. By contrast out of the total *Fortune* list only 12% of the firms declined in their earnings per share. While on the subject of growth rates for earnings per share, we note that during this decade some leading conglomerates posted almost fantastic increases shown as follows:

Company	Percent Increase in Earnings per Share 1957–1967
Occidental Petroleum	56.83
Avnet	49.83
Ling-Temco-Vought	38.96
Gulf and Western	35.85
Litton	33.01

By contrast some of the better known firms amenable to merging included some of the poorest performers:

Company	Percent Increase in Earnings per Share 1957–1967
St. Regis	0.77
Sharon Steel	6.55
Westinghouse Air Brake	− 0.75
Jones and Laughlin	− 2.60
Newport News Shipping	− 0.13
Allis-Chalmers	− 14.36

Although a large proportion of the merged companies give ample evidence of the regression syndrome, it is important to note that this does not imply that these firms are all money losers; for example, during the last 13 years, *Fortune*'s 500 lists a total of 78 companies that lost money for one or more years. Although it might seem logical to expect that a major portion of these firms would be absorbed by more successful companies, actually only 19 companies (24%) were so acquired. This percentage is about the same as that for the entire *Fortune* listing, since out of the 750-plus companies listed in *Fortune*'s tabulation over this period, approximately 209 or one-fourth have disappeared through merger. In other words, money losers are not particularly sought out for merger and there is sound logic to support this contention. In the older, more conventional mergers the acquisition was accomplished through an exchange of common stock or by outright cash purchase. Relatively few of the current rash of mergers are so financed. The most typical financing at present is through subordinated debentures or cumulative convertible preferred stock. It must be stressed that both types of securities are subject to relatively fixed annual charges. Consequently, the acquired firm must continue to earn at a rate sufficiently high to meet all these bond and preferred stock obligations and, in addition, to provide a "surplus" which is added to the acquiring company's net income. This is the leverage factor, or trading on the equity, which is certainly good business practice during periods of prosperity but can become an impossible burden in business reverses.

The third broad factor prompting some mergers—money manipulation—is obviously quite closely associated with the second factor, the recognition of hyperdepressed investment opportunities. The following illustrations, hopefully, will focus on a few recent entrepreneureal *coups des forces* underlying some interesting mergers.

NEWPORT NEWS SHIPBUILDING AND DRY DOCK COMPANY

Late in 1968 Newport News Shipbuilding and Dry Dock Company stockholders voted in a special meeting to sell their company to Tenneco for about $123 million of securities. At that time Newport News invested capital was approximately $90 million. Simple arithmetic indicates that Tenneco was thus willing to pay a premium of $33 million or approximately 37%. The package deal provided for the exchange of each Newport News share into one-half share of Tenneco common and $60 of 7%, 25-year debenture. Since Tenneco was then selling on the New York Stock Exchange at about $27 per share, this deal was equivalent to about $72 per share of Newport News stock. Before the merger proposal, Newport News common stock was selling at between $55 and $57. At the successful termination of merger negotiations, Newport News stock spurted $13.13 in a single day, indicating investor recognition of a sizable merger bonus.

Although the reaction by Newport News stockholders was fairly obvious (they were supposedly making a killing), the motivation underlying Tenneco's generosity is less obvious. Since the package deal given Newport News stockholders would cost (interest and dividends):

$100.2 of debentures at 7%	$7,000,000
850,000 Tenneco shares at $1.28	1,100,000
Annual cost of Newport acquisition	$8,100,000

it is difficult to see Tenneco's strategy. In the relatively "good" year of 1967 Newport News earned $6,598,000, a sum inadequate to cover the annual dividend and interest obligation now assumed by Tenneco.

Although the immediate causal factors probably do not seem to warrant this juncture, it should be pointed out that (a) Newport News was debt free, thus permitting the leverage maneuver; (b) Newport News facilities were acquired years ago and consequently were undervalued in the light of 1968's inflation; (c) Newport News sales to assets ratio was at $2.20, whereas Tenneco's ratio was only $0.50. This acquisition would up somewhat the firm's assets productivity, and (d) the shipbuilding industry had gone through a 20-year catharsis and presumably was close to rock bottom with nowhere to go but up.

JONES AND LAUGHLIN STEEL CORPORATION

Ling-Temco-Vought's acquisition of Jones and Laughlin Steel illustrates still another aspect of merger money manipulation. In May 1968 Ling-Temco-Vought obtained a 63% interest in Jones and Laughlin through a cash tender offer of $85 per share for 5,000,000 shares of common stock. This was an amazing offer since during the previous five months Jones and Laughlin stock ranged between $45 and $50 per share. Consequently, the tender offer was equivalent to a bonus of about $35 per share for an aggregate of $175 million. This tactic is almost identical with that used by Ling-Temco-Vought in its acquisition of Wilson and Company when a tender offer for 750,000 shares was made at $62.50, which was $13 above the prevailing market price.

In justification it is important to note that Jones and Laughlin's common stock did seem to be undervalued on the market. At the time of tender it had a book value of $85.29 per share as contrasted with the $50 market price. Financial analysts also noted that Jones and Laughlin had an estimated cash flow per share of $12.75, the largest in the industry. "U. S. Steel Corp., for example, was shown with a book value of $59.48, and a $39 market price and a cash flow of $9.74." [1]

In hindsight the Jones and Laughlin gambit turned out to be nothing but grief for LTV. In less than two years two unexpected strikes occurred while the industry enjoyed comparative labor peace. In addition, modernization problems, steel price cutting, and other headaches, helped plunge earnings to the point in which dividends could not be covered in three of the last five quarters. Coupled with the generally depressed stock market, Jones and Laughlin shares plummeted to the extent that paper losses to LTV were calculated at about $289 million. In turn LTV stock, which just three years ago reached a peak of $170, slumped to a low of $7 per share. To compound matters the Justice Department instituted antitrust actions to force LTV to sell its Jones and Laughlin stock.

LTV in both its Jones and Laughlin and Wilson ventures used cash as the acquisition media. However, it is equally important to note that LTV's invested capital position is extremely light. In 1966, when LTV ranked 168 in sales, it placed 423 in size of invested capital. In 1967 the respective rankings were 38 and 159, whereas in 1969 they were 14 and 179. In *Fortune's* 1970 listing LTV shows only $268 million in invested capital (as contrasted, for example, with Standard Oil's (New Jersey) $10,092 million and General Motor's $10,228 million).

[1] *Business Week,* 104 (May 18, 1968).

Ling-Temco-Vought's financing strategy stresses long-term borrowing. In May 1970 the company had a $1500 million outstanding debt—a significantly high ratio in comparison to its invested capital. Together with its reliance on borrowings, LTV, perhaps of necessity, seems committed to a policy of working with minority interests. On acquiring control of Wilson and Company, LTV spun-off sizable minority interests through public sales, thus reducing its ownership interest but at the same time obtaining needed cash. The same technique was used successfully in its Braniff subsidiary (once 80% owned), its National Car component (once 55% owned), and its Computer Technology subsidiary (once 70% owned). In the Jones and Laughlin instance the 63% interest could be easily reduced somewhat in order to raise needed cash.

CONTRASTING STRATEGIES

The first two illustrations focus on two extreme financing strategies frequently used in conglomeration. In the first instance no cash is needed and ownership is only partially diluted. The stress is on acceptance by the stockholders of the merged firm of a major portion of their investment's value in the form of debentures. This requires a convincing of these stockholders that they have a good deal—a significant bonus plus an increased annual return.

In the second instance stockholder acceptance is achieved more directly through a sizable immediate profit in the cash tender offer. This is most appealing to the profit-conscious investor. However, it now becomes necessary to borrow huge sums from professional lenders and, consequently, a different type of convincing is necessary.

In the Tenneco illustration the financial pressures are basically internal since the debenture holders, at least initially, are also company stockholders. In LTV's case the lenders are largely institutions and so LTV could be subjected to significant external financial pressures. For example, when LTV borrowed $70 million to finance the Wilson takeover, $40 million was provided as a two-year loan by a consortium of British bankers and $30 million came from American investors scattered among 34 institutions, none of whom assumed a major role. The second loan was also on a relatively short-term basis. As a concomitant of LTV heavy-borrowing strategy, its conglomerate structure tends to be quite fluid and components are disposed of when bond repayment pressures become severe.

While on the subject of money manipulation, it must be reemphasized that a booming economy and spiraling stock market prices facilitate merging. Invariably the firm making the offer has experienced a progressive increase in the market valuation of its common shares. Consequently, any stock exchange offer that it makes will appear quite generous. As stated previously, these merger bonuses ranged between 20 and 40%. The following examples are illustrations.

Gulf and Western's late 1968 abortive bid for control of Sinclair Oil Corporation raised Sinclair's market price from approximately $78 to over $105 per share in about two weeks. This was an increase of about 35%, prompted by no other reason than the belief that merging Sinclair into Gulf and Western would miraculously vitalize Sinclair's performance.

In some instances the suspicion is that the merger bonus evidenced in the stock market price differential is aimed at holders of large blocks of stock. Teledyne's November 1968, $50-a-share tender offer for all 2,-570,898 outstanding shares of Ryan Aeronautical Company stock could be an example. Before the offer Ryan Aeronautical stock had moved in the $30 to $35 range. The 40% or so hike in the tender offer purchase price would in this case mean an appreciation between $4 and $5 million in the 10% ownership interest held by T. Claude Ryan, chairman of the corporation. Windfalls of this sort are almost beyond rejection.

The Glen Alden Corporation's purchase of 945,126 Schenley Industries' shares from Lewis S. Rosenstiel for $75.6 million in cash and promissory notes could be another such instance. This was equal to a price of about $80 per share. During the preliminary stock price shuffling which preceded Glen Alden's takeover of Schenley, Schenley's stock was selling between $43 and $52 per share. It does not seem to be overly cynical to assume that the markup of at least 60% was less than a subtle inducement to win over the major holders of Schenley stock. Relative to the Glen Alden-Schenley takeover, Glen Alden's 1968 proxy statement disclosed that the Federal Trade Commission "wishes to examine possible antitrust and related aspects." The proxy statement also indicated that there were some 18 legal actions instituted by stockholders charging that the $5 million paid in finders fees for the Schenley acquisition were excessive and that the terms given Mr. Rosenstiel for his stock were much more favorable than those given other stockholders in the tender offer.

Sometimes this generosity boomerangs. One of the largest proposed mergers, the $1.5 billion Xerox Corporation's bid to acquire C.I.T. Financial Corporation, fell apart just six weeks after it was first announced. Xerox, the largest manufacturer of office copying equipment, proposed a stock swap of one Xerox share for every 3⅞ shares of C.I.T. stock. On the basis of C.I.T. common share prices before merger negotiations this meant that about $180 worth of C.I.T. stock would now be converted into a share of Xerox stock selling at about $290. This sizable differential, in excess of $100 per unit, represented a premium of more than 50%. As was to be expected, C.I.T. common stock quickly reflected this generous consideration by zooming from the mid-$40 range to $60 a share. What the experts failed to anticipate was a strong negative reaction by holders of Xerox stock. Within two days Xerox stock dropped more than $20 and within a week the stock was selling at 10% less than it was the day before the merger proposal announcement. This unusual negative response by Xerox stockholders was equivalent to a decrease in the market valuation of Xerox stock of over $500 million. Pessimism inducing this 10% drop in Xerox stock prices stemmed largely from the feeling that this acquisition would seriously lower Xerox's growth rate. In mid-November 1968, just six weeks after the proposal was first made public, Xerox and C.I.T. jointly announced that the merger negotiations were terminated by mutual agreement. Immediately, C.I.T. stock dropped to its premerger level and Xerox bounced back to its premerger level.

The fourth motivational factor, managerial megalomania, is understandably difficult to prove or even to illustrate. As a starting point, consider that virtually every one of the newer conglomerates was or is the handiwork of a single indomitable entrepreneur; this is quite vividly shown in Tables 7-2, 7-3, and 7-4. In practically every instance the propelling force in these and almost all conglomerates was, or is, a self-made business leader. Whether these talented and strong-willed men are trying to prove themselves or whether they are compulsive in their drive has not been established adequately by business analysts, business philosophers, or social psychologists. Meanwhile the merger binge continues.

7

MERGERS AND THE
MANAGEMENT REVOLUTION

A quarter of a century ago James Burnham wrote about the shift in organizational control away from the old-style, owner-dominated hierarchical pattern to a new-style, broader-based technocratic-, professional-manager structure.[1] Burnham's *Managerial Revolution* postulated that the key variable or strategic factor in a technologically oriented society is the person who can identify technological needs and then fill them effectively. Obviously this person must himself have a technical competency if he is to develop and exercise his organizing capabilities in such an environment.

In other words, the essence of Burnham's thesis is something all managers and management theorists have known for a long time, namely, that the locus of control has shifted from owner-entrepreneurs to paid professional managers. The reasons for this evolutionary transition are so obvious they need not be enumerated here. However, and this is the significant point, Burnham premises a production- or product-oriented concept of industrial organization. In this context professional managers could be equated with supertechnicians and functional experts who are intimately acquainted with a specific product line or a related family of product lines.

In its narrower connotations Burnham's thesis would have meaning in mergers insofar as technician-managers would necessarily displace the less technically qualified owner-entrepreneurs. Since presumably the supply of dynamic supertalented technician-managers is very limited,

[1] James Burnham, *The Managerial Revolution*, The John Day Company, New York, 1941.

these scarce but essential experts would best be utilized if smaller firms joined together in larger ventures. If we assume a product-oriented industrial structure, this would justify or at least explain many mergers based on backward and forward integration, on horizontal integration, and particularly on diversification stressing by-product utilization, product-line expansion, plant capacity maximization, and broader use of available technical knowhow. The preponderance of these types of mergers during the first half of this century corroborates the increasing role of the technician-professional managers in effective merging.

The current conglomerate thrust certainly does not ignore this vital role of the technician-professional managers. In fact, with the accelerating tempo in technological advancement, the value of this kind of manager is even more universally recognized both in pay and in prestige. In the area of pay average salaries for chief executives in the top 500 American industrial firms are now edging beyond the $250,000 per year level, increasing annually at about 5 to 7%. Table 7-1 shows that at General Motors the top five executives, each a technician-manager, averaged $586,000 in 1968. That year the top six technician-managers at Ford Motor Company averaged $482,660 in salaries and bonuses. These figures do not include fringe items such as stock options, insurance policies, dividends, and appreciation of the company's stock owned by these executives.

Table 7-1

	1968		
General Motors Corporation	Salary	Other Payments	Total Compensation
James M. Roche, Chairman	$225,000	$427,500	$652,500
George Russell, Vice-Chairman	202,500	386,250	588,750
Edward N. Cole, President	202,500	386,250	588,750
Edward D. Rollert, Exec. V.-P.	180,000	367,500	547,500
Roger M. Kyes, Exec. V.-P.	180,000	367,500	547,500
Ford Motor Company			
Henry Ford II, Chairman	$200,000	$400,000	$600,000
Semen E. Knudsen, President	180,952	400,000	580,952
Arjay Miller, Vice-Chairman	175,000	295,000	470,000
Lee A. Iacocca, Exec. V.-P.	150,000	295,000	445,000
Robert Stevenson, Exec. V.-P.	150,000	260,000	410,000
J. Edward Lundy, Exec. V.-P.	140,000	250,000	390,000

In the area of prestige the growing stature of the manager-executive is reflected, for example, in the tremendous increase in the number of such individuals included in *Who's Who in America* listings. In the first volume (1899–1900) approximately 150 industrialists were among the total 8602 names listed in this first tabulation. Virtually all of these 150 industrialists were old-school entrepreneurs or industrial-financiers. In the current 1970-1971 Volume 36 of *Who's Who in America* about one-third of the 65,000 plus listings are business leaders, most of whom could be called technician-managers. On the basis of these facts it seems evident that today's social and financial elite includes a very large proportion of technician-professional managers.

However, even as the pay, prestige, image, and acceptance of professional managers reaches loftier heights, it seems that a new breed is coming into prominence. For lack of a better term we might tentatively refer to this new breed as the macromanagers. They do not seem to be concerned primarily with making a better product or in reducing costs through increased scale of operation or in maximizing profits through oligopolistic tactics. Rather, they seem to be far more concerned in welding together a multipurpose enterprise. Supposedly they seek the benefits of diverse venture, adhering to and perhaps even exaggerating that worn-thin adage that warns against putting all of one's eggs into a single basket. Corollary to this reasoning is the very common-sense realization that massive corporate size also means massive financial, political, and technical impact.

The conglomerate surge, at least superficially, seems to go one step beyond Burnham's thesis that the strategic force in modern industrial enterprise is the supertechnician-professional manager. The growing incidence of conglomerates whose propelling force is a single individual, a professional manager *but* a nontechnician, focuses upon this presumed changing need. A quick glance at the roster of leading conglomerates and the men who have welded these neocorporations supports this contention. Table 7-2 lists 50 of the better known conglomerates that have emerged within the last decade. Although it might be somewhat of an exaggeration, it has been said that each of these neocorporations was the brain child of one man's imagination and drive. Tracing the educational and experience backgrounds of these eminent leaders, it is rather astounding to note that they, as a group, are definitely not in the pattern prescribed by James Burnham's *Managerial Revolution*. A number of this group have not even been adequately recognized to be listed in *Who's Who in America*. Undoubtedly, the very recentness and the meteoric speed with which these neoentrepreneurs attained eminence accounts for this void in listing. Nevertheless, it also points to the fact that

Table 7-2 Fifty "First Generation" Conglomerates

1969 Fortune Rank	Company	Dominant Force
25	Ling-Temco-Vought	James J. Ling
40	Litton Industries	Charles B. Thornton
48	Occidental Petroleum	Armand Hammer
69	Gulf & Western	Charles G. Bluhdorn
94	Ogden Corp.	Ralph E. Ablon
100	Boise Cascade	R. V. Hansberger
110	Norton Simon	Norton Simon
113	AMK Corp.	Eli M. Black
124	Teledyne	Henry E. Singleton
143	White Consolidated Industries	E. S. Reddig
144	Glen Alden	Meshulam Riklis
		Albert List
153	Colt Industries	George A. Strichman
	(Penn Texas)	(Leopold Silberstein)
161	Dresser Industries	John Lawrence
163	U. S. Industries	John Billera
176	Kidde (Walter)	Fred R. Sullivan
235	Crane Co.	Thomas M. Evans
252	Indian Head	James E. Robinson
		Robert W. Lear
266	Evans Products	Monford A. Orloff
267	National Industries	Stanley Yarmuth
		(Bernard H. Barnett)
277	"Automatic" Sprinkler	Harry E. Figgie, Jr.
287	Walter (Jim)	J. W. Walter
		J. O. Alston
310	Norris Industries	Kenneth T. Norris
326	Bangor Punta	N. M. Salgo
350	General Instrument	Martin H. Benedek
354	Avnet, Inc.	Lester Avnet
358	Great Western United	William M. White, Jr.
365	Maremont Corp.	Arnold H. Maremont
368	Fuqua	J. B. Fuqua
373	Questor	Reuben W. Askanase
380	City Investing Co.	R. W. Dowling
		George T. Scharffenberger
389	General Host	Richard C. Pistell
401	Sanders Associates	R. C. Sanders
410	Bath Industries	William D. Kyle, Jr.

Table 7-2   Fifty "First Generation" Conglomerates (Continued)

1969 Fortune Rank	Company	Dominant Force
Unlisted (Random)	Leasco Data Processing Equipment Co.	Saul P. Steinberg
	U.S. Smelting	Jack Wilder
		Martin Horwitz
	B.V.D. Co.	Sol Kittay
	Saturn Industries	J. R. Driscoll
		J. F. McKinney
	TransAmerica	H. R. Brower
		J. R. Beckett
	Seilon, Inc.	Edward Lamb
	BSF Co.	Victor Muscat
	Merritt-Chapman & Scott	Louis Wolfson
	Haven Industries	D. E. Liederman
		Neil Rosenstein
	U. S. Hoffman Machinery	Harold Roth
	International Controls Corp.	Robert L. Vesco
	NVF	Victor Posner
	Perfect Film & Chemical Co.	Martin S. Ackerman
	Beck Industries	Newton Glekel
	MSL Industries	J. T. Zoline
	VTR	Frederic Gould
	Liquidonics Industries	N. Norman Muller
	Monogram Industries	Martin Stone
	Electronic Data Systems	H. Ross Perot
	Resorts International	James Crosby
	Gould-National Batteries Inc.	William T. Ylvisaker

these unlisted successes did not progress to the top in the manner presumably prescribed by the *Managerial Revolution*. Practically none of the neoentrepreneurs are technician-professional managers.

This contention is bolstered by scanning further this sample of 50 new industrial leaders, noting that only about half have earned college degrees. This is in complete variance with recent studies of large-scale industrial corporate leaders' educational backgrounds. It has been pointed out that in the sphere of business over 83% of today's top leaders have earned a first degree and about 25% have earned advanced degrees.[2]

[2] Stanley C. Vance, "Higher Education for the Executive Elite," *California Management Review*, **VIII**, 4, 21–30 (summer 1966).

Yet in the current small sample of 50 new conglomerate founders, only about half have earned college degrees and less than 10% have advanced degrees.

This significant deviation could be interpreted in several ways. On the basis of so small a sample it would be rash to conclude that a college education is a waste of time for one aspiring to get to the top in large-scale enterprise just as it would be equally rash to simply shrug off this phenomenon as a fluke. The examples set by these captains of conglomerates give added credence to the theory that leadership is a self-developed attribute rather than something that automatically accompanies a sheepskin. Perhaps real leadership talent stems from an indomitable drive, together with the ability to size up a promising situation, to recognize where and when action is needed, and when to take the required risks. Although the conventional education process adds to one's fund of facts and figures and expands vocabulary proficiency resulting in higher I.Q.'s, it also dulls the acquisitive instincts and risk-taking propensities. Following this negative reasoning, one might say that a conventional college grooming trains talented youngsters for filling business bureaucracy posts and in typical bureaucratic fashion these degree recipients "play it safe," "go by the book," "never rock the boat." They fulfill their prescribed duties to the letter, but the letter is always in lower-case; it is never a big, bold, prominent capital letter. The run-of-the-mill degree holders tend to perform competently in the carefully specified routine channels but rarely do they venture into the unknown or undefined. With typical bureaucratic caution they tend to bypass all problems and situations that seem to require going beyond standard operating procedure. Yet by definition and the exception principle it is top management's prime job to solve problems when no answer is found in "the book," and to chart courses of action even when no ready "road map" exists.

Although this is not to be interpreted as an attack on modern higher education, it might be the proper time for a value analysis to determine if our hallowed halls of ivy are really fashioning leaders or merely mass-producing a plethora of conformist bureaucrats. Presumably a deeper analysis could show that as conglomerates age, they too will tend to conform and superaggressive individualist-types will give way once again to Burnham's technician-professional managers. However, we are limited timewise for testing purposes since even second generation conglomerates such as Textron, Burlington Industries, FMC, and General Tire (see Table 7-3) have had less than 20 years experience. Yet it could be significant to note that in the relatively small sample of second-generation conglomerates, the education index of top executives is notably higher than that characterizing the 50 new conglomerates

(Table 7-2). Along this same line of reasoning, it should be noted also in Table 7-4 that old-line firms (Singer, ITT, Grace, Georgia-Pacific, Tenneco) which have quite recently adapted to conglomeration show far more conventional educational patterns in their top leaders. Practically all the chief executives, chairmen, and presidents of these revamped and revitalized firms have earned college degrees.

These last two observations—the fact that old-line firms venturing into conglomeration have college-degree leaders and that a higher incidence of college degrees is found in second-generation conglomerate top

Table 7-3   Some Leading Second-Generation Conglomerates

1969 Fortune Rank	Company	Initiating Force	Current Leadership
27	General Dynamics	John Jay Hopkins	Chairman and President Roger Lewis
47	Textron	Royal Little	Chairman R. C. Thompson, Jr. President G. W. Miller
52	Burlington Industries	James S. Love	Chairman H. E. Rauch Vice Chairman J. C. Cowan, Jr. Chairman, Executive Committee E. R. Zane President C. F. Myers, Jr.
65	FMC	Paul L. Davies	Hon. Chairman J. D. Crummey Chairman J. M. Hait Vice Chairman B. J. Carter President J. M. Pope
78	AVCO Corp.	Victor Emmanuel	Chairman K. R. Wilson, Jr. Chairman, Executive Committee C. H. Blaik Vice Chairman R. Harrington President J. R. Kerr
97	General Tire	William O'Neil	Chairman T. F. O'Neil Hon. Chairman L. A. McQueen Chairman, Executive Committee J. O'Neil President M. G. O'Neil

Table 7-4   Some Currently Conglomerating "Established" Firms

1969 Fortune Rank	Company	Dominant Force
11	International Tel. & Tel.	Harold S. Geneen
20	Radio Corp. of America	David Sarnoff
29	North American Rockwell	Willard F. Rockwell, Jr.
38	Armour	William W. Prince
39	Tenneco Inc.	Gardiner Symonds
43	Singer Co.	Donald P. Kircher
45	Grace (W. R.)	J. Peter Grace
68	Signal Cos.	S. B. Mosher
74	Reynolds Industries	Bowman Gray
85	American Brands	Robert B. Walker
101	Georgia Pacific	Owen R. Cheatam
140	Studebaker-Worthington	R. H. Guthrie F. J. Nunlist
142	Northwest Industries	Ben W. Heineman
170	National Distillers	John E. Bierwirth
189	Whittaker	William R. Whittaker
261	Times Mirror	Norman Chandler
347	Fairchild C & I	Sherman M. Fairchild
422	General Signal	Nathan R. Owen
T1	Penn-Central	S. T. Saunders A. E. Perlman
T12	Greyhound Corp.	Gerald H. Trautman
R6	Marcor	R. E. Brooker
	Hughes Tool Co.	Howard Hughes

executives—point to a dichotomy regarding the commonly held notion that a higher education degree is becoming more and more a critical factor for business success.

Another very pertinent observation in the sample of 50 conglomerate leaders, as listed in Table 7-2, is the fact that they have had relatively little experience in lower-level managerial positions in which they could demonstrate their technical competencies. Typically, in large-scale industrial enterprise, it takes between 20 and 30 years for an individual to move to the top executive posts. By contrast the new builders of conglomerates spent only from 5 to 10 years progressing to the top in the typical organizational sequencing before becoming the chief executive. If this fact is accepted, then the concept of leadership by professional managers needs reviewing because professional managers are supposed to acquire their competency through long years of experience, shortened in some cases by intensive education. Yet here we have a situation in which the experience factor is minimal and the education prerequisite is less than standard.

This relatively short in-firm management development period seems to confirm that risk-taking rather than routine bureaucratic performance is the hallmark of the neoentrepreneur. Restlessness and a determination to progress upward characterize this group of conglomerate captains. If we assume that our enterprise system not only tolerates but even favors the risk-taker as versus the bureaucratic professional manager, then Burnham's thesis is even more seriously questioned.

Another point of interest is worth stressing: these conglomerate captains rarely relinquish ultimate control until forced to do so. They almost never rely on committees and even curtail the functions of their boards of directors. "Almost all acquisition companies are highly personalized organizations," says Martin Stone, president of Monogram Industries, a Los Angeles conglomerate. (When executives of the company, which once specialized in aircraft toilets, launched their successful acquisition program, security analysts began calling Monogram "those wonderful men and their flying latrines.") [3] Not a single new conglomerate uses the Office-of-the-President concept of top authority even though the conglomerate's complexity and diversity would seem to warrant such an approach. Despite the confederation character of most conglomerates, seldom is there even a semblance of collegiality in the boardroom or the executive committee. In two-thirds of the new conglomerate cases the *leader* either holds more than one official title, or there simply is no meaningful second-in-command. For example, John Lawrence is chairman, president, and chief executive officer at Dresser Industries; Armand Hammer is, likewise, chairman, president, and chief executive officer at Occidental Petroleum. Although Franklin A. Lindsay is president of ITEK, there is no chairman.

In many instances, even though a company has the conventional hierarchical rankings, effective control is still a one-man thing. (Note Norton Simon's dynamic, even if titleless, position at Norton Simon Industries.) Meshulam Riklis holds only the chairman's post at Glen Alden and similarly Sherman Fairchild is chairman at Fairchild Camera and Instrument, but there is no question about where control is vested. "Automatic" Sprinkler's Harry E. Figgie, Jr., chairman and chief executive officer, at the first reversal in the company's history, fired with one fell

[3] *The Wall Street Journal,* 8 (August 12, 1968).

swoop the company president and four presidents of divisions. At Walter M. Kidde and Company, Fred R. Sullivan, Chairman and Chief Executive Officer, assumed the roles of president and chief operating officer when Kidde's president, Franc M. Ricciardi, left the company.

In the last column of Table 7-3 note what has taken place in second-generation titular ranking. The six-company sample less than a decade ago had no more than *one* readily recognizable and almost absolute head per company. With the passing of these forceful neoentrepreneurs the six companies in question have fragmented top leadership into a multiplicity of functions and titles so that the original six leaders have now expanded to at least 19 superstrata executives. The fragmentation of the once almost absolute authority is much greater than appears in such summary statistics; at Textron, for example, Royal Little was unquestionably *the* sole source of major decisions. Subsequent to his leaving the top post, the once officer-devoid board of directors has changed somewhat from a two to nine officer-director and outside-director balance to a four to eight ratio. There are now 13 vice-presidents and, most significantly, Textron has established the new post of divisional president of which there are 11 out of Textron's 34 divisions. It does seem inevitable that much of the formerly centralized authority has been or very soon will be given to the major operating divisions.

On the basis of this and related bits of evidence it might be concluded that the neoentrepreneurs with macromanager capabilities are a rare breed indeed, and that upon their death or retirement they tend to be replaced by the more conventional, or even prosaic, professional managers, as was postulated by Burnham. This refocuses on the inadequately researched contention that the new conglomerate captains are but a fleeting phenomenon in the longer run course of business enterprise.

In addition to the fragmentation of top-level control so recently concentrated in the conglomerating founder, there are other very visible manifestations of a return to professional manager or even to bureaucratic conformity. Nearly every person listed in the current leadership column in Table 7-3 is a college graduate and a long-time team member in his respective corporation. His background includes a finely honed technical competency in at least one functional field and a managerial experience extending back to one, two, or even three decades. Not one of these new leaders in the second-generation conglomerates can be termed a managerial maverick. On the contrary they are members of the business establishment and their business behavior can be almost predicted. These Pavlovian professional managers will do what they are supposed to do as predicated by their grooming, the expectations of the business community, and their response to peer-pressures.

The contrast in top leadership types is shown graphically in Table 7-5, which contrasts the relative significance of 12 selected aspects, or traits, in four corporate categories. On the basis of the 12 selected management-related items, it is obvious that the men generating the momentum in the new multiindustry ventures are much different from those in

Table 7-5   Relative Significance of Selected Management Aspects in Four Corporate Categories

	Conglomerating Firms			
	First Generation $n=50$	Second Generation $n=6$	Old Line $n=25$	Major Non-Conglomerates $n=25$
Education	°°	°°°°	°°°°	°°°°°
Ivy League	°	°°	°°°°	°°°°
Elitist	°	°°	°°°°°	°°°°°
Founding families	°	°°	°°°°	°°°
Who's Who	°°	°°°°	°°°°°	°°°°°
Civic participation	°°	°°°	°°°°°	°°°°°
Image	°	°°	°°°°	°°°°°
Corporate Interlock	°	°°	°°°	°°°°°
Management Experience	°	°°°°°	°°°	°°°°°
Executive Committee: O. P.	°	°°°°	°°	°°°°°
Collegiality	°	°°°	°°	°°°°
Ownership	°°°	°°	°°°°	°°

Key: °—Little; °°—some; °°°—average; °°°°—much; °°°°°—very much

the other three categories. This is particularly contrasted between the new conglomerators and the heads of major nonconglomerated firms that is, those so frequently considered the establishment. This group tends toward the high-image, well educated, socially prominent, civically active, scientific, and professional management types. The new conglomerators, relatively speaking, are not of this ilk. They do, however, bring to mind the almost forgotten breed of entrepreneurs, the Henry Fords, John D. Rockefellers, J. P. Morgans—the men who built our enterprise system. Focusing on only two basic traits, elitism and education, the contrast is most marked. The new conglomerators with very few exceptions have not come from American aristocracy. The Mayflower Society and the DAR will find few recruits in this group of dynamic enterprisers. Perhaps this is significant: these are "have nots" with little time or interest for the frills of life because they have a major mission to fulfill.

This lack of elitist traits was classically highlighted at an eventful (May 27, 1970) White House dinner, given by President Nixon for the very top of our nation's business leaders. One of the guests, Mr. Isidore M. Cohen, president of Joseph H. Cohen & Sons, a subsidiary of the conglomerate Rapid-American Corporation made the news media headlines by his disestablishmentarian behavior. Perhaps feeling like a conglomerate illegitimate among the lineaged Establishment representatives, Mr. Cohen ranted extemporaneously for 12 minutes, expressing his nonbelonging. In a subsequent interview he stressed that he could not figure out why he and his firm should have been invited to this gathering of the elite monied clan.

"The minute I walked in (the White House) I knew I was in trouble." Mr. Cohen continued. "There I was in a gray suit and blue shirt and all these other guys were standing around in black or dark suits and white shirts. I was the only blue shirt in the house. And I'm only five-foot-three. I don't think there was another person there under six-foot." [4]

Although Mr. Cohen's preference for blue shirts and his much-below-average physical stature certainly do not typify all conglomerators, the feeling of nonbelonging in elite surroundings is probably well put.

Coupled with the lack of elitism is the already stressed much lower incidence of college degrees. In distinct contrast to the so-called business establishment, Ivy League representation among the new conglomerators is conspicuous by its absence. It may be noted that this educational disparity seems to be partly corrected in second-generation conglomerate firms. However, the small sample size in this category makes inference tenuous.

In summary, it may be somewhat premature to pass judgment on leader types and leadership effectiveness in conglomerates. If more of our older established firms should engage in conglomeration, and if second- and third-generation conglomerate leaderships revert to the conventional patterns, then the maverick managements typifying the newer conglomerates could be just a passing fancy. If, on the other hand, this new breed of dynamic leaders sets the prototype of the neoentrepreneur, then the almost universally accepted thesis that professional managers of the James Burnham variety will take over must be reappraised. This reappraisal is a function of the future since many of the most visible conglomerates are less than 10 years old.

Some critics have caustically referred to the new conglomerate cap-

[4] *The Wall Street Journal*, May 29, 1970, p. 1.

tains as multimillion dollar poker players, ostensibly implying that the equity-thin conglomerates are more a gamble than an investment. Perhaps this is the key point in the analysis: the extensive use of borrowed funds in conglomerating very likely does call for a different type of decision maker, one who takes long shots and seeks to parlay one win into a series.

As has been repeatedly stated, the big question is, "How permanent is this manifestation of new conglomerate leadership?" If this is a temporary phenomenon induced by a long period of prosperity, a series of three major wars in the last quarter century, a permissiveness pervading our social fabric and our business structure and such other forces, then we might gloss over the current manifestations of conglomerate leadership. If, however, conglomerates are here to stay, then further attention is warranted. Since it is axiomatic in the sphere of nature that like begets like, it is highly probable that if the conglomeration fever becomes epidemic, there will be some very drastic changes in the top and near-top levels of management in parent companies and their subsidiaries. The following illustrations call attention to this very logical concomitant of conglomeration.

TEXTRON, INC.

Frequently termed the first of the modern conglomerates, its architect, Royal Little, founded the company in 1923 as Special Yarns Corporation. In 1944 Royal Little, striving to adapt his company to the new textile technology, renamed his company Textron, suggesting by this new name that this was a textile firm in the forefront with synthetic fibers such as rayon and nylon. The big step forward in Textron's transformation took place in 1955 when Little aggressively captured control of American Woolen Company and its very sizable tax-loss credit. American Woolen was itself the product of an 1899 horizontal merger that combined 27 woolen mills into the "wool trust." The immediate post-Korean War period resulted in a traumatic experience during which American Woolen in a single year (1953) lost nearly one-fourth of its working capital.[5]

Using American Woolen's assets and tax loss credits as the base, Little moved rapidly into a diversification program that currently numbers about 34 divisions with about 120 plants. Interestingly enough just about 10 years after the American Woolen acquisition, Textron finally disposed of the greatly shrunken remnants of American Woolen (the successful division now renamed Amerotron) and got completely out of the textile

[5] Stanley Vance, *American Industries*, Prentice-Hall, Englewood Cliffs, New Jersey, 1955, p. 422.

business. This seems to be an important characteristic of the new conglomerates—they are willing to take great risks in acquiring ailing firms, but they are equally apt to dispose, with no sentimentality, successful divisions and even their original line of business when better opportunities beckon.

Although Royal Little, with 30 years of textile management experience before embarking on conglomeration, certainly meets the definition of Burnham's technically groomed professional manager, his ingress into the conglomerate field raises some questions. For the most part Little stayed in the manufacturing field. The record shows that his success was greatest in the newly acquired units where only a general experience in manufacturing was necessary. When specialized or highly technical expertise was needed in the managers, his success ratio was considerably lower and, generally, the divisions that tended to be most successful were those which, on merger, brought along intact their technical and management staffs. Although this corroborates the contention that modern enterprise requires professional managers, it also proves that the conglomerators themselves are successful because they possess other than the professional manager's conventional talents. Among these talents in Royal Little was the overriding urge to "run the show." Little's handpicked successor, Rupert C. Thompson, Jr., noted that Little "never was much for committees and meetings. 'The minute he wasn't going to run it alone, he left.'" [6]

In addition to the dominance role, the neoentrepreneurs, exemplified in this instance by Royal Little, seem to be lacking in interest regarding production and marketing problems of their myriad components. These neoentrepreneurs seem to be concerned solely with financial structuring rather than with product- or market-structuring. In Royal Little's case, "as the conglomerate Textron began to assume its present shape, Little realized that his real interest had been in putting it together. He didn't care for operations, and so he decided to bring in some people who did." [7] In 1960 Royal Little retired at the age of 64. His successors, Rupert C. Thompson (chairman) and G. William Miller (president), support the thesis that "like begets like." Thompson, a long-time banker and Miller, a Wall Street lawyer, would not qualify, even by stretching one's imagination, as technician-type professional managers. Their competencies are in the legal and financial intricacies which seemingly characterize most conglomerates.

In this, one of the still relatively few instances where a second-generation management has taken over a conglomerate firm, there is no solid

[6] *Fortune*, "How to Manage a Conglomerate," by Stanley H. Brown, 157 (April 1964).

[7] *Ibid.*, p. 156.

evidence that the managerial revolution-type (product-oriented, research-oriented, or market-oriented) professional managers are again in the ascendency. Rather, stress seems to be placed, at Textron at least, on legal-financial integrative forces.

Some analysts, however, believe that Textron has lost its earlier conglomerating momentum and in the future will function in a far more conventional fashion. In recent years the Textron acquisition tempo has slowed to two or three companies a year. The abortive attempt in late 1968 to acquire the merger-determined United Fruit Company seems to corroborate this sentiment that Textron has lost its conglomerating verve and vivacity. If this is so, then the odds mount that Burnham's "law" as to the inevitability of professional managers might be confirmed even in this case, the first of the conglomerate mavericks. This sentiment is strengthened by a closer look at Textron's current control system. In its second generation, Textron puts the onus for profitability, a 25% return on net worth before taxes and corporate charges, on its top operating personnel. The outside directors and generalist top executives provide financial control and guidance to the over-all operations. It is still, however, the technician-manager, in Burnham's context, whose significant job it is to make each of Textron's 34 divisions meet the 25% criterion.

This fact is somewhat concealed by the structure of both the directorate and the top corporate office. The 12 directors include only four "insiders," of whom one is a retired officer of a division. Nevertheless, even four insiders on Textron's board is an improvement since as recently as 1966 there were only two officer-directors. Even more significant is the listing of the 15 officers of vice presidential or higher rank who constitute the headquarters group. Unlisted, as yet, is a relatively new category, the division presidents. This group, now numbering 11 heads of the more important divisions, constitutes the managers in the James Burnham context. It seems logical to assume that ultimately this very vital group of technician-executives, the division presidents, will become even more prominent in Textron's headquarter's hierarchy. This delegation of authority seems to be somewhat at variance with the almost autocratic control once exercised by the company's founder. Perhaps, then, conglomerates once they become big and successful must inevitably revert to the leadership of technician-managers.

LING-TEMCO-VOUGHT

Ling-Temco-Vought also discussed in Chapter 8 illustrates how a conglomerate can succeed and yet exert a minimum of direct control over its component parts. The headquarters group consists of only 18 officers who oversee the activities of 10 subsidiaries whose annual sales volume exceeds $3.8 billion. Each of these 18 officers sits on the boards of at least three subsidiaries. In a sense these 10 LTV subsidiaries have "inside-type" boards of directors and as John L. Cockrill, vice-president for administration, has stated, "the LTV directors serving on subsidiary boards take a more active role in the subsidiaries than do outside directors of other corporations." [8]

In several instances the LTV directors who serve on the subsidiary boards have had a long-time association with that component in a managerial capacity; for example, Roscoe G. Haynie, chairman of LTV's executive committee, sits on the boards of the three Wilson Subsidiaries: Wilson and Company (meatpacking), Wilson Pharmaceutical and Chemical Company, and Wilson Sporting Goods Company. "He probably is as knowledgeable as anyone of the operations of these subsidiaries because he was chairman of Wilson and Company Inc., which was split into separate operations last year after its merger with LTV." [9]

Ling-Temco-Vought's top decision makers, it would appear, meet Burnham's modern manager prescriptions and so should be termed technician-managers. At Textron, on the contrary, only a single vice-president joins the chairman and the president on the firm's 12-man board.

These two quite divergent illustrations have been presented to show that among the conglomerates there is no complete unanimity as to the role of the top executives and board members. Textron is at one end and Ling-Temco-Vought is at the other end of a corporate control continuum, with several hundred conglomerates ranging somewhere within these seemingly irreconcilable extremes.

[8] *Business Week*, 81 (November 30, 1968).
[9] *Ibid.*, p. 82.

8

MANAGEMENT ACQUIESCENCE

Midas-mania, a result of the inevitable spurt in stock market valuations of merging firms' securities, has tended to obscure what is probably an even more important consideration of the merger movement. In almost every instance when two or more firms join their identities and their capabilities, a change takes place at the decision-making apex. Despite textbook stress on the all-vital significance of leadership in enterprise, very little attention has been focused on the extent, character, meaning, or legality of the very obvious changes in top leadership following recent mergers. Most analyses or references that have been made in regard to this subject focus almost exclusively on *one man*. Thus Textron's actions, philosophy, and accomplishments have invariably been attributed to Royal Little. Armand Hammer gets most of the credit for Occidental Petroleum's remarkable progress. Charles B. Thornton at Litton Industries, Henry E. Singleton at Teledyne, H. S. Geneen at ITT and James A. Ling at Ling-Temco-Vought all epitomize these stalwarts of merging and conglomerating. Yet a small amount of reflection should tell us that, considering today's macroorganizations, it is highly unlikely that one person, no matter how gifted, dedicated, or charming, can singlehandedly maneuver a merger. The insinuation that merger epitomizers are charismatically endowed needs validation. The only tangible evidence lauding these neoentrepreneurs is in the form of journalistic paeans, which incidentally could be attributed to the Madison Avenue types on the merger-hero's payroll.

An analysis free of both halo-complex and unwarranted cynicism is sorely needed. With this in mind this chapter seeks to obtain a better understanding about how professional managers respond to merger overtures or merger threats. Serious questions should be asked concerning the roles played by these top managers and directors of firms that capitulate to merger. Was their acquiescence prompted by a conviction that the merger is the best course of action for all concerned? Perhaps the ready acquiescence by so many managers and directors follows from their lack of interest or lack of a meaningful voice in decision making. We must not overlook the possibility of ulterior motives such as personal gain. In any event the firm agreeing to be merged is giving away something of value—its autonomy and, perhaps, even its identity.

Survival is a prime principle of life. Consequently, it makes sense to assume that every existing firm will strive to preserve its identity and its relative sovereignty against all takeover threats. What happens when a courted company spurns the aggressor's advances? The first two examples of the following manpower adjustments at top managerial levels will illustrate the self-preservation instinct inherent in corporate organizations.

BATH INDUSTRIES, INC.

In early 1968 Bath Industries proposed a merger with Congoleum-Nairn providing for the exchange of one share Series A $5 convertible preferred Bath Industries stock for every three shares of Congoleum common. The Bath preferred would have an involuntary liquidating value of $100 a share and would be convertible into Bath common at a ratio to be determined subsequently and be set by the common stock's market value just before the merger's effective date.

In May 1968 Congoleum's board of directors backed away from the proposal. Their reluctance was based on doubts about Bath's future profitability as expressed in a study by Boston Consulting Group. This study stressed Bath's reliance on major Navy contracts which appeared to be phasing out. In concluding, the report stated that "Bath wouldn't add to the debt capacity, might be a drain on funds and might reflect unfavorably on Congoleum's image . . . [and noted that] there is no significant synergy between Congoleum and Bath."[1]

Dillon, Read and Company employed as a consulting group by Congoleum's directors consequently turned negative because of the doubts regarding Bath's future earning power and its ability to meet the preferred stock requirements. It recommended that Congoleum's directors should *not* vote in favor of the merger nor recommend favorable action to the stockholders.

[1] *The Wall Street Journal*, 8 (September 9, 1968).

In rebuttal Bath Industries hired Kidder, Peabody and Company to review the situation. Kidder, Peabody's report was the reverse of Dillon Read's, stressing that the merger terms were reasonable and that Bath does possess capabilities to compete effectively for shipbuilding and ship modernization contracts but that there can obviously be no guarantee that such business will continue.

Earlier in 1968 Bath Industries acquired 42% of Congoleum's stock. When Congoleum's board turned recalcitrant and 9 of its 15 directors voted against the merger, a special board meeting was held and all 9 opposing directors were ousted. After they were replaced by Bath representatives, the new Bath-named board reinstituted merger proceedings.

Congoleum-Nairn is an example of a reluctant bride being clubbed into submission Neanderthal-style. Not all tough and direct actions are equally successful.

THE WESTINGHOUSE AIR BRAKE COMPANY,
AMERICAN STANDARD, INC. AND CRANE COMPANY

The hassle among these companies is a good example of a strong force being nullified by an even stronger counterforce. Thomas Mellon Evans, characterized by some of his closest associates as "quite shy and proper on the personal side but on the business side he's extremely bellicose-rough, hard-driving, a tough guy," [2] was the strong force seeking control of Westinghouse Air Brake. His Crane Company had acquired nearly a million and a half shares or 31% of Westinghouse Air Brake's common stock. In a typical situation when an aggressor has 31% of the outstanding stock, merger is almost inevitable. In this instance the strong counterforce, American Standard, succeeded after a long, costly and bitter battle in preventing the takeover of Westinghouse Air Brake by the Crane Company. At the final autonomous Westinghouse Air Brake annual meeting, Crane Company did succeed in having three of its representatives elected to the Westinghouse Air Brake board. This victory, however, was quickly nullified by Westinghouse Air Brake's refusal to seat the duly elected Crane representatives.

To make a long and tedious story short, the rugged entrepreneur, Thomas M. Evans, finally capitulated and sold his Westinghouse Air Brake (WABCO) stock, by then converted into 730,312 shares of American Standard preferred stock, for $76 million. This sale incidentally represented the largest single-block trade on the records of the New York Stock Exchange. This action also precipitated a series of legal maneuvers

[2] *The Wall Street Journal,* 18 (May 16, 1968).

relating to the disposition of the profit resulting from this huge sale.

In this illustration ultimate capitulation by Westinghouse Air Brake to one or other of the aggressors seems to have been a foregone conclusion. Perhaps its lethargic performance was the propelling force. Between 1955 and 1968 the company had slipped in *Fortune*'s listing in all respects, dropping, for example, from 196 to 265 in sales and from 148 to 221 in assets.

From Wabco management's point of view it was fairly evident that if Evans and Crane won the battle, the probabilities were strong that Evans' dominant personality would restructure the acquired firm along very definite lines; for example, at both Evans' major enterprises, the Crane Company and the H. K. Porter Company, only two officer-directors were on each board. Despite the numerical preponderance of non-employee directors at Crane and Porter, there seems to be evidence of one-man rule. By contrast American Standard's five officer-directors and eight nonemployee directors seemed to provide Wabco's board a safer haven.

This inference is supported by Evans' record in his previously acquired firms and by his tactics in the present case. Westinghouse Air Brake's chairman, A. King McCord, during the deliberations accused Evans of unethically trying to induce him to support Crane's proposal. He told his stockholders that Evans promised that McCord would receive an option to purchase Crane stock and benefits after retirement, possibly by consulting arrangement. The Wabco executive also told a court that the stock options dangled before him "might" in 10 years be worth $200,000 or $300,000. "I was shocked . . . I told him [Mr. Evans] that it was entirely improper and that I did not wish to discuss this any more. Mr. Evans quipped afterwards: I guess [the offer] was inappropriate enough." [3]

An unsettling feeling was undoubtedly lurking in the background in Westinghouse Air Brake management's ranks that Crane's victory would mean a drastic housecleaning at Wabco. In 1966, after Crane bought Glenfield and Kennedy Holdings, Crane's president, D. C. Fabiani, is quoted as saying: "After we took over, there were a lot of firings. It involved cutting the payroll very substantially because a lot of people had been kept on with nothing to do." [4]

The firing pattern is evident in previous Evans' acquisitions. At Crane several vice presidents were fired immediately after he became chairman. At H. K. Porter also the executive turnover has been rather high.

[3] *The Wall Street Journal*, 1 (August 28, 1968).
[4] *The Wall Street Journal*, 18 (May 16, 1968).

In a five-year period, only three out of eight division general managers retained their posts and in the turnover spots some managers were replaced not once but several times.

Porter doesn't deny that many executives are simply fired, abruptly and without apology, because they don't meet Mr. Evans' exacting standards for profit performance. "We are totally ruthless with people who can't handle the job," says J. Stuart Morrow (Porter's president).[5]

With recent precedent in mind it seems logical for Westinghouse Air Brake's management group to have been wary of Crane's offer. Incidentally, a year after the merger with American Standard, the original 80-man executive force at Wabco remained almost intact with not a single firing. Returning to the topic of the "special" offer to Wabco's chairman by Evans, this is not an isolated instance. The following illustration expands on this theme and injects several other related aspects.

SCHENLEY INDUSTRIES INC.

Schenley, the personal fief of Lewis S. Rosenstiel, who founded the firm in 1933 soon after prohibition's repeal, became a real merger prospect in 1965. The company's performance for the preceding decade had been lackadaisical and Rosenstiel, then in his mid-70's was beset with various personal problems including legal marital tiffs with his fourth wife, 31 years his junior. Whatever the causes, Rosenstiel seemed "to want out" of Schenley Industries.

Early in 1965 Glen Alden Corporation made the first of a series of attempts to take over Schenley Industries. It took more than two years for Glen Alden to accomplish the merger and only after it had acquired 88.1% of Schenley stock by private purchase from Rosenstiel and by a public tender offer to Schenley stockholders. In the private transaction Rosenstiel sold 945,126 Schenley shares to Glen Alden at $80 a share. As an interesting concomitant of this sale, Glen Alden agreed to pay $5 million in finders' fees to Joseph Lubin, an accountant, and Jack Rosen, a lawyer. Presumably these individuals "contributed materially to the consummation of the agreement with Mr. Rosenstiel."[6] This very generous payment, equal to the 1967 common stock dividend of $1.00 per share, led to stockholder dissatisfaction and legal actions. At the 1968 annual meeting (September 26), "irate stockholders variously portrayed Glen Alden management as 'making a bundle,' 'wallowing in money,' and

---

[5] Ibid.
[6] The Wall Street Journal, 5 (September 17, 1968).

'looking after themselves' at the expense of the company." [7] The proxy statement also indicated that there were 18 pending legal actions related to Glen Alden's takeover of Schenley.

Of even more immediate significance is one of the "motivational inducements" Glen Alden tendered Schenley's founder, Lewis S. Rosenstiel. The 76-year-old outgoing chairman was retained under contract "in full service" for the next year at his current salary of $250,000 and as an adviser thereafter. This munificent gesture illustrates how some mergers can be expedited through "sweeteners" offered to the acquired firm's top management, and in this instance the special deal given Schenley's chairman presumably facilitated the merger. In the previous illustration Mr. Evans' offer to Wabco's chairman, McCord, precipitated charges of unethical persuasion. Obviously the courts and our public will have to decide just how far aggressive action of this sort will be tolerated.

Throughout the two-year merger negotiations, Schenley's management, except for Mr. Rosenstiel, played only an incidental role. There was virtually no comment by individual board members or members of the management team. If there were any dissenting board or management views, scant public attention was given. With Glen Alden's assumption of control, Schenley's board of directors, formerly nine officer-directors and five nonemployee directors, was now reconstituted to include three Glen Alden officers, two Schenley officers, and two outside directors. This low outside-director representation would seem to indicate that Glen Alden will run its recent acquisition as an integrated subsidiary rather than as a semiautonomous division.

LING-TEMCO-VOUGHT

Ling-Temco-Vought's cash tender offer of $85 per share of Jones and Laughlin Steel Corporation's common stock illustrates still another situation. Although this offer was about $35 or 70% above the recent market price just before the tender, more was involved than just this hefty premium. As part of the total package James J. Ling offered to place his firm's holding of Jones and Laughlin stock (eventually 63% of Jones and Laughlin's outstanding common) into a voting trust controlled by three J & L managers and two LTV representatives. The trust was to continue until early 1971. This three-year period of grace would give the key J & L executives, all of whom were only five or six years from retirement, an opportunity to be integrated into their new posts or to exit

[7] *The Wall Street Journal*, 8 (September 27, 1968).

graciously. It also, in Mr. Ling's words, "was to assure management of continuity and to show our good faith in present management." [8] In addition, both companies exchanged directors, three J & L men being elevated to LTV's board and vice versa.

Together with the generous financial and managerial arrangements, another factor might have prompted Jones and Laughlin's management to agree to the merger. Ling-Temco-Vought's basic philosophy in conglomeration has been described by the term "project redeployment." [9] As a result of this practice LTV merges into itself the company it controls and operates it as a subsidiary; however, a minority of the stock outstanding remains in public ownership and is traded freely on the market. This technique has served to establish stock market quotations quite favorable to LTV. Together with this financial factor project redeployment also implies a public sharing of pertinent data and a measure of autonomy within the subsidiaries.

SUMMARY

The preceding four illustrations are just a small sample of the various management-wooing techniques used by acquisitive firms. Each suitor seems to have his own inimitable style. In this example the four techniques, succinctly stated, emphasize the use of club, competitor, cash, and contract.

1. In the Bath Industries episode the rebellious Congoleum-Nairn directors were summarily dealt with. Bath Industries' strategy could be termed a frontal attack with no very subtle maneuvering, no holds barred, and no quarter given. There is nothing wrong with this technique, assuming that the aggressor has adequate resources to run the captured enterprise after the takeover. If, however, the recalcitrants continue to hold a very strong minority stock position, intraorganizational strife is very likely. Even more tenuous a victory will be won if the winner does not have adequate management talent to replace most of the top managers associated with the deposed management. Sound logic should warn the winner that this old-guard group would very likely not be hypermotivated and for the next several years could constitute an enclave of potential revolt.

2. Fleeing to a competing suitor is just as common a practice. Presumably, as in the Westinghouse Air Brake situation, this is more than just picking the lesser of two evils. When a firm urgently needs assis-

[8] *Business Week,* 104 (May 18, 1968).
[9] *The Wall Street Journal,* 22 (May 13, 1968).

tance because of a chronic regression syndrome, it is not fighting merger per se, but rather the imposition of a particular partner. The motives for this reluctance will vary but the reaction is singular. Nevertheless, if the objectionable suitor should win, as in the NVF Corporation takeover of Sharon Steel Corporation (despite the Sharon Steel management's extremely strong preference to join with Cyclops Corporation), then the previously discussed strategy (the club) will very likely be used. If, on the other hand, the firm to be merged succeeds in getting its preference, then the union is far less turbulent. But even acquiescence by a harassed management guarantees nothing. William Wood Prince in his desperate maneuver to keep his Armour and Company out of the clutches of Richard C. Pistell's General Host Corporation tendered his family's 499,-000 Armour shares to "friendly" Greyhound Corporation. Within three months his fellow Chicagoan and presumed ally Gerald H. Trautman, president of Greyhound, helped ease Prince out of the chairman and chief executive posts he had held for over 12 years.

If the acquiescing management obtains a strong financial stake in the new firm, the probabilities for a frictionless merger increase. Even more significant, if the capitulating firm's top managers are outstanding in zest and competency and are integrated promptly and properly into the new firm, this willing merger has excellent prospects for success.

3. The Schenley Industries case is far less common in large-scale enterprise simply because of the rapidly declining number of one man- or family-owned firms. However, in the medium-sized and small firm categories, this is probably the most frequently used approach to win consent. Perhaps 90% of all closely held companies agree to merger because the major stockholder has been offered a significant financial inducement. From the seller's point of view there is certainly nothing wrong in getting a better-than-fair price. From the acquiring firm's point of view, particularly if this is a publicly held company with very widely diffused ownership, such a merger might be less than successful. If the merger benefits do not outweigh the stock watering, then obviously such junctures can even be negative. The real danger in many cases is that the courts will eventually become more discerning and penalize participants in these "buddy deals." We can in the next decade anticipate a significant rise in the number and kind of stockholder derivative suits, some of which will question even more severely the special deals given not only to major stockholders but even to the top managers of firms agreeing to a merger. The reaction of some Schenley Industries (and also Glen Alden) stockholders to the present example is an index of future public reaction to some of these legally and ethically questionable deals.

4. Ling-Temco-Vought's strategy in striving to continue Jones and

Laughlin's current management in the control center for at least a four-
or five-year transition period seems very laudable. There are, of course,
certain limitations in this method. It necessitates use of a representative
type of board of directors. In the majority of consummated mergers,
there is no subsequent representation of the acquired firm on the parent
company's board. Such subordination is natural since the acquired firm
is now a dependency. Presumably, since its directors and executives
were unable to preserve autonomy, they are inadequate to be elevated
to the victor's board. Here merger is equivalent to conquest.

The capture of control of Jones and Laughlin by LTV is at the other
end of the continuum. The exchange of LTV and J & L directors, the
guarantee of management continuation at J & L, the strong outside or
minority stock interest, and the other aspects of "project redeployment"
all indicate that here we have an attempt at confederation and not simply an outright conquest. As in all confederations, whether political, religious, social, or business, there is a very real danger that decentralization, which predicates a major measure of autonomy, can lead to
atomizing and disintegration. Ling-Temco-Vought's experience in the
granting of local autonomy to its recently acquired component parts has
not as yet been tested by time and tribulations.

These four basic techniques for winning over the top management of
an acquired firm—by wielding a heavy club, by fleeing to a competitor,
by the cash palative, and by contractual guarantee—are not always
used alone. More frequently we find combinations of these techniques
together with other inducements in convincing top managers of a given
firm to agree to be merged. Although the specific means to be used can
vary, the objective in every instance is the same, to get the current management of the sought-after firm either to agree willingly or reluctantly
to a merger proposal.

9

MERGER AND MANAGEMENT
TENURE

Management turnover, resulting from merger, is a foregone conclusion
particularly for the older and higher paid executives of the acquired
company. *Business Week*, in a commentary on this subject stated, "If a
man is high-salaried and past 50 (and sees a merger bind coming) he is
foolish not to take firm steps to protect his position." [1] This sound advice
applies primarily to the upper level executives of the publicly held companies that yield to merger pressures. Although only about 30% of the
estimated 6132 mergers consummated in 1969 involved publicly held
firms, these are distinctly the larger companies with consequent greater
impact on displaced managers. In the privately held firms that agree to
be merged, top management is very frequently identical with ownership.
In many instances the owner-manager of the merging firm joins the
board of the parent company, and the second in command and lower
level executives continue to function with minimal interruption at least
during the interim period.

In other mergers involving privately held firms where there is a distinct manifestation of weakness in the top-managerial posts or where a
factional feud has developed, there will obviously be a replacement of
managers. This very frequently occurs when management succession is
impeded either by lack of competent heirs or the fear of loss of control
through prohibitive inheritance taxes.

In the more pertinent publicly held merging companies the threat to
certain management types is far more realistic. There is no tenure, union
security, strong ownership interest, or contractual guarantee of pay or

[1] *Business Week*, 145 (March 16, 1968).

position for most corporate managers. With some few exceptions they can be demoted or dismissed at the whim of the chief executive officer. Considering that in a relatively short time after merger a change in chief executive officers occurs in about two out of every three publicly held merging firms, it is logical for managers of the absorbed firms to anticipate employment problems. The relatively high executive casualty rates are not always evident because in many instances mergers are accompanied by a brief honeymoon period. In all but a few cases the dominant firm even goes to extremes to issue memoranda and news releases stressing the continuance of the old management in the acquired firm. For example, when International Telephone and Telegraph Corporation took over the Sheraton Corporation of America, ITT installed Ernest Henderson III (son of the chairman and founder of the international hotel and motel chain) as president. The elder Henderson died soon after the acquisition. Ernest Henderson III after a brief tenure of less than a year as president of Sheraton (now an ITT subsidiary) was deposed and replaced by Philip L. Lowe, a member of ITT's headquarter's management group.

When Newton Glekel, chairman of Beck Industries, purchased the one-third interest Hugo Slotkin had in Hygrade Food Products, Slotkin continued as chairman of Hygrade, but only for a five-month interim period before being abruptly replaced by Glekel. Similarly, J. Edgar Bennett was retained as president of Lorillard Corporation (after the cigarette maker became a subsidiary of Loew's) for a brief five months. On resigning he stated that there was a conflict of management philosophy with the new management that could only be resolved this way. Numerous comparable cases include: John C. Lobb, president of Crucible Steel Corporation, who continued in his post only a few months after that firm's acquisition by Colt Industries; George Perrault, Jr., chairman and president of Sharon Steel Corporation, was, on that firm's merger into NVF Corporation, first replaced as chairman and then several months later resigned his presidency. Soon after Talley Industries took over General Time, it fired that firm's president, Barton K. Wickstrum, and accepted the resignation of its chairman, Don G. Mitchell.

The Crucible Steel illustration had some interesting sidelights. John Lobb, who himself had less than a two-year tenure as Crucible's chief executive, was credited with axing more than 20 Crucible executives from the payroll. This and similar actions was the subject of a *Business Week* article "Hatchet Man for Deadwood Operations" in which Lobb "draws grudging respect even from his detractors. 'There's no question that Lobb can cut through a company and get rid of fat,' says a former

Crucible officials." [2] Lobb's replacement, Edward Jensen, lasted only a few months and was replaced early in 1970 by Martin N. Ornitz as Crucible's president.[3]

This type of top management manipulation is far more the rule than the exception. Friction frequently develops even in situations where peer corporations merge their forces. The 1967 union between United States Plywood Corporation and Champion Papers provides an illustration of two reputable and well-established firms integrating horizontally. The merger was purportedly between equals—neither firm could be considered the aggressor nor the acquiescer. The board of directors of the new firm, United States Plywood-Champion Papers, was equally divided (10 representatives from each merger peer). Even more significantly the new company set up the equivalent of an Office of the President, dividing the responsibilities between its two top officers, chairman Karl R. Bendetsen (formerly chief executive of Champion Paper) and Gene C. Brewer (previously chief executive at United States Plywood). Supposedly this equal division of authority would permit the efficient use of two equally competent chief executives who had previously run their own shows. The technique should have worked but "It didn't. Both men had to agree on decisions and the inevitable disagreements proved uncomfortable." [4] In the end Brewer surrendered his half of the office to become chief operating officer, and Bendetsen became chief executive officer and the final decision maker for the firm. A few months later John T. Schlick, a director and an executive vice-president heading the United States Plywood group, resigned. Although Mr. Schlick gave the usual "personal reasons" explanation for his resignation, there was considerable speculation that policy differences with the chairman and chief executive officer might have precipitated the move. It should be pointed out that in some respects John Schlick was an architect of this merger since he was Brewer's acquisitions man and had first proposed the merger with Champion Papers.

Within a few months in what appeared to be a Bendetsen-engineered coup, Brewer's post was apparently downgraded in a major reorganization of the merged firm. As a concomitant Brewer announced his resignation as president and chief operating officer.

Mr. Brewer's reasons for resigning as president weren't spelled out. The Company was asked if Mr. Brewer had found himself at odds with Mr. Bendet-

[2] *Business Week*, 80 (September 6, 1969).
[3] *The Wall Street Journal*, 10 (February 4, 1970).
[4] *Fortune*, 52 (April 1968).

sen. Through a spokesman, Mr. Bendetsen replied, "Mr. Brewer is a fine fellow. I admire and respect him, and there was no basic disagreement between us in policy or the management of this company." [5]

Despite his resignation Mr. Brewer was to receive $150,000 annual compensation for the next five years. Together with Brewer's retreat, at least three other top United States Plywood executives were replaced with Bendetsen Champion Paper proteges. As a corollary to this narrative, Gene C. Brewer was early in 1970 elected president of Southwest Forest Industries, a significantly smaller firm.

Sometimes the replacement of top executives of merged firms is accomplished by a subtle abdication or an almost imperceptible phasing out. When Ling-Temco-Vought acquired control of Jones and Laughlin, the chairman and chief executive, Charles M. Beeghly, was retained in his post and was named a director of LTV. He was also designated chairman of LTV's executive committee and one of the five trustees of the voting trust which was set up to run Jones and Laughlin until 1971. Within a few months of this very amicable and rewarding arrangement, late in December 1968 Charles M. Beeghly accepted a position as vice-chairman and trustee of the Richard King Mellon Foundation and vice-president and governor of T. Mellon and Sons. Although he did not then resign his Jones and Laughlin positions, the inference can easily be drawn that the assumption of the new duties would certainly leave him far less time to take an active role in LTV's Jones and Laughlin subsidiary.

LTV's "soft" line very likely followed from its policy of "project redeployment." Too forceful an approach could lead to irritation in the relatively strong minority stockholder camp. Perhaps even more significant was LTV's candid realization that in Jones and Laughlin it had a tremendous commitment in a technically and competitively very complex industry. LTV had immediate need for Jones and Laughlin's technicians.

This line of reasoning permeates many similar mergers. "Sometimes an acquired company retains its autonomy (and personnel) only because the new parent is unfamiliar with the nuts and bolts of its business. 'There's been damn little change,' says an executive for Brown and Root, Inc., the construction company acquired by Dallas' Halliburton Co., an oil well and marine services company. 'We do have a pretty autonomous relationship because we're engineering and construction, and we know what that's all about.'" [6]

[5] *The Wall Street Journal,* 18 (March 21, 1969).
[6] *Business Week,* 51 (April 26, 1969).

Almost the opposite tactic was used in the 1969 takeover of Endicott-Johnson Corporation by the West Virginia industrialist, Bernard P.
McDonough. Just two weeks after he acquired control he began to un-
load both Endicott-Johnson's directors and executives. Eight members of
the old board were forced to resign and were replaced by McDonough's
men. Three top vice-presidents and two high level managers were asked
to resign. Within a few days the employment of at least four other top
level managers of specialized technical functions and about 17 junior executives was terminated. In this instance the justification for the extremely severe management pruning was cost cutting—a hope to pare
about $500,000 from the company's payroll by consolidating the func-
tions under fewer people.

Similar cost-cutting considerations are very often used as justification
for drastic management layoff and plant closure in takeovers. When ITT
took over Sheraton Corporation of America in 1968, it dumped 20 marginal or money-losing properties and reorganized. Quite often the cost-
cutting argument carries overtones of Machiavellian machinations. In
Monogram Industries' tender offer to stockholders of Cleveland-based
National Screw and Manufacturing Company, Monogram's president,
Martin Stone, stated that he intended to retain National's present management after the merger was completed. Consequently, National's officers, including its president Eli A. Channer endorsed the deal and tendered their own stock. "Shortly after the acquisition became effective,
however, Channer came into his office and saw a notice on the bulletin
board that he was retiring. This was the first he had heard about it. Says
a man who was with Channer: 'He was stunned, really shaken.' " [7]
Within a relatively short time the entire National management was
changed with only two younger executives from the premerger regime
remaining with the firm.

The Machiavellian maneuverings in this example seemed to be evident in the appointment of Fred C. Chandler as Channer's successor.
Chandler had been head of National's California operations. It was he
who brought National to Martin Stone's (and Monogram's) attention.

A rapidly increasing fraternity of flunked-out executives have helped
guide their firms into merger partnerships. Paul J. Vaughan who
founded Filmco and subsequently facilitated Filmco's merger into R. J.
Reynolds Tobacco Company resigned his post as president of Filmco
after a relatively brief tenure in the conglomerate stating he wished to
pursue outside interests.

Even more dramatic was the departure, after less than a year, of Rob-

[7] *Ibid.*, p. 52.

ert E. Williams as president and chief executive officer of Youngstown
Sheet and Tube Company and vice-chairman of Lykes-Youngstown Corporation, the holding company. The company announced tersely "that
he elected to take early retirement (at age 57) to devote his time to
other interests."[8] Williams had been president and chief executive officer of Sheet and Tube for five years before the firm's merger into Lykes.
One observer commented: "What's happening there is the merger syndrome. First you have all the nice words about how management will
stay the same and nothing is going to change. Then everything starts
changing."[9]

As is evident in the preceding examples, although the methods and
explanations vary, the dominant group most frequently takes away autonomy from the merging component. Sound logic supports this tactic.
First it can be assumed that practically all second-party firms either
seek or yield to a merger because they are not in the soundest performance positions. It is a distinct rarity when a healthy and prosperous
firm desires to be merged. On the contrary, as was shown in Chapter 5,
it is the companies with serious regression syndrome symptoms that
make up the roster of merged- and merger-prone firms. Although it
might be somewhat harsh to imply that all companies characterized by
the regression syndrome have ineffective managements, there is a strong
direct relationship. Consequently, it would be to the detriment of the
acquiring firm to be saddled, because of a false notion of obligation or
decency, with ineffective managers in the acquired components. There
would be also little cathartic value if all mergers guaranteed employment with unchanged functions, authority, and compensation to every
manager. One of the most propelling reasons for merger, the therapy associated with culling deadwood from the organization, would then have
no meaning. In the better interests of business and society ineffective
managers should be removed, and mergers provide an excellent opportunity for this culling. The big problem, of course, is to differentiate the
incompetent from the qualified. In the earlier eras when vertical and
horizontal mergers were the rule, it was much simpler to judge the technical and managerial worth of the managers of the absorbed companies.
This is an obvious inference because both the acquiring firm and the acquired were engaged in the same line of endeavor. However, current
conglomeration compounds this evaluation of managerial adequacy.
Frankly, could RCA make competent judgments as to the absolute effec-

[8] *The Wall Street Journal*, 8 (April 3, 1970).
[9] *Ibid.*, 5 (April 6, 1970).

tiveness of the Hertz executives when the leading car-rental agency was absorbed by this outstanding electrical and electronics manufacturing firm? Equally perplexing was ITT's appraisal of Avis' top managers. Was Avis second-best because of a second-best management or was Avis' management superb because it did make inroads into the position of the industry leader?

There is still another very important reason for making significant managerial changes at upper executive levels. The probabilities are extremely high that the key executives of the acquired firm will eventually resent being merged. The surest way to prevent dissent, slow-down, or even open revolt is to depose these managers as soon as it is reasonably possible. Niccolai Machiavelli succinctly stated this sentiment in his sixteenth century commentary (*The Prince*) on how the effective political leader should deal with his conquests. In Machiavelli's opinion those who are forced to give up their own autonomy must either be wooed or be crushed and killed. If they are considered absolutely essential to the conqueror, then they should be wooed and their long-run interests should be so meshed with those of the conqueror that these once-independent men would not dare or dream of revolt. A far surer method is to destroy completely the conquered so that revolt possibilities would be reduced to zero. The British author, Anthony Jay, in his interesting book, *Management and Machiavelli*, paraphrases these sentiments by saying, "Senior men in taken-over firms should either be warmly welcomed and encouraged or (be) sacked: because if they are sacked they are powerless, whereas if they are simply downgraded they will remain united and resentful and determined to get their own back." [10] Machiavelli's advice does seem to be heeded in both politics and business where loyalty frequently supersedes competency. Although this crass practice might appear reprehensible to the idealist, it is nevertheless the best assurance of survival and success. As such it might be viewed as an instinct and not simply as a management practice.

Even if we assume that the winning team in a corporate takeover realizes that it should replace all key executives in the acquired firm, such action is not always feasible. Some of the hypermerging firms have been adding 12 more smaller companies annually to their corporate amalgam. In a sense it would be corporate suicide to depose the officers of all such acquisitions. Even our largest corporations, with the best management development programs, could be hardly expected to produce top management talent in such quantities and varied competencies to staff so

[10] Quoted in *Time*, 91 (February 23, 1968).

many new positions. Consequently, it then becomes expedient to use Machiavelli's alternate advice: to woo the indispensable managers, at least temporarily.

Turnover, as a consequence of merger, is not restricted to the top executive group. It was pointed out in Chapter 5 that firms chronically manifesting regression syndrome symptoms and subsequent merging averaged total labor force attrition of about 3% annually. This conclusion is reinforced by a study made by Jon G. Udell, assistant dean and director of research at the Graduate School of Business, University of Wisconsin. In probably the first study of its kind, Dr. Udell, surveying 240 Wisconsin companies acquired by other concerns during the years 1963 through 1967, concludes that the firms acquired domestically had employment rate changes from premerger annual increases of 4.7% to postmerger annual gains of only 1.4%. However, the 24 companies acquired by out-of-state conglomerates which had 11.6% annual employment gains before merger now had 1.8% annual employment declines.

On the national scene, it appears that in the 6100-plus firms that lost their identity and autonomy in 1969 about 2,000,000 employees were directly involved. Of these perhaps 250,000 had some managerial title, including about 50,000 executives. Then, too, the conglomerating firms had to do something about the approximately 50,000 corporate directors of these acquired firms. As a judicious estimate in the postmerger work force adjustments, line employees averaged no more than a 5 to 10% attrition; staff employees faced a 10 to 25% cut; managers had a 20 to 33% replacement; in the executive category between 33 and 50% of the brass were let go and in the corporate boardroom 50 to 90% of the directors were fired. The stress on the term *fired* is in recognition of the legal and ethical responsibility of the board of directors. It is this august group which has the full responsibility "to manage and to control" the affairs of the corporation, acting as trustees for the stockholders. In virtually every instance when a firm manifests chronic regression syndrome symptoms, the fault should be put where it belongs—primarily with inept and apathetic directors and secondarily with incompetent and lackadaisical executives and managers. Even in the less common cases in which highly successful smaller firms agree to merger for any of a variety of reasons, top management probably should be exorcised after the adjustment period. The willingness of these managements to yield their autonomy and identity could indicate a "burned-out genius," weakness, or a recognition of forthcoming inadequacy. There are, however, instances where the reverse strategy, retention of the acquired managements, should be followed. This is distinctly true when the parent firm is lacking a requisite technical competency and when the merger was prompted primarily to purchase such a special technical or managerial talent possessed by the acquired firm.

Table 9-1 provides a rough estimate of labor adjustments which were effected in 1969 following approximately 6100 mergers. Out of about 2,-000,000 employees whose firms lost a large measure of identity and au-

Table 9-1   Estimated Labor Force Adjustments in 1969's Approximately 6100 Mergers

Level	Manpower Involved			
	Total	Terminated	Reused	Scrapped
Line	1,000,000	50,000	30,000	20,000
Staff	750,000	150,000	75,000	75,000
Managers	200,000	50,000	20,000	30,000
Executives	50,000	20,000	10,000	10,000
Directors	50,000	30,000	10,000	20,000
	2,050,000	300,000	145,000	155,000

tonomy because of the mergers, approximately 300,000 or 15% had their jobs terminated within one year. However, roughly half these terminations were rehired by other firms; thus the actual attrition was about 8% of all employees involved. In the rehired category, however, there was a functional degradation particularly in the upper level positions; consequently, the manpower utilization rate was further affected negatively. Note that in the actual manpower scrapping, line employees were barely affected with only about a 2% rate which comes close to the normal attrition rate. However, the other four categories and particularly top executives and directors suffered a disproportionately severe squeezing.

Looking at the merging scene, it is very clear that no single prescription as to employment turnover applies to all mergers. Varying circumstances, individual personality differences, degree of financial control, diversity in corporate philosophy, and numerous other considerations affect the way the takeover firm uses or disposes of the merged firm's managers. The following illustrations emphasize this disparity.

GREAT WESTERN UNITED CORPORATION

Great Western, a semiconglomerate, parlayed within the last several years by 29-year-old William M. White, Jr., from a $100,000 personal investment and a $700,000 loan into a multimillion-dollar venture, is a good example. In less than three years, what had been the 100-year-old Colorado Milling and Elevator Company ($34 million assets) absorbed Great Western Sugar Company ($117 million assets), together with Shakey's (pizzas), Emerald Christmas Tree Company, and California City Development Company.

This juncture of quite different business endeavors focuses on the role that modern professional managers play in facilitating conglomeration. White's financial coups understandably led to resignations by the acquired firms' managers and directors. "Taking orders from what they regarded as a mere child was too much for Great Western's veteran management; within eight months its two top executives quit. Says White: 'You can't meet the problems of the Sixties by the standards of the Thirties.'" [11] Then the article proceeds to support the personnel changes. "All White's companies are well aware that they have been acquired." [12]

Basic to these comments is White's managerial philosophy, "to give responsibility and opportunity to men—that is, let them do their thing. . . . I haven't given an order to Bob Owen and he's been with the company eight months. My job was finding him." [13] The article, *Young Man of Denver Shakes up the System*, goes on to state, "At least one GWU officer suspects that this free-form management philosophy stems partly from White's own inexperience." [14]

This last sentence is probably the crux to the better comprehension of some conglomerators' attitudes toward their managers. When the parent firm lacks production and marketing know-how, there is a distinct propensity to keep the acquired firm's management team intact, but if it is less dependent on the acquired firm for technician-manager needs, then management replacement, selective or even wholesale, can be expected in the merged firm.

MCDONNELL DOUGLAS CORPORATION

The three-year experience of McDonnell Douglas as a merged firm provides an interesting case study. Before the merger Douglas Aircraft Company had a top-executive group of 25 persons of vice-presidential-status or higher. Of this officer group six also served on the company's board of directors which included nine nonemployee directors. After the merger, Douglas contributed only four of its officers and one of its previous nonemployee directors to the new board of directors. Even more

[11] *Forbes*, 22 (August 15, 1968).
[12] *Ibid.*
[13] *Business Week*, 180 (October 19, 1968).
[14] *Ibid.*

significant was the subordination of most of its 25 vice-presidential-status individuals to less prestigious posts. Only six members of this top Douglas team were given comparable posts in the new firm.

By contrast eight of McDonnell's officer-directors, out of a previous 10 such directors, were included on the new board and two were reduced to the rank of vice-president. Then, too, virtually its entire vice-presidential group was moved over to the merged firm. The following data show the dominant McDonnell influence and the subordinate role of Douglas in the new firm.

Premerger

| | Directors | | | Top Management |
	Officer	Outside	Total	
McDonnell	10	2	12	20
Douglas	6	9	15	25

Postmerger

| | Directors | | | Top Management |
	Officer	Outside	Total	
McDonnell	8	2	10	23
Douglas	4	1	5	6

Yet on the basis of the pertinent data for both companies for 1966, the last year of independent operations, Douglas was about twice McDonnell's size when measured on the basis of assets and number of employees. Sales volume and invested capital were almost equal. The big difference is in net income. This is particularly noticeable since Douglas' figures reflect the production problems, financial pressures, and customer gripes Douglas experienced in 1966.

Performance Data, 1966

	Sales	Assets	Net Income	Invested Capital	Employees
McDonnell	1060	386	43.2	190.0	44,285
Douglas	1048	850	(27.6)	175.0	80,200

If, as the McDonnell forces must have concluded, the significant loss of $27.6 million is an index of managerial inefficiency, then downgrading of Douglas' directors and top executives in the merged firm might be justified. If the poor performance was the consequence of extraneous and uncontrollable forces, then Douglas' management paid a heavy price for being simply part of the top decision-making component of a firm capitulating to merger.

Among the severest casualties were D. W. Douglas, Sr., chairman of Douglas Aircraft Company and his son and heir apparent, D. W. Douglas, Jr., the firm's president. Douglas, Sr., was simply dropped from all posts, whereas Douglas, Jr., was retained as a director but "apparently has been put into left field in the merged corporation as vice-president for administration, taking a cut in annual salary from $150,000 to $100,000." [15]

Despite the drastic demotions of the two top officers, the forced exit of 10 directors and the subordination of 19 vice-presidential-level officers, it appears that the dominant McDonnell did not perform all-out surgery. " 'The first year and a half wasn't really a merger,' says Donald W. Douglas, Jr., 51, who had been president of Douglas Aircraft. 'All attention was on Long Beach (in California, where the DC-8 and DC-9 are assembled). As soon as that was behind us we could look at the long-range problem of organizing the company.' " [16]

In this instance even though McDonnell probably had adequate talent to assume effective operations control over Douglas, the choice was to run Douglas as a separate company and not to compress it into the new company.

Looking back, Lewis (McDonnell Douglas's president) is glad things have gone the way they have. "If we had formed the corporate organization right away," he says, "The faces would have been different. Now we know the Douglas people and have confidence in Don (Douglas) and McGowen that we never would have had a year and a half ago." [17]

This commentary, even though it is a partial exception, supports the contention that when "like takes over like" (horizontal merger), heavy attrition can be expected in the absorbed firm's management group. Here, perhaps because of the magnitude of the takeover (1966 sales by Douglas of $1048 million), the special expertise of Douglas' executives in dealing with their customers (the major airline presidents), public opinion, government pressures, or some other reason, a more complete replacement of Douglas managers was not attempted. However, the data on page 95 show that only about one out of every four Douglas top ex-

[15] *Business Week,* 100 (January 11, 1969).
[16] *Ibid.*
[17] *Ibid.*

ecutives was given comparable status in the new firm. Similarly, two-thirds of Douglas's directors were dropped (Douglas, Sr., one vice-president, and eight outside directors). As an interesting sidelight on this radical change in boards of directors' structuring, it should be noted that before the merger 40% of the directors were outsiders (17% at McDonnell and 60% at Douglas) In the new firm, McDonnell Douglas, only 20% of the directors were nonemployees. Although this does not necessarily indicate a trend, it does deserve further study. It could be that Douglas's heavy stress on outside directors did help bog the company in its 1966 problems. Without intending any negative reflection on the nine prominent citizens who formerly served as Douglas' directors, one should ask, was it their advice or lack of advice that initiated or accentuated the company's demise? In all too many instances when there is trouble, it is the firm's chief executive officer and the members of his executive team who bear the entire blame for defeat. Yet, considering the "to manage and to control" mandate which virtually every corporate charter puts on its directors, officer and nonemployee alike, it is simply unbelievable that the courts and the American public so readily exonerate a troubled firm's board of directors.

GULF AND WESTERN INDUSTRIES

Even though a conglomerating firm seemingly subscribes to a given policy regarding the managements of acquired firms, it can, on occasion, use a quite contrary approach. Gulf and Western Industries is a classic example of a conglomerator that tends to retain the key executives of its acquisitions. For example, William Jackson, president of G & W's Bonney Forge Division, who had been with that firm before its being taken over, states the following:

At first we were unsure of what was to happen. Then we were given a bullish green light to move ahead, to move faster than we did before. Jackson says his "autonomy is almost complete." He runs his own sales, manufacturing, and product development; G & W controls capital expenditures.[18]

This is in line with Gulf and Western's policy of keeping a rather small central staff and relying heavily on decentralized operations. At headquarters the parent company has less than 100 employees (including secretaries). Major policy decisions remain in the hands of 6 top officers who together control about 10% of the company's stock. With so lean a corporate staff it almost becomes mandatory that each subsidiary be given a large degree of autonomy and that the managements of newly

[18] *Business Week*, 51 (April 26, 1969).

acquired firms be continued unchanged in their operating and policy capacities. At Gulf and Western this approach has even led to the elevation of a number of chief executives of acquired subsidiaries to the parent board of directors.

Although there is an apparent autonomy given to the various corporate components, Gulf and Western's top policy makers stress a semantic's differentiation between autonomy and autonomous operations. David N. Judelson, president, states the following:

> We don't believe in autonomous operations, nor in a central staff that can run far-flung operations. How do you marry the two ideas? You set up the groups as profit centers, and make the group vice-presidents part of the corporate staff. This may sound like nothing, but it's everything. We have communications—this bridge between operational people in the field, working day to day with the corporate staff. We have the best of two worlds.[19]

There is at least one G & W significant exception to the practice; its Paramount Pictures subsidiary. Before the 1966 takeover Paramount was a moribund company in a rather lackluster industry. Throughout most of 1965 several factions waged a bitter fight for control of the corporation. When Charles Bluhdorn and his Gulf and Western associates finally did get control of Paramount in a $125 million takeover, he installed himself as president and chief executive officer. A Paramount executive, Martin S. Davis, who had served as vice-president and director of advertising and public relations, was installed as executive vice-president and chief operating officer. The next two most important positions were filled by young men brought in from the outside. James J. Burke, 39, formerly with Litton Industries, was made financial vice-president and treasurer and Richard D. Spence, a 29-year old lending officer at Chase Manhattan Bank, was designated vice-president.

Fortune comments on this radical departure from Gulf and Western's usual practice of retaining the acquired firm's top management. "With Bluhdorn and Davis in charge, Paramount usually can decide in a day or two whether to invest in a film production: previously, some potentially lucrative projects evaporated while Paramount waited for a board of directors' vote, which often took weeks. Budgets for films, which used to be most hopeful guesses, now are worked out in such detail that the company can tell whether costs are awry in the first few days of shooting."[20]

Whether or not Gulf and Western's new direction at Paramount Pic-

[19] *Business Week*, 38 (July 5, 1969).
[20] *Fortune*, "Gulf & Western's Rambunctious Conservatism," by William S. Rukeyser 204 (March 1968).

tures will permanently move the moviemaker out of the doldrums remains to be seen. Two years after the merger, the new management reported earnings for the first quarter of the fiscal year to be $26 million as contrasted with earnings of a quarter million dollars in the comparable period just before the merger. *The Wall Street Journal* notes, "Mr. Bluhdorn recalled that conglomerates have been criticized for buying companies without improving them. 'Well,' he said, 'look what we did at Paramount. A new wind is blowing. Paramount was practically out of business two years ago.' " [21]

SINGER COMPANY

As was stated in the previous illustration, standard practice in virtually all cases of merger or conglomeration is to continue the acquired component as an entity but to remove or drastically reduce its autonomy. This is true whether the acquisition becomes a completely absorbed division of the parent or if it continues to function with considerable freedom in operations. In many instances, however, the acquisition is dismembered with the more profitable components being sold off in order to recoup some of the cash expended in the takeover. In a far smaller number of instances, the dismembering is for a somewhat different purpose. Ling-Temco-Vought's division of Wilson and Company into the firm's three basic lines of endeavor—meatpacking, pharmaceuticals, and sporting goods—(facetiously referred to by some financial analysts as meatballs, goofballs, and golf balls) was a logical move. Wilson's organization had, even before the merger with LTV, recognized these as three separate areas. Here dismembering was more akin to reorganizing.

More recently Singer Company's purchase of General Precision Equipment Company, a highly technological manufacturer of aerospace systems, typifies a quite different strategy. Donald P. Kircher, Singer's chief executive officer, experienced considerable opposition from GPE's management which simply was not interested in merger. " 'We didn't even want to talk to him,' admits Donald W. Smith, then president of the firm. 'We had acquisition plans of our own.' " [22] Despite the opposition Singer did acquire GPE and within a short time began to dismember systematically the company. In this merger Singer decided to break up its huge new acquisition (1967 sales $461 million, assets $323 million) by joining GPE's various divisions into related Singer operations. (Before this merger Singer had more than 20 different divisions.) For example, GPE's Kearfott and Librascope defense and space systems groups

[21] *The Wall Street Journal*, 12 (October 31, 1968).
[22] *Dun's Review* 28 (January 1969).

were fused into Singer's HRB-Singer and Metrics divisions. The fusing function was not restricted to the organizational components alone; it was also extended to the key personnel. GPE's president, Donald Smith, was included by Kircher in a newly formed President's Office with the title of chairman of the executive committee. One might speculate that this inclusion of GPE's Smith in the new Singer President's Office follows the "wooing" policy advocated by Machiavelli where the victor sorely needs the services of the vanquished. Premerger Singer had a total of 103,000 employees of whom about 2600 were scientists and engineers. GPE by contrast had at least 6700 scientists and equivalent out of a 27,000-man workforce. Obviously, the effective integration of this high-caliber technical workforce would require special handling.

However, the alternate Machiavellian precept of crushing the opposition was equally manifest. Not only were the GPE divisions dismembered and put in subordinate roles but there was also a severe culling of personnel; for example, the chief of a GPE subdivision was elevated to head the new education group. This and the many other executive changes were in keeping with Kircher's previous policy of removing key executives when necessary. (Of the company's 32 vice-presidents only 10 were with the company when Kircher became president.) Considering their technical competencies, however, the shuffling and reshuffling of GPE personnel need not necessarily have been a good thing. In the words of one top-level manager, "The old joke that goes, 'If my boss calls please get his name,' isn't a joke around here. Every week we get a new bulletin announcing changes in vice presidents." Adds another, "No one has really been hurt yet, but you do get the feeling that GPE is getting pulled asunder." [23]

This commentary is not intended as an evaluation of Singer's tactics in absorbing its GPE acquisition. It does bring out the very obvious inference that different situations warrant different strategies for the integrative process.

BLAW-KNOX COMPANY

As one further and final example of merger impact on management, Blaw-Knox Company's takeover by White Consolidated Industries provides a classic pattern. Blaw-Knox, as shown in Chapter 5, had a significant regression syndrome before its acquisition, slumping from a *Fortune* ranking of 233 in 1955 to a position of 363 in 1967—a drop of 130 positions. Blaw-Knox needed the catharsis of merger.

[23] *Ibid.*, p. 31.

The company's management was quite elated when White Consolidated Industries made overtures. In particular, they were impressed by White's gruff-spoken president, E. S. Reddig, welcoming him as a potential saviour. " 'They thought he was another production man,' says John Thornton, Blaw-Knox's former corporate planning manager, 'because he cursed a lot.' " [24] Management's optimism was perked considerably when Blaw-Knox's chairman twice issued statements to the effect that there would be no major employment changes after the takeover. " 'Your job and mine will continue as in the past,' he announced over a public address system in Blaw-Knox offices and in a subsequent written message to employees." [25] " 'Under no circumstances will there be any changes in personnel or policy,' Snyder's message reportedly said, repeating the sentences for emphasis." [26]

In less than one year the headquarters staff was trimmed from 230 to a mere 40. The company's eight operating divisions were scattered around the country. Within a few months after the merger, several key vice-presidents left the firm and subsequently W. C. Snyder. Blaw-Knox chairman, retired from his active role in the company.

White chairman, Edward Reddig, justifies the heavy-handed treatment by saying his firm favors decentralization, hence the deemphasis on the headquarters staff.

Charles F. Hauck, president of Blaw-Knox now and before the acquisition, confirms White's pre-merger assurances that it planned few job changes; he ascribes the staff reductions that followed the takeover to 'changes in the business climate.' There have been more (personnel) changes than anyone expected.[27]

SUMMARY

Successful merging depends very much on effective absorption of executives and managers into the parent firm. There rarely is a surplus of top technical talent in the taking-over firm. Consequently, at least during an interim period, it is usually expedient to follow a status quo policy in regard to management. The nature and duration of this interim period will vary depending on so many variable factors that no single formula will prove effective in all situations. Even in a given firm with presumably a stated policy for integration of merged-firm managements,

[24] *Business Week*, 50 (April 26, 1969).
[25] *The Wall Street Journal*, 1 (May 15, 1969).
[26] *Business Week*, op. cit., p. 50.
[27] *The Wall Street Journal*, op. cit., p. 1.

policy is frequently stretched to accommodate the realities of practice. Consequently, within the same parent firm it is possible to find the extremes of virtual dismemberment and of almost complete divisional autonomy applied to different takeovers. Despite this variance there does seem to be a sound philosophical base resembling Machiavelli's realistic precepts: Woo the vanquished when it is expedient, otherwise crush and discard these potential troublemakers.

10

RAIDING

During the early 1950's considerable attention was given to the phenomenon of "raiding." Briefly put this was a maneuver in which a financier quietly purchased a large block of stock in a moribund firm and then, usually before that company's management had any inkling of the seriousness of the situation, the raider moved in to take control. The term "raiding" was presumably intended as a slur, implying that the aggressor was unethical and was using legally suspect tactics. In particular the news media at that time focused considerably on a fairly common practice among raiders of selling off the more valuable assets of the captured firm, thus dismembering the raided company. According to the raiders this action had an obvious justification—these were valuable but uneconomically used components. By disposing of such components the rest of the company could, presumably, get back to more profitable performance. If this were so, then the raiders were actually providing a very valuable service, they were removing from the business system what might figuratively be called corporate cripples. The whole nation would, hopefully, benefit by their removal or by this transformation of the sick and the sluggish.

Much of the bitter criticism seemed to issue from old-line-establishment managements which assumed they had an inviolate proprietary right in *their* company. In virtually every instance these self-presumed permanent managements were characterized by poor performance. This poor performance resulted in depressed market prices for the company's common stock which, incidentally, facilitated the raider's takeover. In many cases the very threat of takeover served to give a significant boost to the threatened company's common stock price. In other instances the moribund managements were rudely shocked out of their deep sleep and, to their credit, some rejoined the dynamic business scene.

The allegations as to the legality of raiding, judged nearly a generation later, appear to be nothing more than emotional charges without any basis in fact. The questions of impropriety and unethical actions likewise appear to remain largely without proof. By far the most significant consideration about whether a specific raiding action was good or bad, productive or wasteful was the ability of the raiding firm to compete and prosper. If the raiders did perk up a lagging firm, then the action was defensible, and if uninterested or incompetent managers (and particularly members of the board) were removed by this cataclysmic action, then the raiding was justified. If, however, the raiders were simply interested in the "fast buck," then, obviously, condemnation is in order.

It is interesting to note that less than 20 years ago there was a stigma attached to the raiding technique. Raiders were "bad guys," disrupters of the economic establishment. Yet a dispassionate comparison of raiding techniques and the way many modern mergers are effected show an amazing similarity. Some of our most merger-prone companies, and particularly many of the glamorous conglomerators, use precisely the same tactics as those characterizing raiding. Then, too, the raiding and merging climates are virtually identical. Almost every time the raided firm manifested chronic symptoms of the regression syndrome. Rarely was a healthy, prosperous firm attacked. Hardly any of the raided firms were active in developing new products or in modernizing production facilities. Most had poor dividend records. Invariably the market price of the common stock was significantly below the book value. Considered from this angle it can be inferred that the raiders were simply men of vision who recognized a "good thing when they saw it." These raiders manifested a faith in our economy's future and like true entrepreneurs they were willing to take risks.

From a top-management consideration there is likewise an almost perfect identity between raided and merged firms. It was previously pointed out that in the mergers of the 1960's one finds a remarkably high proportion of outside-type boards of directors in the taken-over firm. Similarly, the boards of the raided companies in the early 1950's had a very high proportion of outside directors. In fact, there was almost an absence of raiding in companies with officer-director-type boards. The inside board is defined here as one with more than two-thirds of its directors coming from the officer-director ranks. An intermediate-type directorate has between 40 and 67% officer-directors, whereas the outside-directorate has less than 40% officer-directors. The similarity between boards of directors of firms raided in the early 1950's and boards of firms merged, acquired, conglomerated, or taken over since 1955 are so obvious that no further comment seems necessary.

The following data for 35 major firms raided during the period 1951–1953 emphasizes this fact.

	Raided Companies	
Board Type	Number	Percent
Inside	1	3
Intermediate	10	28
Outside	24	69
	35	100

From another management angle it is intriguing to note the identity in types between the raiders and merger managers, both are extreme individualists. It is always possible to identify a given raid or a specific merger with a particular individual. In the early 1950's business literature frequently mentioned names such as Louis E. Wolfson, Leopold D. Silberstein, Sidney L. Albert, J. Patrick Lannan, Edward Lamb, and Norton Simon. These and their cohorts were raiders in yesterday's financial vernacular. Each of these raiders was strong-willed, competent, competitive, and willing to take risks. There never was any question as to who was boss in any of the raiding firms. This same commentary has already been made about the men who are initiating the current sequence of mergers. In particular the raiders and the prominent captains of conglomerates (Thornton, Ling, Singleton, Ablon, Riklis, and so on) manifest identical organizational and leadership traits.

During the mid- and late-1950's an almost imperceptible change occurred in the attitude of the public and the press toward raiding-merging-conglomerating. As if mandated by Madison Avenue what just a few years earlier was looked on with suspicion now became acceptable. The first prominent example of this sudden acceptability was Royal Little and Textron. Little's capture of American Woolen Company, together with its huge tax loss carry-forward and its abundant but underemployed assets, could be considered a classic example of raiding. American Woolen certainly did fit the regression syndrome pattern—its management was lackadaisical, its assets were underemployed, its R & D program was non-existent, and the company did have a streak of bad luck. Very likely Royal Little's capture of control and his immediate redeployment of American Woolen's assets (with the subsequent dismemberment and demise of American Woolen) fits unquestioningly the prescription for raiding. Yet there were and are very few references to Little and Textron as being raiders. Perhaps a changing public attitude, the financial community's acceptance, or the phenomenal success of some raiders brought about this shift from being suspect to becoming glamorous. Within the last decade the term raiding, as applied to the takeover technique used by financiers in the early 1950's, has become archaic. The same phenomenon, now viewed as a glamorous and inspired business coup, bears the label *conglomeration*.

Louis E. Wolfson

Louis E. Wolfson was one of the first and best-known of the "raiders." Son of an immigrant junk dealer, Wolfson borrowed $10,000 and engaged in buying and selling government surplus during and after World War II. He expanded by operating a shipyard in Jacksonville, Florida, and in 1948 secured control of Washington, D. C.'s, Capital Transit Company.

In 1951 Wolfson became chairman of Merritt-Chapman and Scott, a construction firm, which he started on a tremendous diversification program. By 1956 his many acquisitions were organized into seven groups: manufacturing, equipment, steel, chemicals, shipbuilding, construction, and personal enterprises. Previously he was engaged in the transportation field through Capital Transit which he sold at a substantial profit early in his raiding career. The scope of Wolfson's activities would today designate him as a prime conglomerator.

Wolfson's prominence as a raider reached its zenith in the period 1955–1958. In 1955 using Merritt-Chapman and its $375 million sales and $132 million net worth as his base, Wolfson made a grandiose grab for control of Montgomery Ward and Company, then run by Sewell Avery. This attempt brought him widespread characterization as a raider; his tactics included a quiet buying up of Montgomery Ward's underpriced stock, and his objective presumably was a $300 million nest egg of idle cash and liquid assets accumulated by Montgomery Ward. Although he was not able to get sufficient proxy votes to control the company and won only three seats on Montgomery Ward's board, Wolfson did make a sizable profit on his investment in Montgomery Ward stock when he later disposed of his shares. Even in defeat raiders, like their successors, the conglomerators, invariably made a profit because the value of the stock they held in the intended acquisition had skyrocketed in anticipation of a merger.

No depth analysis is needed to note the similarities in this raiding episode and in the merger maneuvers of the late 1960's. The tactics and strategies are identical and the objectives are the same. From a managerial point of view the aggressors, raiders, mergers, and conglomerators can be scarcely differentiated. The managements of firms capitulating to raiders in the 1950's had the same "tired blood" characteristics so evident in many acquired companies in the late 1960's mergers. Wolfson, reflecting on joining Montgomery Ward's board, succinctly describes the old-guard's petrified attitude.

"You should have seen that first board meeting," he laughed. Standing up behind his desk, he gave an imitation of the Ward men at the meeting. "Everyone looked like undertakers. This man came in with a dark blue suit and a high collar, the next with a black suit and high collar. And they sat down at the table very properly and very seriously. Each stood up to read his report, then sat down very stiffly. Each report was read to Avery, even though he was just a director by then. He wasn't even head of the company. I nearly bust out laughing and punched Rittmaster (Wolfson's closest adviser) and said, "My God, what have we got into?" But later on, things got more relaxed. Oh, it took a couple of meetings, but we began to get along fine." [1]

Wolfson sold out his minority position in Montgomery Ward in 1956 and turned to other interests. He had been a stockholder in the Hudson Corporation which merged with Nash to form American Motors in 1954 and so he became a stockholder in the new firm. Eventually he increased his holdings to 9% of American Motors stock and attempted to take over the company, first in 1956 and several times subsequently. In the process he had to divest his empire of several of his smaller companies.

Wolfson failed to get control of American Motors and soon thereafter his troubles began to compound. He had sold short a very sizable block of American Motors stock and suffered a severe loss when the stock, instead of falling, rose significantly. Even worse, Merritt-Chapman, the bastion of his empire built by raiding-merging, suffered a $29.7 million loss in 1960 and subsequently began an uninterrupted decline. Sales in 1959 reached $428 million, but by 1968 were down to about $7 million; net income dropped from $9 million to a loss of more than a half million; owners' equity was squeezed from $145 million to less than $60 million.

Worse than the monetary loss was the loss of position and prestige. A series of lawsuits were started by stockholders and federal agencies charging Wolfson with perjury, filing false reports with the SEC, and conspiring to defraud company stockholders. In partial settlement of more than a dozen of these suits, a New York State judge ordered Wolfson to pay Merritt-Chapman $750,000. His salary, which despite his

[1] *Fortune*, "Why Things Went Sour for Louis Wolfson," by Richard Hammer, 161 (September 1961).

firm's troubles totaled $525,000 in 1965 and $453,150 in 1966, was ordered cut. In August 1968 Wolfson was found guilty on other charges; in December he was sentenced to serve four concurrent 18-month terms and fined $32,000. This was in addition to a one-year jail sentence and a $100,000 fine imposed on Wolfson for selling unregistered stock in Continental Enterprises, which he also owned. Late in December 1968 a United States Court of Appeals affirmed the conviction in Continental Enterprises.

This saga of sagging success certainly does not typify all raiding experiences. Neither is there any implication that a similar fate awaits all current-era conglomerators. There is, however, a managerial moral. For the most part the raiders of the early 1950's were freewheeling, ruggedly individualistic types who did not shy away from great risks if they could lead to great success. A prime characteristic of all raiders was the concentration of control in one man—the raider. There were no effective checks and balances, which had a positive feature in that decisions were almost instantaneous. What the raider wanted, he got. A negative aspect of this same trait was the danger that the raider, lacking in technical competency in most if not all of the multitudinous activities engaged in by his empire, could easily make costly blunders in his decisions. Actually, Wolfson's troubles could be traced to a very serious slump in the performance of New York Shipbuilding Company, one of Merritt-Chapman's early acquisitions. It should also be noted that much of the legal onus the courts placed on Wolfson was more the consequence of individual actions than that of corporate actions. Yet in this and comparable raider-merger cases the identity of the raider is meshed too much with that of *his* corporation. In the absence of effective checks and balances the one-man type of control can easily lead to at least arbitrary actions and sometimes even to illegal and unethical actions. Hopefully, the current breed of merger-conglomerators will have learned from observing their predecessors, the raiders, and will be less inclined to act as if the entire corporation is theirs to do with as they will when, in fact, it is publicly owned.

An authoritarian raider could also be unduly susceptible to the backlash from preferential associations with so-called cronies. Alexander Rittmaster became Wolfson's closest adviser in 1949. "Mr. Rittmaster acknowledged that from 1951 to 1966 he received $1,209,000 in compensation acting as financial consultant, director and member of the executive committee of Merritt-Chapman." [2] In the subsequent trials the prosecution scored one of its biggest victories when this same Rittmaster

[2] *The Wall Street Journal,* 8 (June 19, 1968).

reversed his position and pleaded guilty to one count of conspiracy. "His trial was severed from that of the others and he became a key Government witness." [3]

Early in 1969, Rittmaster was sentenced to four months in prison and fined $5000 after pleading guilty. The assistant United States Attorney, prosecuting the Merritt-Chapman case, commended Rittmaster and stated that Wolfson's conviction could not have been obtained without Rittmaster's testimony which was "full, complete, sincere, and truthful."

Louis Wolfson was judged guilty for selling the unregistered stock of Continental Enterprises and received a one-year prison sentence and a $100,000 fine. Late in 1968 he was also found guilty in conspiring to obstruct a Securities and Exchange Commission investigation into sales and purchases of Merritt-Chapman and Scott Corporation stock. For this offense he was sentenced to concurrent 18-month prison terms on each of four counts and was fined $32,000. In a subsequent shareholders' derivative suit initiated by five stockholders against Merritt-Chapman and Scott, a New York State Court ordered Wolfson to repay the Corporation $303,075 of the 1967 salary of $453,075 paid Wolfson by the Corporation. As another sorry aftermath of this episode, Mr. Abe Fortas, an Associate Justice of the Supreme Court, was forced to relinquish his post when it was disclosed that he had been paid $20,000 by the Wolfson Foundation in 1966. Mr. Fortas returned the $20,000 fee after Wolfson was indicted in the Continental Enterprises case. "If Louis Wolfson is to be believed, he could have obtained a Presidential pardon last December. . . . Through political connections, the millionaire industrialist says, he could [have] secured a pardon from President Johnson if he had asked for it. Wolfson says he received this assurance 'from somebody who is as close as anybody could be' to Mr. Johnson." [4] Mr. Wolfson turned down this chance at executive intercession and served his sentences.

Pertinent to the concept of corporate confederation, an extremely significant observation was made by Wolfson at the 1966 annual meeting of his firm. He stated that after the problems were resolved, he was terminating all association with the company and would never again have anything to do with any publicly owned concern. " 'Such businesses,' he asserted, 'no longer suit his taste.' He characterized himself as an individualist who 'can't conform to conformity,' and as a 'misfit in publicly owned corporations,' which he said are run more and more by lawyers and a 'robot type of management.' " [5]

[3] *The Wall Street Journal* (August 9, 1968).
[4] *The Wall Street Journal*, 32 (April 22, 1969).
[5] *The Wall Street Journal* (April 26, 1966).

This comment and a subsequent reference by Wolfson to the effect that in his scheme the delegation of corporate responsibilities had not always been successful point up the importance of managers and management techniques for successful raiding, merging, conglomerating, or just plain running a business. At the end of the Merritt-Chapman trial Wolfson noted, " 'Perhaps what I am guilty of is depending too heavily upon others to accept the responsibility in these specialized areas,' he continued, adding, 'I had the responsibility to run this corporation and made practically every major decision as its chief executive officer.' " [6] In Wolfson's case his apparent inability to continue competent managements in the many subsidiaries led to either autonomous or apathetic control. Inadequate communications between headquarters and the subsidiaries was likewise a factor. Even though the verbal flow of communications might have been voluminous, the inability of Wolfson and his nontechnically trained inner circle to comprehend undoubtedly aggravated the situation. Many other vital management principles such as long-range planning, performance controls, and motivation of technically competent executives outside of the headquarter's staff also seemed to get little attention. This case might be a preview of what can happen to any firm that takes too lightly the precepts of sound management. But there is also the possibility that if Wolfson had been able to weather, in better form, the period of the early 1960's he might still have been able to propel Merritt-Chapman back into the league of big-time conglomerators when a more propitious business climate and a merger-mad public attitude prevailed.

Edward O. Lamb

It is not unusual that many of yesterday's raiders were endowed with charismatic attributes. (Most of them had a gift for winning the confidence of many small investors.) In 1954, when Edward Lamb launched his empire building by seeking control of Air-Way Electric Appliance Corporation, a Toledo vacuum-cleaner firm, he took to the air over a Toledo radio station, which he owned, and gave battle. Evidently statements such as "Air-Way is a splendid company, although the antiquated management has not been able to reform Air-Way's antiquated sales methods" [7] won the confidence of enough investors to give him control of the company. Although he made charges of antiquated management during his proxy fight, Lamb himself did not run Air-Way more efficiently. In the year before the takeover Air-Way earned nearly a half

---

[6] *The Wall Street Journal*, 30 (December 9, 1968).
[7] *The Wall Street Journal*, "Industry In Fighter," **LXVI**, 99, 1.

million dollars on sales of more than $12 million. The next year, under Lamb, the company lost nearly $400,000 on sales of about $15 million. In 1956 the company lost $2.7 million and ever since has been plagued by very spotty performance. This has led critics to praise Lamb's intelligence and ability as a corporate battler while questioning his management ability. "A former official of Air-Way asks 'What company has he successfully run?' " [8]

In 1955 he started a campaign to take over Seiberling Rubber Company and succeeded in doing so seven years later. Again as in virtually all raiding episodes the victim was a rather poorly managed firm with obvious regression syndrome symptoms. Mr. Lamb became interested in Seiberling when he noted that its stock, although selling at $9 a share, had a net asset value of about $23 per share. This was a perfect raider's target especially since the firm had only 587,000 outstanding shares.

True to expected raiding procedure Lamb gave the press and the public a knight-in-white-armor first impression. He elevated H.P. Schrank, executive vice-president and an able technician, as the company's new president and chief executive officer. Although Schrank was given a five-year contract, most of the other Seiberling executives and old-guard directors were quickly removed from the scene.

Performance at Seiberling soon matched Lamb's record at his first major takeover—Air-Way Electric Appliance Company. The Seiberling acquisition lost money in three of the next four years. Lamb then sold Seiberling's tire-making division to Firestone Tire and Rubber Company for $31 million which demonstrates Lamb's raiding genius. Even though his takeovers have turned out to be consistent losers from operations, Lamb has managed to make sizable profits by dismembering the acquisitions and selling off their undervalued assets. Lamb paid about $5 million for his nearly half ownership in Seiberling. Thus the sale of the tire division alone would mean a profit as much as $10 million for Lamb plus his remaining interest in Seiberling's other assets.

The remaining components of Seiberling were then grouped with certain other Lamb holdings to form Seilon. Returns from operations both at Seilon and at Lamb's other operating company, Lamb Industries, continued to be unspectacular. Seilon lost nearly a million dollars in 1967. Lamb Industries became a corporate shell with extensive debts and faced delisting from the American Stock Exchange. In typical raider fashion, however, the buying and selling continued. In mid-1968 Seilon agreed to sell its one-sixth interest in Copolymer Rubber and Chemical Corporation for $5.5 million in cash. Late in 1968 Seilon took control of

[8] *Ibid.*

First Bancorporation, a Nevada one-bank holding company, through an investment of $2.7 million. Early in 1970 Seilon's stockholders voted to sell the firm's most profitable division, Lockwood Corporation, to Alaska Interstate Company (a $20-million sales conglomerate) "in order to pay off $8,093,451 of bank loans of which $7,267,000 was in default." [9] The total price, including assumed liabilities, was just under $10 million. Seilon's profit on this deal was estimated at about $2.4 million. After the sale, Seilon, once an ambitious raider turned conglomerate, had left just two components, Thomson Manufacturing Company and a 36% interest in First Bancorporation.

Returning to the concept of corporate confederation, it is quite evident that most of Lamb's raiding ventures turned out to be highly profitable but to repeat an earlier quoted comment, " 'What company has he successfully run?' " [10] Some very serious blemishes are on his management record. Air-Way went through four presidents in three years after Lamb's takeover. Seilon had four presidents in six years. A similar instability seems to characterize the entire executive group and even the work force. This phenomenon is probably a consequence of Lamb's unfamiliarity with manufacturing industry.

Mr. Lamb's frequently expressed managerial philosophy is to set up a small closely knit staff of young aggressive management people. A good example of this Lamb philosophy is seen in the October 1968 "restructuring" of Seilon when P. N. Wehr, Jr., age 47, resigned as president. The company's 30-year-old chairman and chief executive officer, John H. Hickman (he succeeded Edward Lamb in April 1968), then formed a new "office of the chairman" as the top policy post. " 'As a practical matter, I will be chief administrative officer, as well as chief executive officer and chairman,' he said. 'Our need for operating types has decreased and our need for planning people and for the execution of growth through acquisitions and mergers has grown.' " [11] As members of his office of the chairman, Hickman then named Maxon W. Furness, the 34-year-old assistant to the chairman, Leroy W. Sigler, age 40, vice-president for legal services, and Richard A. Moore, age 30, treasurer and controller. Within less than a year, the 32-year-old chairman, president and chief executive officer, John H. Hickman III, resigned after the company's 1968 loss of about $1 million was followed by a $1.3 million loss in the first six months of 1969. (That year's net loss reached $4.4 million.) The youthful Hickman was succeeded in the president's post by still another youngster, 31-year-old Robert T. Guyton.

[9] *The Wall Street Journal* (February 25, 1970).
[10] *The Wall Street Journal,* "Industry In Fighter," **LXVI**, 99, 1.
[11] *The Wall Street Journal* (October 23, 1968).

Seilon and Lamb's stress on youthful top executives points to significant differences between raiders (yesterday's and today's) and modern mergers and conglomerations. There is evidence, at least in the press, that most modern mergers are serious ventures with long-run operational aspirations. Consequently, they put a premium on managerial and technical competency with the obvious result that youth is conspicuous by its absence in top managerial posts of both the taken-over and taking-over firms. There are, of course, some notable exceptions particularly among the key conglomerators themselves.

Raiders, to the contrary, seem to have little, if any, intention of remaining permanently in the raided firm's line of business. If a fast sale of the previously undervalued assets is the raider's prime objective, then, obviously, investing in competent but costly managerial and technical talent is far beyond the raider's intent. Serious questions should be asked as to the economic and social consequences of this instant attrition and replacement of top managers. If such action does perk up a sluggish management, thereby putting the firm's assets to better use, then the results might be beneficial. However, if this is just a Las Vegas illusion, that value and profits are created by a fast shuffle, then raiding and raiders should be considered suspect. Edward Lamb, who continues in the real control center as vice-chairman of Seilon and its major stockholder, seems to be unable to shift in his thinking and acting from the prototype raider of the 1950's to the new conglomerator of the 1960's and 1970's.

U. S. HOFFMAN MACHINERY CORPORATION

The rise and fall of U. S. Hoffman Machinery Corporation illustrates the significance of risks inherent in most raiding episodes. Late in 1953 a group of financiers, led by Herbert Malkin and Hyman Marcus, captured control of the company. One of the tantalizing objectives was the rather sizable accounts receivable and cash held by U. S. Hoffman. In its bid for control the financial group paid approximately $20 per share. After their successful raid they were disappointed to find that the liquidation value of the stock was only in the $13 to $14 range. More than $7 million of current assets consisted of installment contracts which would most likely be defaulted the moment the company went out of business. This discovery led the raiders to take another risk to try to stay in business. They decided to get rid of the manufacturing facilities and to use subcontractors. Although the raiders in this instance did not liquidate the firm, they did liquidate the fixed assets. Because of this move, 1954 became a very prosperous year. The company reduced current liabilities from $22 million to $6 million; it paid off $13 million in bank loans and showed a profit of $600,000 versus a 1953 loss of nearly a million dollars. Management then split the stock three for one and the price of the common stock zoomed to $33 per share. This was nearly a 400% increase over the price the raiders had paid for their investment.

Performance continued at a high level through 1956 when the company earned over a million dollars on sales of nearly $91 million. The company expanded, diversifying in several directions including vending machines, metal containers, dry-cleaning and laundry equipment, movie screens, pneumatic conveying equipment, gray-iron castings, military ordnance and other products. Although it was never referred to as such, this was a conglomerate.

In less than eight years, however, the company was in dire straits. Beginning with 1957, the firm had suffered an unbroken string of annual losses. (In 1964 losses totaled $2.2 million on sales of $16.6 million compared with $1.0 million profit on $91 million sales in 1956). Two of its principal subsidiaries were bankrupt. The company had an accumulated deficit of $20 million and deficiency in net assets of $2.3 million. The New York Stock Exchange delisted U. S. Hoffman securities in 1962 because its earnings and assets did not meet exchange requirements. Its corporate headquarters in Newark, (New Jersey) were closed and the courts put a 10% weekly garnishee on the $50,000 annual salary of Harold Roth who was then chairman, president, and chief executive officer of U. S. Hoffman. Mr. Roth owned about 15% of the company's stock and was its largest stockholder.

The decline in U. S. Hoffman's performance "came largely from the disposal of most of its subsidiaries in order, management said, to raise cash or to divest unprofitable operations. This system trimming, however, failed to put the company back in the black." [12]

The catastrophe was preceded by a series of very questionable maneuvers involving sales of U. S. Hoffman assets to other Roth-controlled enterprises, particularly Continental Vending Machine Corporation and Hoffman International Corporation (listed on the American Stock Exchange) which U. S. Hoffman had spun off in 1958. There was considerable shifting back and forth of assets and subsidiaries.

The bubble burst in 1963 when the American Stock Exchange suspended trading in Continental Vending stock. The Securities and Exchange Commission subsequently forced the company into bankruptcy charging "that Mr. Roth and his associates had siphoned off some $4 million in cash through a Roth-controlled affiliate, Valley Commer-

[12] *The Wall Street Journal*, 26 (July 27, 1965).

cial Corp." [13] The court-appointed trustee then filed a $45 million civil damage suit against Roth and his associates, including U. S. Hoffman.

This illustration forcibly brings out a very significant characteristic found in all raids and in many of today's mergers. The raider, and raider-type conglomerator, meshes his own personal financial interests with those of his firm so that it is almost impossible to see any lines of demarcation. Consequently, the progress of his empire moves in unison with that of the raider (or raiding-type conglomerator). This is fine on the upswing but can be disastrous in adversity.

CURTIS PUBLISHING COMPANY

In today's financial parlance the terms "raider" and "raiding" are virtually archaic. However, we must not assume that we have done away with raiders and raiding techniques simply because we have dropped a few words from our business vocabulary. The phenomenon which was prevalent two decades ago is even more prevalent today. The only difference is that we now euphemistically call the technique and the participants by less derogatory terms.

One of the more current examples of raiding in the late 1960's is the debacle at Curtis Publishing Company. In 1954 the company ranked 181st in *Fortune*'s listing of major industrial firms. Sales were in the $180 million bracket; assets were in excess of $91 million. The company was a pillar of stability from its inception until 1961 when it had its first loss of $4.2 million. The next six years (with one exception) were also loss-heavy so that in the period 1961–1968 the company lost nearly $60 million. By 1969, because of its steadily decreasing sales and equity, the company no longer ranked even among the nation's top 1000 firms.

In 1962 the Curtis and Bok families, which had been in control, were replaced by a group of Wall Streeters led by Treves and Company and including J. R. Williston and Beane, Carl M. Loeb, and Rhoades and Company. Called by any other name—takeover, reorganization, financial coup—this was still a raid, or it soon became one.

In 1964 a classic "palace revolution" took place at Curtis and involved at least 17 of the company's top executives and editors, led by Clay Blair, Jr., editor-in-chief of Curtis Magazines, and Marvin D. Kantor, chairman of the Curtis Magazines Division. The immediate cause for the revolt was the continued losses at Curtis ($18.9 million in 1962, $3.4 million in 1963, and $14 million in 1964) and the objective was to depose the firm's chairman, Matthew J. Culligan. The revolt fizzled because

[13] *Ibid.*

Serge Semenenko, the flamboyant Boston financier who had headed a six-bank group that refinanced $35 million of Curtis' debt, continued to support Culligan. What apparently happened at this point was that one group of raiders superseded another group.

Mr. Semenenko's impact on Curtis Publishing during this period was very much like that of a raider. Although Semenenko's bank, First National of Boston, advanced almost one-third of the $35 million, "as a concomitant, in addition to an interest rate one full percentage point above the prime rate, First National Bank of Boston received an additional one-fourth of one per cent for acting as agent for the bank." [14]

Other questionable acts occurred such as Curtis' obligation to keep hefty balances, which earned no interest, in the bank and the switching of $38 million of the company's pension funds to an affiliate of First National of Boston. "Mr. Semenenko allegedly profited personally from this association. He bought a considerable block of Curtis stock at depressed prices. Subsequently, after a significant ore strike on some Curtis Company land, Semenenko sold his holdings at a profit." [15]

Ironically, Mr. Culligan was ousted in 1965, just when Curtis showed a profit of almost $11 million. On the surface this performance reversal gave Curtis the distinction of having the best rate of return among *Fortune's* listed firms. Curtis in 1965 earned a phenomenal 53% on its invested capital. There is, however, a slight hitch in this record since the company had experienced a significant capital shrinkage during the past three years and thus the computational base was misleading. More significantly, all the profit came from the sale of $35 million worth of Curtis' best assets. These sales served also to conceal an operating loss for the year of $3.4 million. The significant point about this commentary was that Culligan and, supposedly, his sponsor, Semenenko, were using typical raiding techniques to dismember Curtis Publishing. Presumably this was a matter of exigency, of dire need; nevertheless the raiding label applies. Judging dispassionately, one might ask what the outcome might have been if these valuable assets had not been sold. It is very obvious that as a troubled firm begins to dispose of its best assets, its problems will likely multiply.

This is precisely what happened at Curtis Publishing. In April 1968 a 36-year-old financier, Martin S. Ackerman, seemingly came to Curtis' rescue by providing a much-needed loan of $5 million through his personally controlled Perfect Film and Chemicals Corporation. Almost immediately there was a series of slashes in Curtis Publishing activities

[14] Stanley C. Vance, *The Corporate Director*, Dow Jones-Irwin, 1968, p. 51.
[15] *Ibid.*, p. 52.

and a selling-off of still more assets. It is intriguing to note the raiding pattern in the asset sell-offs; for example, the profitable magazine distribution and subscription procurement subsidiaries were sold to Perfect Film and Chemical for $12.5 million. Perfect also got four Curtis magazines: *Saturday Evening Post, Holiday, Status,* and *Jack and Jill.* "Although Perfect took title to the magazines and all their assets, Curtis was left with the liability of fulfilling the magazines' subscriptions and the responsibility for any legal actions and tax claims." [16] Assuming these facts, Ackerman's actions involving Curtis Publishing and Perfect Film are in the best raiding tradition.

Many other episodes supported this contention such as the switching of auditors from Price Waterhouse and Company which, in Ackerman's words, had done an outstanding job to Touché, Ross, Bailey and Smart, the firm which serves Perfect Film as auditors.

When Curtis Publishing purchased *Status* magazine in August 1968 distribution of *Status* was switched from Independent News Company to Curtis Circulation Company, a subsidiary of Perfect Film.

More recently Ackerman engineered an investment involving $3.5 million of *Saturday Evening Post* cash to obtain 4% of the stock in LIN Broadcasting Company and then took over as president and chief executive officer. In 1967 LIN earned only $56,000 and, on the basis of its $3.5 million investment and 4% control in LIN, this would represent a return of considerably less than 1% on the *Post's* investment. The LIN stock for which *Saturday Evening Post* paid $44 per share in a private deal was quoted just five weeks later at $18 per share. Assuming the legality of this action, much is still reminiscent of the earlier raiders.

In February 1969 Ackerman engineered a transference of $6 million out of the Curtis Pension Plan and Trust on the flimsy contention that this huge sum was surplus and not needed to meet actuarial obligations. One million of this sum was then used as working capital and $5 million was put into *Saturday Evening Post.* When the Curtis Council of Unions instituted a suit charging that Ackerman and his two associate trustees "misappropriated, fraudulently converted, and dissipated" $6 million from the Pension Plan and Trust, Ackerman threatened to close down the printing plant. He further demanded that the suit be dropped and that he be allowed to withdraw another $4 million from the "surplus funds" of the pension reserves. " 'It'll be put up or shut up,' " he said. " 'What do you want, the suit or jobs?' " [17] This move into the company's pension fund by Ackerman is a good example of a conventional raiding

---

[16] *The Wall Street Journal,* 28 (February 7, 1969).
[17] *The Wall Street Journal,* 6 (March 3, 1969).

technique. Initially the pension fund had been very ably managed by
U. S. Trust Company of New York. The soundness of this earlier trustee's management is evident in the fact that the fund actually did show a
surplus. Then upon taking over the company. Ackerman replaced U. S.
Trust with the Fidelity Bank of Philadelphia as trustee. Again, late in
1968 Fidelity Bank was dropped as the Pension Fund's trustee and control over the fund was vested in Ackerman and two of his closest colleagues G. B. McCombs, the company's executive vice-president, and
E. Eugene Mason, the company's secretary. For all practical purposes,
Ackerman then had complete control over the employees' pension fund.
This action, in addition to illustrating a not-so-subtle raiding technique,
also calls attention to the imperative need for removing corporate
executives and directors from the administration of all tempting morsels
such as employee pension funds.

On February 3, 1969 two preferred stockholders filed charges alleging
a series of improprieties since Martin S. Ackerman became Curtis' president while remaining chairman and president of Perfect Film and
Chemical Corporation. One of the complainants alleged that Ackerman,
Perfect Film, and former and present directors "'entered into a plan,
scheme, and conspiracy to liquidate Curtis by causing to sell or dispose
of its principal assets and businesses.' Part of the plan, he charges, was
that Curtis would sell some assets to Perfect Film for 'wholly inadequate
considerations.'" [18] The other suit charged Ackerman with "illegal, op-
pressive and fraudulent actions that have misapplied and wasted more
than $45 million of Curtis' assets." [19]

On February 6, 1969 the Trustees of Cyrus H. K. Curtis estate, which
holds about 32% of Curtis Publishing common stock and 22% of its preferred (Mr. Ackerman personally owns only 100 or 200 shares), asked for
Ackerman's resignation. There is an interesting, and perhaps pathetic,
commentary on the role of the dissident but silent directors in this and
similar cases. It was pointed out that the two Curtis Estate representatives on the board "unanimously voted to approve most of the actions
proposed by Mr. Ackerman since he took the Curtis helm last April.
But, this source explained, "'the directors were bamboozled. They went
along (with Mr. Ackerman), but they still don't know what they approved and what they didn't approve. He'd say he was doing one thing,
and then he'd do another.'" [20] Subsequently it was pointed out that for
more than a half-year, no written minutes of Curtis board meetings had
been submitted to the directors themselves. Nor were they regularly

[18] *The Wall Street Journal*, 4 (February 4, 1969).
[19] *Ibid.*
[20] *The Wall Street Journal*, 28 (February 7, 1969).

supplied with financial information or copies of the sales contracts involving disposal of Curtis' assets.

From a leadership point of view it does seem obvious that Ackerman's 10-month tenure showed all the characteristics of raiding. The old-guard directors and executives were in a deep sleep. The chronic manifestation of regression syndrome symptoms attests to this inference. Even subsequent to Ackerman's takeover, the old-guard directors seemed to have been passive onlookers to the dismemberment of their organization. It seems that the only way directors under Ackerman could express their disagreement was to resign. In the nine-month period, eight directors quit the board. Only one director at that time had served more than two years.

Relative to the board of directors, there is an interesting episode involving Lewis D. Gilbert, the perennial gadfly at corporate annual meetings. Mr. Gilbert attended the 1968 Curtis Publishing annual meeting—his first such attendance at Curtis since 1941. (Considering that Mr. Gilbert attends several hundred corporate annual meetings yearly and keeping in mind Curtis' pathetic performance for almost a decade, the 27-year absence implies agreement on Gilbert's part with Curtis' top policy makers.) At this meeting Gilbert objected to inside directors (officers serving also as board members) receiving a $50 fee for attending board meetings. In 1969 there were two officer-directors, together with 11 outside directors on the board. At a time when Curtis Publishing Company was averaging nearly $10 million losses per year, the $50 fee paid to officer-directors per meeting (a maximum outlay of $1200 per year) does seem to be nitpicking. Perhaps this is one of the talents of the gifted raider: to channel criticism onto extraneous matters, thus reducing surveillance and questioning of the more germane activities.

Turnover in the directorate ranks was matched by a comparable instability in other management areas. Four different chief editors held office between 1961 and 1964. There were six chief executive officers in a seven-year period. However, the saddest commentary on dismemberment through raiding, as seen at Curtis Publishing, was the attrition among employees: the workforce shriveled from 8500 in 1964 to about 2000 in 1969. Even this drastically shrunken workforce remained in a tenuous position. On March 3, 1969, after a meeting of the board, Ackerman resigned as Curtis' president and chief executive officer. At the annual meeting in May a completely new board of directors was voted in with the Curtis Estate winning nine out of eleven directorships up for election.

This fairly recent experience at Curtis Publishing Company provides incontestable proof that although the terms "raider" and "raiding" may no longer be found in the financial lexicon, raiders and raiding by other names are very much at work. Times, mores, and the attitude of the press certainly have changed. For example, Ackerman's fiasco in arbitrarily cutting the *Post*'s subscription list from 6.8 million to 3 million has been glamorized by some news media commentators as his strategic attempt to turn the *Post* from a "mass" to a "class" magazine. Ackerman's reference to himself serving as Curtis Publishing's unpaid chief executive has likewise been rather favorably presented in the press. This dedication, minus salary, has elicited from Ackerman the publicized comment that "If I do a good job, I think someone will find it in their heart to compensate me."

The new view of raiders and their tactics is fittingly expressed in an excellent analysis in *Business Week*. "When Martin S. Ackerman killed off the *Saturday Evening Post* last week, it might not have enhanced his stature as a publisher, but his nine-month association with the magazine has demonstrated his proficiency as a razzle-dazzle financial operator. . . . Ackerman is a prize specimen of the new breed of financial operators who, blessed with a flair for putting deals together, have become celebrities on the United States corporate scene." [21]

SUMMARY

Some of the better-known examples of corporate takeovers which only a decade ago were termed raids are listed below:

Corporation	Raider
New York Central Railroad	Robert R. Young
Thor Corporation	Arnold Maremont
Van Norman Company	Herbert I. Segal
International Telephone & Telegraph	J. Patrick Lannan
New York-New Haven and Hartford R.R.	
Pennsylvania Coal & Coke Company	Leopold D. Silberstein
Niles-Bement-Pond	
Air Way Electric Appliance	Edward Lamb
Ohio Match	Norton Simon
Hunt Foods	
Merritt-Chapman and Scott	Louis E. Wolfson
New York Shipbuilding	
Belllanca Aircraft	Sidney L. Albert
Waltham Watch	
Colt Manufacturing Company	David A. Goodkind

[21] *Business Week*, "Ackerman Looks Beyond the Post," 26 (January 18, 1969).

A casual check of the raided companies will show that in every instance before the raid, the firm had had a rather miserable performance record. However, even though the company was sick, it was not generally beyond restoration. In every instance the book value of the common stock was significantly higher than the market price. Also, because of ultracautious accounting techniques, the balance sheet frequently did not reveal valuable hidden assets. In such cases the raiders probably did have a good argument in claiming that they were performing a needed economic service by putting such idle resources to productive use.

Perhaps in the 1970's the debate over the good and bad of raiding will have only an historical interest. Yet, if there is substance in the allegation that many of today's mergers, and particularly conglomerations, are simply raids under the guise of a new name, then it could be worthwhile to glance backward and note the historical similarities. Both yesterday's raiders and their current counterparts sought and still seek the following:

1. Sick but not dying firms
2. Firms whose assets are undervalued
3. Companies in which management does not control more than 25 to 30% of the voting stock
4. Companies with a board of directors having a preponderance of outside directors
5. Companies with long-entrenched but lackluster managements
6. Companies in growth industries with below average records in these industries
7. Companies with relatively few shares of common stock

Bearing in mind these conditions it would be almost impossible to differentiate between the raids of the 1950's and today's more flamboyant raids. There is a new generation of raiders or raider-conglomerators, but their tactics and objectives remain the same. The one big difference is that today the men and firms engaged in what might figuratively be called necrophagous corporate functions are now respected and glamorized. The pendulum of public acceptance has definitely reversed its swing.

11

DIRECTORS IN A
CONGLOMERATE ERA

Following a merger, adjustments in the labor force and in supervisory personnel generally come slowly and only if the new firm is keenly concerned with improving efficiency. At the upper managerial levels and particularly at the very top, changes come faster and more frequently. Some of these changes in directorate composition take place for financial reasons, some from personal considerations, but all reflect a change in the organization's control center—the board of directors. At the lower organizational levels many of the merger-initiated changes are imperceptible. At the upper levels, executive and directorate, the changes tend to be more visible and more publicized. This probably is as it should be considering that it is the board of directors that sets the corporate course. The course an individual corporation elects to follow might have only incidental impact on business and society, but if the trailblazing firm is joined by enough equally adventuresome firms, the consequences can be significant. With this supposition in mind it seems quite important that we learn more about the men who are remaking our corporate system.

The following analysis is restricted to boards of directors. As a fundamental premise it is assumed that *every* member of a board is rationally selected and that he fulfills a vital need. Consequently, the composition of a board tells us much about the character of that board. If, for example, in a typical 14-man board there are 12 bankers, then this board is concerned primarily with money matters; if, on the other hand, there are 12 lawyers, then this is a firm beset with legal dealings. A company with an exclusively officer-director constituency can reflect the strong arm of an authoritarian leader, but an all-officer board can also indicate that this is a working board made up exclusively of men who contribute significantly to the company's operating needs. Conversely, a predominantly nonemployee board can be symptomatic of authoritarianism, particularly if the outsiders have minimal competency matched by an equally low interest level. The point being emphasized is this: corporate board structure affects corporate performance. Although it might be somewhat premature to pass judgment on the effectiveness of the more recent mergers, we can nevertheless view the new firms' board structures and note the more apparent trends.

Since there is no truly authoritative merger definition or compilation, it becomes very necessary to narrow the area of analysis. In this instance the investigation will deal only with the largest of mergers on the supposition that their impact is greatest not only operationally and financially but also from a precedent-setting point of view. *The Fortune Directory*, a ranking of the 500 largest United States industrial corporations, provides an authoritative source of information. The directorate dichotomy of officer-director and nonemployee-director boards supplies the necessary quantitative yardsticks for comparison purposes.

As a first step in the analysis it should be interesting to compare, on a corporate structure basis, the two parties to the merger: the acquiescing firm and the aggressor. In the period 1967 through 1968 there were at least 40 mergers of currently or previously *Fortune*-listed firms. From this group of 40 of our biggest corporations only four had boards of directors where half or more of the board consisted of officer-directors (for example, Glidden, Schenley, Stanley Warner, and Rockwell-Standard). By contrast virtually all the remaining merged firms have had predominantly nonemployee boards. In many cases the acquired firm had, in addition to its chairman and president, none or at best one other officer on the company's board (Wilson, Mack Truck, Blaw Knox, Rayonnier, E. W. Bliss, Island Creek Coal, Woodward Iron, Westinghouse Air Brake, Crucible Steel, etc.).

Among these 40 firms absorbed by merger the board had an average composition of 4.3 officers or former officers serving as directors and 8.0 nonemployee directors. This is equivalent to 35% inside control versus 65% outside control. These data contrast sharply with the typical manufacturing firm's board composition as tabulated by the National Industrial Conference Board in its most recent compilation. The NICB found that the typical manufacturing firm had a board averaging 12 members but with 42% of all board seats occupied by officers and 8% occupied by former officers.[1] Thus the typical board would have a 6 to 6

---

[1] *Corporate Directorship Practices*, National Industrial Conference Board, SPB 125, 1967, 6.

balance between company men and noncompany men serving as directors. By itself, the average 4.3 inside director versus 8.0 outside director balance for acquired firms can lead to an understatement. Actually, in the 40 company sample, only three firms had boards with a greater than 50% inside representation. Thirty-seven merged firms, consequently, had less than 50% such representation. Even more significant is the fact that 25 of these firms had less than one-third of their board seats filled by officers or former officers.

Since the absorbed firms had a disproportionate representation of outside directors, almost a two-to-one ratio as compared with the all-manufacturing balance of a one-to-one ratio, it is obvious that the outside influence on boards of directors is a sign of weakness—an easy mark for aggressive merger-minded companies. However, it would be unwarranted to assume that the lopsidedly outside-director type firms are always captured by the inside-type firms. Before any such inference can be made, it is necessary to get the facts. If the boards of the companies that swallowed up the 40 firms in this sample are analyzed on a director-type basis, the results will show a 8.3 inside-type director plus 7.6 outside-type director balance. Although this does not mean that the aggressor firms can be termed overwhelmingly inside type, they are certainly different in structure from their acquisitions.

On the basis of this evidence it seems reasonable to make an inference, namely, that the surest route to merger as the compliant party is to put top control in an outside board of directors. This inference gets support from logic and empirical analysis. The argument presented proceeds logically as follows: Every director must serve a real corporate *need*. A board which tolerates lackadaisical performance by even one board member soon finds its one deadbeat joined by additional deadwood. An apathetic board soon becomes an acquiescent board. The day of reckoning can be delayed or even averted if a strong dictator or benevolent despot takes complete and vigorous control. We have quite a few instances in some of our largest corporations where this strong-man type of leadership has led and continues to lead to outstanding performance. These exceptional firms attain eminence in large measure because the rank and file follow unquestioningly the dictates of a qualified and dynamic leader. But the odds are against any long-term resurgence of one-man control-concentration despite the remarkable success of neoentrepreneurs such as Charles B. Thornton, Harry E. Figgie, Jr., Henry Singleton, or Meshulam Riklis. These strong-man types lead to a cult of the personality, here aptly termed the cult of the chief executive officer. A number of these "men of gold" have already turned out to be "men of clay" (such as Louis E. Wolfson, William Zeckendorff, Victor

Muscat). In an era of high-intensity democracy the cult of the chief executive officer seems to be quite anachronistic. In the more stable, older corporations the growing number of Offices of the President, where presumably top authority and responsibility are shared by a team of three to five key executives, attests to the repudiation of the cult of the chief executive officer.

An obvious impersonality and intangibility occur in all arguments based on averages. Thus, although the evidence is incontestable that outside-director-type boards in large-scale manufacturing tend to be more merger prone, the inference needs vitalizing. It can be put into a meaningful and realistic context only when related to real live people and their corporations. The analysis which follows is such an attempt.

In any people-oriented situation, as the group expands the ramifications increase in a supergeometric order. Consequently, it is imperative that at least the analysis begin with an illustration of an aggressive acquisition-minded firm that has a relatively small board of directors.

TELEDYNE, INC.

Teledyne, founded just eight years ago, is an excellent example. In the short span of its existence Teledyne has acquired over 100 small firms and has moved steadily upward in the ranks of our biggest corporations. (*Fortune* placed it in the 84 spot in the 1969 listing.) Perhaps because of its relatively recent origin, Teledyne's board is very much like that used by so many of our earliest entrepreneur-type directorates. Even today despite its size (1969 sales: $1300 million, assets: $944 million, and 53,000 employees), top control is vested in a board of only six members:

Henry E. Singleton, chairman
George A. Roberts, president
Robert B. Sprague, vice-president

George Kozmetsky, former
executive vice-president
Arthur Rock
Claude E. Shannon

The significant thing about the board of this extremely dynamic firm is that the board actually manages and controls the company. Although the "to manage and to control" prescription appears in the charter of virtually every major corporation, there are a declining number of instances where this legal responsibility is strictly fulfilled. At Teledyne the character of the board implies effective managing and controlling. Every member of this board performs a meaningful function—all have been with Teledyne from its inception. Although three board members could technically be called outsiders, semantics should not cloud the issue. Every Teledyne director is a working member of the board.

George Kozmetsky, now dean of the College of Business Administration at the University of Texas, is a Teledyne cofounder and one of its principal stockholders. Arthur Rock was likewise involved in the original financing. Claude E. Shannon, an eminent scientist in the fields of mathematics and information theory, provides technological counsel. All the board members hold advanced academic degrees in technical fields and are presumably eminently qualified to run a space-age conglomerate.

This focus on Teledyne shows that the entrepreneur inside-type board of directors can perform most effectively in today's merger-oriented business environment. Considering the number and variety of acquired firms it is remarkable that only one of the merged firms (Sprague Engineering) has placed a member on Teledyne's board. It is equally remarkable that considering financing needs, no outside banker has usurped a board seat. With the maze of legal technicalities involved in the myriad mergers it is also a sign of strength that Teledyne has avoided adding lawyers to its board.

What of the future? It is very likely that Teledyne will be forced to modify its board because of further growth and increasing technical, financial, and political problems. The nature of the change will be determined by these problems and by the composite philosophy of Teledyne's current dynamic leadership.

"AUTOMATIC" SPRINKLER CORPORATION OF AMERICA

At the opposite end of the board structure continuum is "Automatic" Sprinkler Corporation of America. This recently launched conglomerate (1964) is very much the product of one man's imagination and aggressiveness. Harry E. Figgie, Jr., Chairman, President, and Chief-Executive Officer, is the epitome of the autocratic finance-oriented entrepreneur. His 13-member board includes only three company officers, Figgie, a division president, and the vice-president finance. The 1967 Annual Report stresses that all the board members except three are outsiders, yet the Company says this board is "in every sense a working board. Meeting once each month, the directors not only contribute their broad knowledge to operating problems and financial matters, but their record of help in sales, personnel and acquisitions has also been outstanding."[2] We must point out that in this loyal and supposedly working board at least six members are long-time associates of Figgie's, either from his earlier career at Booz, Allen and Hamilton or from "Automatic" Sprinkler's early financing.

---

[2] "Automatic" Sprinkler, *Annual Report*, 1967, p. 40.

The meteoric rise of Figgie's firm is a matter of record. The 1969 *Fortune* listing gives it a rank of 277 with sales of $325 million, assets of $211 million, and a workforce of 16,000. It would seem that two diametrically different board structures, Teledyne's and "Automatic" Sprinkler's, can be equally conducive to success in the new conglomerate era. However, there is one slight joker to this conclusion. Both firms have operated in a climate of unprecedented prosperity. There had been no drastic catharsis in the business community since 1960. With "Automatic" Sprinkler the commotion following the release of the company's 1968 first-half earnings report could indicate heavier clobbering to come. The announcement that earnings had plummeted from a previous 93 cents a share to a low of 17 cents a share toppled the common stock from a $74 per share price to $18 per share. The sharp drop in the approximately 50 to 1 price-earnings multiplier reflected the financial community's loss of faith in what then appeared to be a high-flyer with acrophobia.

From a board structure point of view it is important to note that at this first reversal Figgie took prompt and autocratic action; he fired two of his former Booz, Allen and Hamilton associates including James J. Gilligan who was his number two man, a director and also vice-president finance. Also fired were the presidents of the company's Vandalarm, Essick, Powhatan, Scott Aviation, and Baifield Divisions. This autocratic action, the firing of six executives with presidential titles or equivalent, reflects on the inadequacy of the corporate structure. Despite the titles with presumably some measure of authority, "Automatic" Sprinkler's 24 divisions headed by presidents do not have a single representative on the board. In theory they should communicate through other channels—operations review committees and the like. Nevertheless, without adequate divisional representation on the board, the operating heads tend to have limited contact with top-policy making, and the top-policy makers in turn tend to have insufficient information.

"Automatic" Sprinklers' troubles continued even after Figgie's determined and Draconic edicts abolishing all semblance of corporate confederation. Despite further talk of continued conglomeration and a somewhat change in the earning's picture, the firm's stock market quotation plummeted further, reaching a 1969–1970 low of 6. In what could have been interpreted as an attempt to shed the negative corporate image, "Automatic" Sprinkler late in 1969 changed its name to A-T-O, Inc., the firm's New York Stock Exchange symbol. Mr. Figgie's reason for this change was his contention that the company had grown from a small concern engaged primarily in fire protection systems to a widely diversified company.

This single negative experience should not be misconstrued as an indictment against all boards that completely divorce the operational aspects from the policy-making function. Textron, probably the first of the new conglomerates, follows a rigid policy of separating the two groups. It theorizes that inclusion of division heads on a board will invariably lead to a wheeling and dealing in order to get divisional preferential treatment to the detriment of over-all objectives. Consequently, Textron includes only three officers in its 13-man board.

GULF AND WESTERN INDUSTRIES

A board including division heads as directors has been referred to derogatorily as a "legislature." As Textron's representatives claim, many weaknesses can exist in this practice. Nevertheless there seems to be a growing number not only of the newer conglomerates but also of the more dynamic older firms which subscribe to the use of a legislature as the top policy-making forum. Gulf and Western Industries, ranked 69 in *Fortune*'s 1969 listing, is one illustration. In 1961 Gulf and Western had a nine-man board of which five were definitely officers and two others, although holding officer title, also held full-time positions outside the company. With its rapid growth Gulf and Western also modified its board structure into the legislature type. The 1967 Annual Report shows the following:

12 officer directors (7 general officers, 5 divisional heads)
 5 outside directors
17 directors

By mid-1968 Gulf and Western had made several additional major acquisitions including E. W. Bliss, Consolidated Cigar, and Universal American. The June 1968 Proxy Statement relative to the proposal to annex Allis-Chalmers Manufacturing Company, Associates Investment Company, and Brown Company listed the Gulf and Western board composition as the following:

18 officer directors (6 general officers, 12 divisional heads)
 5 outside directors
23 directors

The divisional-head officer-directors represented 11 of Gulf and Western's more important acquired components. The more than doubling of these divisional representatives on the board seems to be a move toward a legislature-type board. Considering the size and importance of the three firms proposed for merger in this recent Gulf and Western proxy

(Allis-Chalmers, Brown, Associates Investment), it is almost a certainty that these acquisitions will likewise get proper representation on Gulf and Western's board. This adequate and proportionate boardroom representation for all of a parent company's subsidiaries and divisions can lead to complications in top-level control. First, it takes more than a King Solomon to determine equity and adequacy in proportionate representation on the board of a hyperdynamic conglomerate. In addition, the very size of these representative boards of directors can result in slow motion and stalemate. Partisan politics, sometimes leading to civil war, must be expected.

On the other hand, it is highly probable that a legislature-type board will be a better informed board. The divisional representatives, assuming that they head up semiautonomous profit centers, must invariably "put all their cards on the table." Figuratively, keeping a trump card hidden would be quite difficult and dangerous when dealing with one's peers. Although amenities and even filibusters can slow deliberations, a technically conversant group of peers can, when prompted, make exceptional progress. Then, too, there is an immeasurable value in the pride factor within the entire division when its chief is considered important enough to sit on the board. Whether these factors plus the many other advantages outweigh the very real limitations of directorate democracy is a matter for individual board resolution.

WALTER KIDDE AND COMPANY

The trend toward elevating certain key executives to the board as representatives of major divisions frequently replacing less essential outside directors is evident in numerous other conglomerate firms such as Walter Kidde and Company. In 1963 the 10-man board was equally divided, 5 to 5, between actively functioning officers and nonemployees. By 1969 this director mix had shifted to an almost completely inside-type directorate. Of the nine directors five were central office top executives and the remaining four represented important Kidde acquisitions (Globe Security, Fenwal, Inc., Weber Aircraft, and the Lighting division). These four recently appointed divisional-representative directors could indicate a move by Kidde toward the legislature-type board.

LING-TEMCO-VOUGHT, INC.

Ling-Temco-Vought provides a final illustration of what could be the board pattern of tomorrow's dynamic conglomerate. As recently as 1965 the Ling-Temco-Vought board included 5 officer-directors and 11 nonemployees. Only one of the inside directors could be termed a divisional representative. However, by 1968 the board contained

9 officer directors (3 general officers, 6 divisional heads)
<u>10</u> outside directors
19 directors

With the acquisition of Jones and Laughlin Steel Corporation, an even more positive move toward the legislature-type board was taken by Ling-Temco-Vought. In the merger proposal it was agreed that three LTV officials were to serve on the steel company's board and three top executives of Jones and Laughlin were to be added to LTV's board. In July 1968 three Jones and Laughlin representatives were named as LTV directors (Charles M. Beeghly, J and L's chairman and chief executive officer; William J. Stephens, president and chief operating officer; and H. Stuart Harrison, a J and L director).

The legislature effect in this board restructuring is obvious. It becomes even more evident if those outside directors who perform important economic services for LTV are considered as quasi-inside directors. Although they technically do not head divisions, they certainly function in very vital capacities. By analogy their services are comparable to the services of the divisional-head officer-directors; for example, as noted in the April 1968 Proxy Statement, Lehman Brothers was paid a total of $1,278,000 for services rendered LTV during 1967. Mr. William H. Osborn, Jr., a partner in Lehman Brothers, is also a director of Ling-Temco-Vought. Although Mr. Osborn is certainly not an LTV official, his performance is equivalent to that of a division head. By stretching the imagination, Mr. Osborn could be viewed as the head of a hypothetical LTV underwriting division.

Mr. Osborn's function was paralleled by that of Mr. Gustave L. Levy, a partner in Goldman, Sachs and Company. Mr. Levy's prime employer, Goldman, Sachs, was also paid a huge fee, $427,085 in 1967, for underwriting services. Consequently, the analogy could be extended to include Mr. Levy as a quasidivisional head. At least one additional bit of information is pertinent to this duality in roles performed by Mr. Osborn and Mr. Levy. Their major employers, Lehman Brothers and Goldman, Sachs, also acted as comanagers for an exchange of LTV 5% subordinate debentures for Greatamerica Corporation common stock. The fee, contingent here on the volume of shares exchanged, was set at a minimum of $400,000 but could reach $1,251,350.

This focus on the Lehman Brothers-Goldman, Sachs role in LTV financing is not meant to stir controversy as to the proper boardroom behavior of outside directors. Yet the charade of supposedly "public" directors who are actively engaged in negotiating deals between the host company and the director's prime employers needs to be exposed. Only by shutting one's eyes and fleeing into fantasy can such dual-loyal outside directors be termed protectors of the general investing public, particularly when they are performing important business functions in some instances just as important as those of division presidents.

At Ling-Temco-Vought the use of outside directors in this quasifunctional head capacity is not restricted to the underwriting function alone. Mr. Troy V. Post, a director of the company until June 1967, was the principal stockholder of Greatamerica Corporation before LTV's acquisition of Greatamerica in February 1968. As a consequence of this dual role Mr. Post could be considered as a quasi-inside director, performing in the acquisition's department.

Among other LTV outside directors whose impeccable public interest could be questioned are Mr. James H. Bond who has an 8% interest in Investment Bankers, the firm which owns and leases the LTV Tower, the company headquarters, for an annual rental of $1,188,000. (In September 1968 LTV announced the sale of the building for $16 million to a Bahamas-based investment fund.) Mr. A. D. Martin, Mr. L. T. Potter, and Mr. Bond, together with LTV's two top executives, Mr. James J. Ling and Mr. Clyde Skeen, are also on the boards of banks which do substantial business with the corporation.

At LTV the concept of top corporate control has still another interesting facet, presaging a more widespread future use of corporate officers as corporate directors. The headquarters group consists of only 18 executives who exercise close control over the 10 major subsidiaries that are engaged in a great variety of business activities. "Each officer sits on the boards of at least three subsidiaries and these groups meet every other month to review operations and advise management. John L. Cockrill, vice-president for administration, says that the LTV (officer) directors serving on subsidiary boards take 'a more active role' in the subsidiaries than do outside directors of other corporations." [3]

It should be noted that in LTV's ultimate hour of tribulation (on May 17, 1970), when James J. Ling, the conglomerate's founder and driving force, resigned as the firm's chairman and chief executive, the board was restructured along "inside" director lines. First, the number of directors was cut from 20 to 14. Although the number of functionally active directors on the board had previously been evenly split 10 to 10, the reconstituted board was made up of eight officers and only six outsiders, prominent among whom were the Goldman, Sachs and Lehman rep-

[3] *Business Week*, 81 (November 30, 1968).

resentatives. Commenting on this restructuring, Ling noted that the reorganized board is comprised of directors, all of whom have or represent substantial holdings in LTV stock, debt securities, or both.

Two months later when Ling resigned as president the board was even further modified to a 9 to 5 pro-insider balance with the resignation of Robert H. Stewart II (an outside banker) as LTV chairman and the appointment of C. Edward Acker, executive vice president of Braniff Airways, to that top post. Meanwhile the headquarters officers continued their previously active roles as LTV representatives on the boards of the several subsidiaries.

Again, while these dual roles, outside directors on the parent board and headquarter officers on the subsidiary board, might be criticized, this is not the current intent. Rather, the point is to emphasize that in the imminent future, conglomerates and revamped dynamic older firms will undoubtedly restructure their boards in the light of corporate needs. The era of pontificators as corporate directors seems to be at an end. Action-oriented firms need willing and working directors. The legislature-type board, despite some inherent imperfections, seems to be superbly structured for the needs of tomorrow's aggressive multidimensional conglomerate firm.

SUMMARY

The five illustrations seem to confirm the conclusion that the corporate board of directors is subject to evolutionary change. Every board is meant to meet specific needs. When needs change or when a board is proven to be inadequate, then the inexorable economic forces will restructure that board. Sometimes the restructuring is simply a matter of changing the personnel.

This newest need seems to focus on functional and divisional top officers who also serve on the firm's board of directors. The first category, the functional directors, seems to be in growing demand in conglomerates since certain fundamental areas of organizational activity essential to all the corporate components must have a measure of authority commensurate with their importance. Similarly, heads of the company's more important divisions likewise fulfill increasingly more critical roles in highly diversified enterprises. It becomes almost imperative in large-scale, multiindustry endeavor that the top council, the board of directors, includes an increasing number of these vital executives.

12

SYNERGY

In a very interesting empirical analysis on "Why Do Mergers Miscarry?", John Kitching summarizes the sentiments of executives of 22 companies that acquired a total of 181 companies during the period of 1960–1965. The data show the following:

Table 12-1   Which Types of Acquisition Have the Highest Incidence of Failure? [a]

Acquisition Type	Percent of Total	Percent of Failures
Vertical	3	0
Horizontal	25	11
Concentric marketing	13	25
Concentric technology	14	21
Conglomerate	45	42

[a] John Kitching, "Why Do Mergers Miscarry?" *Harvard Business Review,* 91 (November–December 1967).

No sophisticated statistical verification seems necessary to conclude that it is the concentric marketing type of merger that has the highest probability of failure. Concentric technology-type mergers noticeably are next most likely to fail. At the other end vertical and horizontal integration seem to offer the best possibilities for success.

Assuming the validity of these data it is interesting to speculate why there is such evident disparity in the success-failure ratios of different type mergers. Kitching advances an interesting theme when he points

133

out that in 84% of the failures the acquired firm had less than 2% of the parent company's sales at the time of acquisition. This leads to an inference that far too frequently the absorbed firm is submerged in the mass of the bigger firm and is forgotten. Kitching quotes a sentiment frequently felt by managers of such small and submerged acquisitions that the acquired firm "was so small no one in corporate headquarters could get interested in it." In far too many cases the acquiring firm seems to believe that a mystical synergy will guarantee performance improvement. In the currently popular context synergy is interpreted as "two plus two equals something greater than four." In the corporate field it is a very strong faith that assumes that the product of two firms in joint venture will always be greater than the results obtained by these firms working independently. This truism does get some support in those mergers where economies of scale whether production, marketing, advertising, or financing can be effected. It might also come about if the managements of the junctured firms complement or even activate each other. Then too a firm manifesting regression syndrome symptoms might be helped by a firm that has an abundance of highly competent managers. But, and this is the significant point, synergism is not a mystical addition of $2+2$ is greater than 4; neither is it something for nothing; nor is it inherent in every merger. Actually, the dictionary definition of synergism says it is "The doctrine that the human will cooperates with Divine grace in the work of regeneration." [1] Far too many mergers, where the acquired firm becomes an incidental part of the parent firm, seem to rely on this theological definition of synergism. At a subsequent date they learn to their corporate regret that there is no demonstrable correlation between prayers and profits.

The disproportionate failures in the two concentric-type categories of mergers as evidenced in Table 12-1 seem to follow from this faith in a too frequently nonexistent synergy. The acquisition-prone firm believes, sometimes with good reason, that it knows its present market and the potential of its available technologies. It is understandable that this assurance can be easily extended to encompass related markets and technologies. As a consequence of this overconfidence the expansion-minded firm underestimates the complexities in the related but different product lines and in the similar but not identical production techniques. What is obviously lacking is the following:

1. Competent management to run the acquired concentric component.

2. Adequate organization and communications to integrate completely the acquisition into the parent firm.

[1] *The Oxford Universal Dictionary,* Oxford University Press, p. 2113, (1955 edition).

3. A sufficient reserve of money and talent to carry the meged firm through a fairly extensive adjustment period.

By contrast to the concentric failures horizontal mergers seem to do best. The managerial implications are obvious. The parent firm, presumably, knows its business and has adequate competent managers of its own who can be used in key roles within the acquired firm. Replacement of obsolescent managers in the acquired firm is very frequently a vital necessity. Then too it is sometimes essential to depose even highly qualified managers in the merged unit. When the acquiring firm does have ample talent to replace incompetent or undesirable leadership in the acquired firm, the horizontal merger's prospects for success tend to be rather high.

Similarly, vertical mergers, both backward and forward, will more likely tend to be successful when the products and technologies are intimately related and the acquiring firm possesses an abundance of technically competent talent with transferrable skills. Remember, however, that as the levels of vertical integration increase, the chances that a given firm has enough men with adequate competencies to fill all managerial posts decreases markedly.

In far too many instances, synergy is axiomatically associated with any and all mergers. The faith factor and sometimes the feeling that large aggregates of money, cleverly manipulated, will always bring synergy into play have led to many casualties.

There are several reasons why some previous mergers seem to have attained synergistic benefits. A steadily climbing economy during the last two decades virtually guaranteed annual increments in sales and assets. Financial finagling in which fixed, interest-bearing obligations replaced owner's equity has likewise given a false portrayal in many cases. A reduction in the relative number of common shares tends to enhance earnings per share prospects. Despite these negative features, some measure of synergism is frequently attained in a merger particularly when a "fat but lazy" firm yields to merger. Putting underemployed assets to more productive use is the most common means of getting this synergistic effect. There are many good illustrations of this accomplishment; in fact, *every* merger assumes that the merging partners will do just this.

Outside the financial sphere synergism might be simulated or even be generated by manpower manipulation. Invariably the juncturing of the firms also means a consolidation of both boards of directors. The new board, however, is almost always so structured that it includes only 50 to 60% of the merging companies' directors. Generally, the acquiring firm keeps most of its directors on the new board and adds one, two, or three members from the acquired firm's board. This could be the fountainhead of synergy *if* in the restructuring process only the most qualified and most useful individuals were named to the new board.

In similar fashion a catharsis at the executive level could produce or accentuate the synergistic phenomenon. In every organization, at every level, there is a propensity for deadwood to accumulate and to stay put. It is a nautical phenomenon that violent storms can serve to cleanse the sea of driftwood, tossing it high onto the seacoast sands where this useless wood can bleach and decompose. Mergers can lead to corporate weather disturbances with consequent violent upheaval and the ejection of much useless manpower. The resultant savings in wages and salaries can sometimes be viewed as a synergistic benefit. More significantly the merger jolt can bring the moribund back to life.

The term *synergy,* like so many other fadist phrases, is invariably assumed but never proven. Proof of synergy requires factual analysis, which is tedious, boring, and assiduously avoided by almost all users of the term. If as the popular conception of synergy implies, the juncture of two firms produces results greater than the sum of results of these two firms functioning independently, then the existence or nonexistence of synergy should be fairly easy to prove. There are, however, at least five very important considerations to remember.

1. Accounting idiosyncrasies must be kept to a minimum. For example, shifts in inventory valuation methods, from LIFO to FIFO or reverse, or in reporting windfall gains or losses can distort performance data.

2. Financial factors must be kept in proper perspective. The use of debentures and preferred stock in many mergers can distort comparability.

3. Subsequent and previous mergers and sell-offs must be properly included in the analysis. In far too many instances what appears to be a synergistic gain is simply the result of improperly including figures of newly merged firms in the current period but failing to do so in the base data. This gimmickry, or as it more fittingly should be called, this falsifying of comparisons, is why so many glamour mergers seem to accomplish such fantastic growth.

4. Extraneous forces such as business cycle fluctuations, longer-term trend characteristics, inflationary impact, international tensions, and similar factors must not be overlooked. Meaningful adjustments must be made for all such extraneous forces, otherwise causality is inevitably attributed to the mystical synergy.

5. Efficiency improvements by capable executives applying conven-

tional scientific management techniques must be considered. Too frequently the effects of modernization, research and development or culling deadwood personnel, are mislabeled as synergy.

U. S. PLYWOOD-CHAMPION PAPERS INC.

The following case illustration stresses the significance of some of the previously mentioned factors in tempering one's views on synergy. U. S. Plywood Corporation and Champion Papers were officially merged on March, 1, 1967. There was sound logic in this juncture since Champion Paper was one of the leading printing and converting paper manufacturers and U. S. Plywood was a leader in products for the construction industry. The merger provided a measure of diversification, yet both parties had much in common as to raw materials, technology, and marketing.

Both partners, because of the character of their operations, were large landowners. The combined valuation of the timberlands in 1966 was almost $84 million, representing ownership of 1,175,576 acres. At an acreage price of $70 per acre this is probably an understatement of the real value of this tree-growing acreage. This implication is borne out by the fact that in 1967, the first year of the merger, the company sold certain timber and timberland holdings for $5,500,000, which resulted in a related profit of $3,680,000. In this one instance it would seem that the timberland valuation on the company's books would represent only about one-fourth the true market value. This undervalued asset could be easily manipulated to affect reported performance data.

This is certainly not an indictment of U. S. Plywood-Champion Paper, since the firm has actually manifested the opposite trait—expanding its holdings rather than disinvesting. In 1967 this expansion raised timberland valuation to $103 million and acreage to 1,420,202. The point stressed here is that what too frequently is assumed to be the mystical force of merger synergy can be nothing more than increased profits through sale of undervalued assets.

Regarding the second note of caution, the influence of financial factors, this merger likewise provides an interesting case. Although holders of U. S. Plywood common stock were not affected by the merger, Champion Paper common stock owners received for each old share, one share of $1.20 cumulative convertible preference stock plus four-tenths of a share of common stock in the new company. The net effect of this exchange would be a significant decrease in the common stock equity account together with a sizable decrease in the currently outstanding number of shares. However, the transference is into convertible preference stock; consequently the very real possibility remains that the preferred stock will be converted. To illustrate, before the merger U. S. Plywood's common stock had a book value of about $28.80, whereas Champion Paper's common stock had a book value of about $29.10. As a consequence of the merger, since Champion Paper stockholders received both a share of cumulative preference stock and only four-tenths of a share of common stock, this meant that the number of shares of common stock would be considerably less than that of the combined common stock of both firms. The result is an obvious increase in book value of common stock to $34.50 per share. This, of course, is a financial figment since ultimately the preference stock might be converted into common stock. Nevertheless there is the semblance of mystical synergy, particularly when dividends per share increase. In this instance the 1967 Annual Report shows total dividends paid on common stock decreasing from $17,-805,000 to $16,694,000 despite the fact that dividends *per share* actually increased from $1.40 to $1.50. Certainly this is not illegal nor unethical, but it does create a false sense of synergy.

The third caution previously mentioned stresses the significance of previous and subsequent mergers for precise analysis. In the five years before this union, U. S. Plywood had acquired Cascades Plywood Corporation (for 815,514 shares of common stock), McCloud River Lumber Company (for $41,000,000), Canadian Collieries Resources (for $21,-000,000), West Coast Plywood Corporation (for 109,000 shares of common stock), the Dee, Oregon Division of the Edward Hines Lumber Company (for $8,000,000), and the Del Mar Industries and Union Lumber Company (for 85,000 shares of common stock). Similarly, Champion Paper had acquired a number of companies including Carpenter Paper Company, Whitaker Paper Company, and Sample-Durick Company. These three firms alone before the merger had combined net worths of nearly $38 million and combined sales of $158 million. Obviously these premergers must be kept in mind for any meaningful analysis of performance.

Then, too, future acquisitions are even more important. In this instance, during the first half of 1968 alone, U. S. Plywood-Champion Papers negotiated acquisition of Drexel Enterprises (1967 sales of $78.4 million) and several smaller firms: Arrow Transportation Company, Tennessee Valley Sand and Gravel Company, and Berman Forest Products. These transactions involved payment of 1,296,000 shares of $1.20 cumulative preference stock and 1,300,025 shares of common stock. Other important acquisitions occurred in 1969 when Birmingham Ornamental Iron Company and Trend Industries were merged into U. S. Plywood-

Champion. Ignoring these and future acquisitions could easily lead to distorted conclusions.

The frequency of acquisitions and proposed acquisitions creates an almost impossible situation for the precise-minded analysts. In this instance, for example, in mid-November 1968, U. S. Plywood-Champion Papers and Johns-Manville Corporation announced exploratory discussions toward a possible merger. Three weeks later they terminated discussions. Assuming that a merger had been consummated, this would have pooled Johns-Manville's $510 million-plus sales with U. S. Plywood-Champion's more than $1050 million sales. Undoubtedly, the specific financing agreement could have affected the apparent and published performance records.

The significance of extraneous forces must likewise be properly weighted. The 1967 Annual Report states that "Since the effective date of the merger on March 1, 1967, our company has made excellent progress in many respects although adverse conditions in certain of our building materials markets tended to obscure our growth and consolidation. The sharp decline in housing starts during the first half of 1967 and softness in certain of our paper markets during the second half caused our earnings to decline 16.7 per cent from the previous record year." [2] Fluctuation in seasonal and cyclical business conditions certainly must be taken into account. The caution, not only in this case but in every instance, is that causality should be realistically pegged and should not be attributed to a mystical synergy.

By 1968 the factors which had depressed U. S. Plywood-Champion Papers sales performance in 1967 were almost completely reversed. For example, plywood prices had skyrocketed to $144 per thousand square feet, the highest levels ever reached. This boom which about doubled the price of plywood and lumber in a single year was induced by extraneous forces and was in no way the result of this particular firm's extraordinary efforts or of that evasive synergistic force. Consequently, just as negative performance caused by acts of God or of Government must be documented for realistic evaluation, so too similar extraneous influence must be weighted to tone down attribution of causality in the overly superb performances. This is further demonstrated by the fact that in 1970 forest-product prices had once again settled back from their 1968 highs to what might even be considered below normal levels, and the merged company's performance was again noticeably affected.

Perhaps the simplest test to see if synergy really did come about

[2] U. S. Plywood-Champion Papers, Inc., *Annual Report*, p. 5 (1967).

from the U. S. Plywood and Champion Paper merger would be to plot profit performance before and after the merger, as in Figure 12-1. The pertinent data are adjusted for the inflationary spiral during this period and for all mergers in which the U. S. Plywood and Champion Paper components were involved during the period.

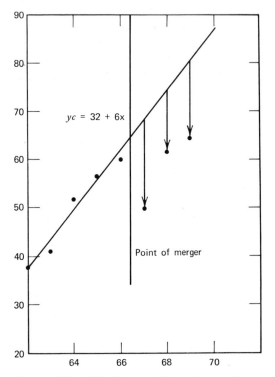

Figure 12-1 U.S. Plywood-Champion profit expectation, adjusted for price changes, 1969 = 100.

The profit trend line, computed by regression analysis, shows how the firm's profits should rise on the basis of premerger performance. Thus in 1969 the company should theoretically have earned about $80 million. Yet the actual net income was only $64 million. Similarly, 1967 and 1968 results were considerably below the trend expectation. Actually, it appears as if the newly merged firm has set a new profit trend line *at* a considerably lower level. The only inference that can be made on the basis of this graphic presentation is that if there is such a phenomenon as synergy in merger, then up to this point in U. S. Plywood-Champion's career all that we have seen is a negative or reverse synergy.

The final of the five factors which must be accounted for before synergy can be assumed in any merger is the improved productivity resulting from better use of personnel and facilities. For U. S. Plywood-Champion Papers the productivity gains, although presumed, are less obvious than in other classic examples. Consequently, this manifestation of improved efficiency, higher productivity, and better performance is illustrated by more pertinent examples.

ALLIS-CHALMERS MANUFACTURING COMPANY

In the period 1954–1969 Allis-Chalmers dropped from 54 to 140 in *Fortune's* annual ranking. In the meantime one of its biggest competitors, International Harvester, dropped slightly from 23 to 31, whereas another competitor, Caterpillar Tractor, climbed from 75 to 42.

This measure of the regression syndrome is more fully illustrated in the following comparison showing the percentage changes in these three firms between 1956 and 1969.

Firm	Sales	Assets	Net Income	Employees
Allis-Chalmers	+50	+58	−26	−26
Caterpillar Tractor	+282	+400	+310	+91
International Harvester	+128	+99	+15	+33

The contrast is much too marked to shrug off as a consequence of chance. Allis-Chalmers' long record of poor performance but coupled with prospects of possible improvement led to a series of merger overtures. Among the more active suitors were Ling-Temco-Vought, General Dynamics, Signal Companies, City Investing Company, Gulf and Western Industries, and White Consolidated Industries. Although ultimate merger might be inevitable considering that the most current acquisition-minded suitor, White Consolidated, had accumulated a total of 3,-248,000 shares out of slightly more than 10 million shares outstanding, Allis-Chalmers nevertheless made serious attempts to rectify its position. Late in 1968 the then newly elected president, David C. Scott, announced a severe reorganization involving the following:

1. Closure of three of its five major construction machinery facilities.
2. Consolidating of its seven farm equipment plants into four.
3. Release of 5000 nonproduction workers out of approximately 18,-000 such employees.

4. A cut in the corporate staff from 1510 to 132 people.

5. A total of 22 key personnel changes including dropping the chairman and also the chief financial officer.

6. Decentralizing by more than doubling the number of profit centers to 30, arranged in seven operating groups.

These drastic moves would seem to indicate that Allis-Chalmers, under its new president, David C. Scott, who also assumed the chief executive officer's post and the chairmanship, was serious in striving to retain its identity and its autonomy. Mr. Scott, in a previous executive capacity at Colt Industries, had helped build that conglomerate using somewhat similarly severe pruning. At Colt Industries, however, the credit for successful venture seems by implication to have been the result of conglomerate synergism—this was simply hard-fisted business realism.

In addition, Scott launched Allis-Chalmers on its own diversification program, incurring the anger of White Industries which charged that such acquisitions through stock exchange served to dilute the White Industries equity position. Mr. Scott, striving to put his firm on a firm footing, also proposed selling 450,000 shares of convertible preferred, which eventually could have been turned into 1.8 million additional shares of common stock.

These maneuvers were almost mandated by the very poor performance of the company in 1968. Coupled with the operating loss were the extremely sizable expenses related to closing down the inefficient and excess plants and the elimination of slow-moving inventories. As a consequence Allis-Chalmers had a massive pretax loss of $122 million for the year. This was reduced by tax credits to $54 million, still a significant figure.

However, as a concomitant of the efficiency moves, the firm's president predicted reasonable profits for the next year. His optimism was based on the fact that the inefficient plants and deadwood personnel had been eliminated. As a consequence, it was estimated that $6 million would be saved annually from reducing salary costs by firing over 5000 excess nonproduction personnel. Allis-Chalmers actually made a profit in 1969 of $18.4 million on sales of $805 million.

This illustration is not intended as condemnation of Allis-Chalmers despite its unprecedented $122 million loss. Rather, the focus is on the difference, if any, between conventional cost cutting and merger synergism. There does seem to be a remarkable identity.

In Allis-Chalmers' case the drastic drive to cut costs to give new life to the floundering firm does have a relationship to merger, but in a negative sort of way. Allis-Chalmers' leadership is striving to prevent merger, yet it is using the incisive cost cutting, the major surgery, so frequently associated with postmerger reorganization. Perhaps the real synergistic value follows simply from the merciless elimination of deadwood personnel, outmoded products, antiquated equipment and archaic technology. In an alert, progressive firm this therapy comes continuously or at least intermittently from dynamic leadership. In a static situation there seems to be no alternative except takeover or the very serious threat thereof.

HAMILTON LIFE INSURANCE COMPANY

The concept of synergy applies presumably not only to manufacturing enterprise but to all organized endeavor. The rise and fall of Philip J. Goldberg and Hamilton Life Insurance Company illustrate the universality of this concept. Within a seven-year period from its founding in 1959, Hamilton Life grew under the guidance of Goldberg into a firm with $500 million of life insurance in force. Typical of many messianic leaders who believe they can create synergy by their faith and steel wills, Goldberg has been quoted: " 'I feel that God tapped us on the shoulder when he directed our steps toward life insurance as a career,' he likes to say in his frequent lectures to agent groups. 'To me, we are all His financial ministers, doing for man's worldly needs what the priest, rabbi and minister do for his spiritual needs.' " [3]

In this quotation, the faith-facet of synergy is very well illustrated. But, faith alone is seldom sufficient to achieve the mystical multiplication of a "loaf of bread and a new fish" into a meal satiating the hunger of a multitude. The Age of Miracles is probably a thing of the past—in corporations as well as in churches.

Goldberg, in his synergistic zeal, had a vision that one insurance company could not perform as well as an amalgam of several different but related companies, all working in tandem. "Under a central system, a number of companies would have one actuary, one accounting firm, one printing plant and one data-processing plant. In addition, Mr. Goldberg reasoned, if an agent couldn't sell a prospect a policy in Company A, he could offer him one in Company B or Company C." [4]

However, as Hamilton's decline (its stock traded for $16 over the counter in mid-1966 and for only $1.50 two years later) attests, messianic zeal is not enough to generate synergy. There is an absolute neces-

---

[3] *The Wall Street Journal*, "Money Woes Hobble Hamilton Life, Once Led by Super-Salesman with a Preacher's Zeal," by Edward P. Foldessy, 28 (March 20, 1968).
[4] *Ibid.*

sity for technical know-how, for competency not only in one sphere but in all related areas. Hamilton was accused, for example, of poor quality underwriting, that is, it wrote too much risky insurance at too low a premium. Richard E. Stewart, New York state insurance superintendent, is quoted, "You can't write a group contract on an old ladies' home for the same premium you charge on a group of Cub Scouts." [5] Yet Hamilton did hand out some bargains such as charging only $88 a year for a $10,000 policy with life coverage. Even elementary arithmetic shows that assuming a 15-year life expectancy in this case, premiums would cover no more than 15% of the policy obligation. A group policy of this type would require several subscribers well below the 60-year level to balance a single sexagenarian's actuarial impact. In too many instances Hamilton evidently did not read the actuarial message accurately.

Poor judgment or incompetency at the top policy level is generally accompanied by top-management instability. A wished-for synergy will never take place in an environment of managerial instability. Yet at Hamilton Life, between 1962 and 1967, eight men held the chairmanship, and five different presidents presided. In a single three-year period more than 40 individuals were added and dropped from the company's 15-man board of directors.

One of the more prominent casualties was Jackie Robinson, the talented baseball hero who became Hamilton Life's cochairman. Robinson commented that "Getting involved with Hamilton Life was not one of my wisest business decisions." Paraphrasing these words, it might also be stated that Hamilton Life's getting involved with Jackie Robinson and with every other nontechnician and noninsurance oriented executive or director was not one of Hamilton's wisest business decisions. This is certainly not a personal criticism of Jackie Robinson, but it is an assertion that synergy can come only from technical competency plus inspired leadership.

Hamilton Life seems to be a good example where the faith factor essential for synergistic creation was obviously present. However, few if any of the many other ingredients requisite for this mystical multiplication seem to have accompanied Goldberg's religious zeal.

MARTIN MARIETTA

The accompanying reprint from an advertisement appearing in April 1970 in a number of leading business periodicals is an excellent example of synergy misrepresentation. On the surface the unsuspecting reader can easily get the impression that in the one-year period Martin Mariet-

[5] *Ibid.*

ta's sales zoomed by 44% from $682 million to $981 million. This is obviously not so, since in 1969 Martin Marietta acquired 82.7% of Harvey Aluminum Company whose total fiscal 1969 sales volume of $189,567,000 then seems to be included in the parent's tabulations. Yet *no* comparable figure is included in the parent's 1968 data. Consequently, the actual growth in sales is considerably less.

Martin Marietta

Financial Highlights		December 31
	1969	1968
Sales		
Cement and Lime	$115,217,000	$106,656,000
Chemical	106,630,000	100,026,000
Rock Products	71,337,000	63,479,000
Aluminum	189,567,000	—
Aerospace	498,693,000	411,865,000
Total	$981,444,000	$682,026,000
Earnings		
Cement and Lime	$ 11,693,000	$ 10,116,000
Chemical	7,333,000	7,908,000
Rock Products	5,863,000	7,001,000
Aluminum	7,517,000	—
Aerospace	16,729,000	14,447,000
Total	49,135,000	39,472,000
Other income and deductions:		
The Bunker-Ramo Corporation	3,350,000	2,739,000
Other income—net	994,000	2,606,000
Earnings before interest	53,479,000	44,817,000
Interest net of federal income taxes	9,297,000	4,586,000
Total net earnings	$ 44,182,000	$ 40,321,000
Per Common Share		
Net Earnings assuming no dilution	$ 2.21	$ 2.08
Net Earnings assuming full dilution	2.10	2.05
Total Assets	$906,498,000	$641,865,000
Other Data		
Average number of common shares outstanding	19,859,990	19,183,270
Number of shareholders	82,823	74,443
Number of employees	32,000	26,700

Even more misleading is the stress put on the supposed synergistic effect on total net earnings which at $44.2 million appear to be a growth of about 10% over the previous year. Again the previous year's data ignore the aluminum-producing subsidiary's contribution which incidentally was listed in Moody's as $15.4 million for 1969. Actually, if Harvey Aluminum's profit contribution were not included in either year, Martin Marietta's total net earnings for 1969 seems to have declined by nearly 10%.

Similarly, the increase in total assets, jumping from $642 million to $907 million, seems to be almost entirely accounted for by the lumping of Harvey Aluminum assets ($286 million in 1969) into the parent's account. The number of common shares outstanding, listed as 19.2 million in 1968 and only 19.9 million in 1969, gives the reader the impression that Harvey Aluminum was acquired by Martin Marietta at virtually no cost and little if any exchange of stock. Yet the merger offer, extended through December 22, 1969, set the exchange rate at 1.4 company shares for each share of Harvey stock. Harvey Aluminum had a premerger capitalization of 6,607,102 shares in 1969. A far more realistic presentation admitting conversion and dilution would show a significantly increased number of common shares. In addition, the more than doubling of the interest charges shows that in acquiring Harvey Aluminum, Martin Marietta assumed nearly $90 million in long-term obligations.

This commentary is certainly not intended to focus unpleasantly on Martin Marietta but rather upon the too-prevalent belief that synergy always follows mergers.

SUMMARY

The American public has been smitten by the cliché appeal of the term synergy, purportedly emanating from most mergers. As emphasized in the preceding paragraphs, this synergy is supposed to be a mystical multiplication through merger. Presumably, the act of merger by itself guarantees improved performance. In actuality, improved performance which sometimes does follow mergers is far more a function of cold-blooded managerial cost cutting than that of mystical synergism. Then, too, what often appears to be synergistic multiplication is simply financial finagling or concomitants of upward business cycles. On the other hand, mergers and even merger threats have in some cases served to jolt complacent managements into dynamic action. Synergy, however, seems to be more a matter of determined and competent management rather than some mystical force inherent in merger.

13

INSTANT GROWTH

Among the more intriguing phenomena in the current state of corporate conglomeration is the brashness of what figuratively might be termed "Little David" companies challenging giant "Goliath" corporations. This phenomenon seems to run counter to the assumption that bigness in business is invincible. In fact, much of the anti-Big Business agitation of the last several decades was predicated on the thesis that unless checked by Government, the big companies will eventually take over our economic system. Consequently, it is surprising to have an increasing number of once-assumed impregnable corporate headquarters invaded by unknown conglomerators. Not all of these "little guy" assaults on Establishment firms have been successful. Nevertheless the increasing incidence of this sort of challenge, previously unknown in our enterprise system, deserves comment.

Like the Biblical David, most of the conglomerators in this category have very unimpressive resources for combat. Their "slingshots" would appear to be totally inadequate in a contest with the heavily armed Goliaths. (This weapons-resource limitation will be stressed in the subsequent illustrations.) Then too the Davids are pathetically lacking in battle experience. Although Goliath was a seasoned veteran, David had, up to the critical contest, been completely involved in pastoral pursuits. Also, there was the age factor or generation gap. Similarly, today's corporate Davids have leaders generally in their 30's or early 40's, whereas the Goliaths invariably have top executives in their very late 50's or in the 60's. The directors of the challenged bigger firms tend, on the average, to be in the 60 to 75 year range, whereas directors in conglomerates are generally in the 40 to 55 age bracket.

In technical and managerial experience there is likewise an obvious disparity. Virtually none of the challengers have had meaningful technical experience and only modest managerial backgrounds. By contrast the defenders are staffed with seasoned veterans. Considering the odds against the weak, unseasoned, poorly outfitted conglomerate-prone corporate Davids, it is indeed surprising that so many have come forth to toss pebbles at the seemingly unbeatable Goliaths. The following situations highlight a number of the more prominent fairly recent David-Goliath contests.

LEASCO DATA PROCESSING EQUIPMENT

In June 1968 Leasco Data Processing Equipment Corporation announced a plan to tender an offer to acquire at least 51% control of Reliance Insurance Company. At that time Leasco held 138,000 common shares or less than 3% of Reliance stock. The tender provided for a $55 principle amount of Leasco convertible subordinated debentures paying $2 a year together with a one-half warrant. A full warrant is entitled over a 10-year period to purchase one share of Leasco common at $87. Among other more interesting aspects of this proposal were the following:

1. On the day of the proposal Leasco traded at $84.625 and Reliance traded at $59.875. Consequently from a straight dollar point of view this offer is rather unimpressive.

2. Reliance, the to-be-merged firm, earned $18 million in 1967, whereas Leasco, the tender-maker, earned less than one-tenth that figure.

3. Reliance had paid dividends since 1858 while Leasco has never paid a cash dividend.

4. Reliance stock had been trading for quite some time in the 30 to 42 range at a P/E ratio of about 10. By contrast Leasco's 1967–1968 price range gyrated from 34 to 146, reaching a fantastic P/E ratio of over 100.

5. Although 51 institutional investors owned 478,000 shares or almost 9% of Reliance common, there were only eight institutional investors of Leasco stock with holdings totaling about 72,000 shares.

6. Reliance Insurance had assets of $685 million and an owners' equity per share of approximately $50, whereas Leasco Data Processing had only $14.24 equity per share.

These data raise serious questions as to why Reliance Insurance should show even a surface amenability to overtures from a much smaller, less successful, high-flyer firm. Yet within two months another "small-fry" firm, Data Processing Financial and General Corporation, entered the fight to acquire Reliance Insurance. This second computer-leasing company was equally minus performance merit. Data Processing had been earning between $1.35 and $1.85 during the past two years, yet its stock reached the $184 range for a P/E ratio up to 140. It had never paid a dividend and had an equity per share of only $7.08.

After several months of higgling and haggling Reliance Insurance capitulated to the overtures of the first aggressor, Leasco Data Processing. In the meantime, however, the merger offer was sweetened slightly; Leasco offered to buy 70,000 Reliance Class A shares (convertible into 790,000 common shares) from three of Reliance Insurance's outside directors. The selling price was $720 per Class A share. Certain management concessions were also made to Reliance; for example, Mr. Roberts, its chief executive officer and the company's only inside director (one officer-director and 16 outside directors), would remain as head of the acquired firm. Also Reliance's current management would continue to name a majority of the Reliance Insurance division's board of directors.

It would be most difficult, if not impossible, for one standing on the periphery to assay the merits and the maneuvering associated with this case. Why a long-established, successful, reputable insurance firm such as Reliance should even condescend to discuss merger with so brash an upstart as Leasco is a matter for conjecture or for the courts to decide. The alternative of the court action is precisely what two Reliance Insurance holders elected. In August 1968 parallel legal actions were instituted in United States District Court and the State Court in New York against Reliance, its current and certain past directors, Leasco, and the brokerage firm of Carter, Berlind and Weill. (This brokerage firm had acted as finder for Leasco while at the same time it was said Carter, Berlind and Weill owned 30% of Reliance's common stock.)

Nearly two years after the merger Leasco was the subject of a House Antitrust Subcommittee series of hearings held to determine if there was a need for a law to curb conglomerate mergers such as Leasco's absorption of Reliance Insurance. As a side issue it was brought out that to maintain secrecy Reliance was referred to by the code name "Raquel" taken from Raquel Welch, the movie actress. The rationale for a code name symbolizing sex incarnate and Reliance Insurance's finer attributes was never really explained, but the firm's 30-year old chairman conceded that one purpose for acquiring Reliance was to obtain the insurance company's $38 million in surplus funds which could be used for future acquisitions.

Just a few months after Leasco achieved its objective by acquiring 98% of Reliance Insurance Company stock, it gave serious indications that it intended to take over Chemical Bank New York Trust Company, the nation's sixth largest Commercial Bank. Leasco, even after its absorption of Reliance Insurance, was still much a miniature when compared with Chemical Bank and its nearly $9 billion in assets. The very audacity of this maneuver stunned most financial analysts and prompted countermeasures by Chemical Bank. For example, it agreed in principle to acquire Realtime Systems, a time-sharing computer service, thus putting an antitrust block to Leasco's takeover attempt. The brashness of Leasco's gesture also seemed to stir the investment and banking sectors into action. Chemical Bank's officials vehemently denied that they were even considering the proposal. William S. Renchard, the bank's chairman, stressed that there were "absolutely no negotiations in progress." Steinberg in turn stated that he would never take over a bank whose management was in a hostile mood.

This particular grab by a newcomer conglomerate for control of one of our most substantial and prestigious financial institutions failed within several weeks. Despite Leasco's retreat it almost concurrently gave evidence that it would continue to seek another bank for merger purposes. There were reports and denials that Leasco was interested in Franklin National Bank, based in Mineola, New York. Franklin National, one of the nation's fastest growing commercial banks, has assets of about $3 billion.

UNIVERSITY COMPUTING COMPANY

In May 1968 University Computing Company, a tiny Dallas-based computer service, made an unsuccessful tender offer for 750,000 shares of Western Union Telegraph Company stock at $44 per share. Western Union stock was then selling at $37 per share. The remarkable thing about this move by University Computing was its daring or, perhaps, its audacity. University Computing had sales in 1967 of only $16.6 million as contrasted with Western Union's $320 million. Despite its miniscule size, its nondividend record, its meager cash resources ($6.09 million), and its modest earnings ($2.5 million in 1967), University Computing proposed a tender offer whose price tag was approximately $33 million.

While Western Union's management was successfully staving off this affront, it became involved in a merger proposal with another very small, untested firm—Computer Sciences Corporation. This second venture came to an unexpected end in August 1968 when American Telephone and Telegraph suspended negotiations with Western Union regarding the sale of its TWX public teletypewriter network. The suspension of negotiations for the TWX sale seemed to be intimately related to the proposed Computer Sciences merger.

Once again evaluation is difficult; it is not easy to discern the merger-propelling forces. Yet one merger trait is quite evident. In the previous illustration it was pointed out that the acquiescing firm had only one officer-director on its 17-member board of directors. The same pattern is discernible in this second case; Western Union has only two officer-directors on its 12-man board. In both these and comparable instances the aggressor firms appear to have rather small boards whose membership is invariably and intimately associated with active control of the dynamic company.

ELECTRONIC SPECIALTY COMPANY

The list of superambitious giant-toppling upstarts could be extended to quite some length. In August 1968 Electronic Specialty Company was engaged in serious merger discussions with Carpenter Steel Company. This juncture would have put the Carpenter-Electronic Specialty joint venture among our country's top 500 firms. In the midst of this discussion an unexpected intruder, International Controls, suddenly made a counteroffer: a $39-a-share tender to ELS stockholders. (The shares had been selling in the $25 to $28 range at a P/E multiplier of about 16.)

The unexpected aggressor, International Controls, had 1967 sales of $6.8 million, earning 31 cents per share. Electronic Specialty, by contrast, had sales of $112.4 million and earned $1.42 per share. Nevertheless, bolstered by $25 million from foreign investors, International Controls' tender offer was a real threat to ELS. Although all the reasons prompting this move are certainly not aboveboard, a significant factor was probably ELS's debt-free status with borrowing potential estimated at $20 million or more.

In the several-months battle for control, a turning point came when Electronic Specialty's chairman, William H. Burgess, and its president, C. Ray Harmon, despite their very vocal objections to the merger tender offer, submitted their own shares: Burgess sold his 125,000 shares at the $39 per share offer (for a sale nearly $5 million) and Harmon sold his 26,000 shares. Interestingly, before the tender offer, International Controls held only 38,100 shares of Electronic Specialty or about one-fourth the number of shares held by that firm's two top officers. Commenting on ELS's management's bitter battle to repulse his takeover attempt, Robert Vesco, 32-year old president and chairman of International Controls, tersely stated "He has our $5 million (for stock Burgess tendered to ICC at $39 a share) and $150,000 a year. He is just sitting back laughing." [1]

[1] *The Oregonian*, Portland, Oregon, 7 (October 9, 1968).

Early in 1969 after gaining a 55% stock interest in ELS, the aggressive conglomerator, International Controls, elected six of its representatives to ELS's seven-man board of directors.

NATIONAL SUGAR REFINING COMPANY

The preceding examples typify a fairly frequent exception to the rule, that is, the case of the little fish swallowing the bigger fish. The surprise is even greater when the little fish aggressor is of minnow dimensions, yet moves with piranha voracity. In June 1968 Haven Industries proposed a tender offer for at least 51% of National Sugar Refining Company stock. National Sugar, the second largest sugar refining company in the United States, had sales of $200 million 10 years ago but now has a sales volume of about $120 million. Net income has recently ranged between $1 to $2 million.

National Sugar could very well serve as an excellent example of a firm showing all the symptoms of the regression syndrome. Its progressive decline is evident in that it no longer ranks among *Fortune*'s 500, whereas in 1954 it ranked 214 in sales, 422 in assets, 398 in net income and 457 in number of employees. In absolute figures performance compares as follows:

	1968	1954
Sales (million)	$117	$145
Assets (million)	58	43
Net income (million)	0.6	1.9
Employees	1000	2750

The aggressive Haven Industries, formerly New Haven Clock Company, had 1967 revenue of less than $1 million and net income of $51,-344. Haven Industries, incorporated late in 1961, is certainly not a well-known company. In response to the initial offer, "While directors of National Sugar didn't take a stand on Haven's proposal, they said that 'available public information on Haven Industries is meager, *it having emerged from bankruptcy only last fall.*' " [2] (Italics by author). Haven Industries had been suspended from trading on the American Stock Exchange in 1963 and is now seeking resumption of trading on the American Exchange. This presents quite an anomaly; a nonlisted, recently bankrupt, and delisted firm seeking to get control of a venerable but somewhat ailing corporate giant.

[2] *The Wall Street Journal,* 7 (June 5, 1968).

An amazing aspect of this maneuver was the fact that Haven Industries' offer seemed to be cashless—the proposal offered for each National Sugar common share a combination of 5.5 Haven common shares, a new Haven $15 principle amount 4% convertible subordinated debenture due 1988 and two warrants. In a half-page advertisement in the February 17, 1969 issue of *The Wall Street Journal*, National Sugar's management pointed out among other facts, the following:

The book value per share of National Sugar common is $24.19 per share (after allowing for conversion of preferred stock) while the book value per share of Haven common is only 23¢ per share. The Haven stock being offered to you has been badly diluted by the sale of cheap stock and is subject to further dilution. Last year, Haven sold 2,856,250 shares of its stock on the exercise of options and warrants at a price of 16 cents per share: The average market price for those shares at dates of exercise was about $6.80. . . .

"Based on the pro forma statements contained in the Prospectus, if Haven acquired 51% of National Sugar, the National Sugar stockholders would have contributed
(a) 97% of Haven's revenues;
(b) almost all the earning power; and
(c) 75% of Haven's net equity.
For this they would get less than half of the Haven stock, even assuming conversion of all the debentures.[3]

Soon after Haven's tender offer, two real estate investors, Sol Goldman and Alex DiLorenzo, Jr., entered the arena by acquiring approximately a 33% stock interest. Previously, the Havemeyer interests held about 29% of the stock. The big question even to the initiated financial analyst was "what would anyone want with National Sugar?" It had acquired a reputation for poor management and commensurate poor performance. But prominent among its negative assets was a $13.6 million tax-loss carry-forward, $9 million of which was to expire in another year. With such an incentive, negative although it might be from a performance point of view, the three-way battle for control becomes somewhat more understandable. Common stock price quotations for National Sugar are likewise better comprehended. In May National Sugar was trading at $18 a share; by July the price had spurted to $52 a share but subsequently dropped to about $40.

In March 1969 Haven Industries, which by then held slightly more than 50% of National Sugar's outstanding shares, won five seats on the eight-man board. Haven's chief executive, Neil S. Rosenstein, was then elected chairman of the sugar refiner. The Haven Industries' Chairman's

---

3 *The Wall Street Journal*, 15 (February 17, 1969).

Letter in the 1968 Annual Report, reproduced as a paid advertisement in the June 24, 1969 issue of *The Wall Street Journal,* stresses that through acquisitions in a single year Haven expanded in sales from under $1 million to more than $122 million and in net assets from $3.3 million to $65 million.

Like so many of the present mergers National Sugar's dilemma highlights the role of the neoentrepreneur. The company had for quite some time been in a relaxed-management status. Havemeyer family interests had long been dominant in setting company policy. The combination of a lackadaisical management, together with depressed sugar prices, inevitably culminated in National Sugar's doldrum status and its eventual loss of autonomy and identity.

COLLINS RADIO COMPANY

Still another example is Electronic Data Systems (1968 sales of $8 million) attempt to take over Collins Radio Company (1968 sales of $447 million) in a cashless coup. EDS offered to swap $65 worth (at then current market prices) of its stock for each share of Collins Radio stock, then selling at about $50. The joker in this deal was the fact that Collins Radio was then selling at a P/E figure of just under 12, whereas EDS stock, which was selling at $48 per share, had a P/E ratio of a fantastic 342. To emphasize this point EDS stock's P/E ratio of 342 meant that it was supposedly selling at 342 times that of last year's earnings. In this context it should be pointed out that H. Ross Perot, Electronic Data's president, chairman, and founder, owned more than 80% of the company's 11.5 million outstanding shares. With such a concentration in ownership the 342 P/E figure might be suspect since the likelihood of a free interplay of stock price-setting forces is extremely low.

PAN AMERICAN AIRWAYS, INC.

Equally brash was the attempt by Resorts International, a New York-based firm that owns a gambling casino, two resort hotels, and part of tiny Paradise Island in the Bahamas, to take over Pan American Airways. Resorts International, together with its founder-chairman, James Crosby, acquired 7% of Pan American's outstanding stock from Gulf and Western Industries and from pension trusts administered by Chase Manhattan Bank. Resorts also acquired an option to buy another 2.7% of Pan American stock for a total of about 3.3 million shares.

If the merger had been consummated, it would have joined a firm with revenues of about $30 million annually with the giant Pan American's billion dollar plus annual revenue. This merger possibility of micro and macro was rather short-lived. The White House, the Civil Aeronautics Board, the Securities and Exchange Commission, and even the American Stock Exchange took prompt action. The Exchange halted trading in Resorts stock for more than a month, accusing the company of leaving vital questions unanswered in its proxy statement relative to the intended purchase of the Pan American Shares. The SEC charged Resorts was in violation of Section 14a of the Securities Exchange Act which requires specific proxy statement information; for example, the SEC claimed that Resorts failed to reveal that it was to pay Kleiner, Bell & Company, a Los Angeles brokerage firm, $1 million in cash plus warrants to purchase 75,000 Resorts Class A stock at $40 per share. This was a finders fee for Kleiner, Bell's services in leading Resorts to Gulf and Western Industries.

The rather fast and severe congressional reaction to the possibility of Resorts International's takeover of Pan American seemed to follow from a fear that common carriers should not be run by companies with significant noncarrier interests. Three fairly recent examples of airlines being taken over by nontransportation companies are Braniff Airways by Ling-Temco-Vought, Frontier Airlines by General Tire and Rubber, and Air West by Howard Hughes. Congressman Harley O. Staggers introduced legislation noting that in a parallel field there were numerous proposed acquisitions of railroads by holding companies and that railroads themselves have formed holding companies in attempts at diversifying. He questioned "how far . . . they represent a serious intent to discharge common carrier duties or how far they might change to be simply erections of financial empires for other purposes." [4]

Other legislative proposals would set a maximum permissible ownership by a single interest of 5% in any common carrier's stock. As a consequence early in April 1969 Resorts International announced that it was cutting its Pan Am purchase plan to 4.8%.

SHARON STEEL CORPORATION

The list of little Davids with big aspirations could be extended to quite some length. Late in 1968 NVF Corporation (formerly National Vulcanized Fibre) made public a bid to acquire Sharon Steel Corporation, a firm six times NVF's size. Sharon Steel's sales had topped the $200 million mark, and NVF had sales in the $30 million range. On the basis of earnings Sharon Steel's $4.1 million for the first half of 1968 was

[4] *Business Week*, 40 (March 15, 1969).

approximately twenty times NVF's earnings. Commenting on the proposal, Mr. George Perrault, Jr., Sharon's chairman, president, and chief executive officer, stated "The first time I heard of NVF was today (the day the proposal was announced). I think he (Mr. Posner, chairman of NVF) is putting the cart before the horse." [5]

Rather than capitulate to NVF Sharon Steel's management went so far as to endorse merging with another small-fry firm, Cyclops Corporation, a specialty steel producer. Despite this strong resistance by Sharon Steel, NVF, through its tender offer, did succeed in getting approximately 90% of the steelmakers' common stock and control of the company.

SUMMARY

These seven accounts of little Davids swinging a mighty powerful sling could be easily expanded to several score. In December 1968 AMK Corporation in a pooling of interests merger, took over the nation's fourth largest meatpacker, John Morrell and Company. Morrell's sales that year were $800 million, whereas AMK had sales of slightly more than $40 million. A year later AMK was a serious contender for the takeover of the United Fruit Company whose sales were at the $400 million level. Late in 1968 Loew's Theatres, with assets around one-seventh of those of Lorillard Corporation, absorbed that major cigarette maker. In September 1968 Hecla Mining Company, a relatively small firm with sales of about $20 million, announced its plans to acquire U. S. Smelting, Refining and Mining Company whose sales were in excess of $123 million. Ironically just a short time before, U. S. Smelting had made an abortive bid to take over Cudahy and Company (sales in excess of $320 million) and Clevite Corporation (sales nearly $200 million).

From these examples it is evident that major corporations can become vulnerable to takeover not only by peer-corporations but even by the very small firm whose leaders possess vision, determination, and other entrepreneurial traits.

[5] *The Wall Street Journal*, 26 (September 23, 1968).

14

MERGER CONSTRAINTS

Mergers, particularly of the conglomerate type, are frequently inhibited by three types of constraints: legal, financial, and managerial. The legal category of constraints, although traceable to the Sherman Antitrust Act of 1890, is, for all practical purposes, rooted in Section 7 of the Clayton Act. This classic legislation stated that a merger is illegal if it "may substantially lessen competiton or tend to create a monopoly."

During the 50-plus years that this legislation has been in force the prime focus has been on the acquisition by one company of a *competitor* company's common stock. This rather restricted focus was quite natural since before World War II virtually all mergers were either vertical or horizontal in character. With the major consolidation movement that took place after World War II, it became obvious that the Clayton Act needed redefining or redoing. Consequently, in 1950 the Celler-Kefauver Amendment to the Clayton Act's Section 7 was passed. The intent was to plug the serious loopholes that allowed the merging of firms with nonrelated products, processes, or markets. The 1950 Amendment stressed that the law was concerned fundamentally with the combination of two companies more so than in the techniques used in the combining. This new interpretation added a new dimension, stressing that the law is a rather comprehensive regulatory scheme whose limits are set by circumstances and can consequently be changed.

SUPREME COURT DECISIONS

Over the last dozen years there has been a series of redefinitions or restatements of the Clayton Act's Section 7; for example in 1962 the will of Congress in stimulating competition by means of decentralization and through small, locally owned businesses was emphasized in the Supreme

157

Court's Brown Shoe Company ruling. This was a momentous decision since it reversed a long line of previous Supreme Court decisions. The same idea was restated in the United States versus Aluminum Company of America case when the presence of small but significant competitors was deemed an economic necessity.

Other significant interpretations of the Clayton Act's Section 7 include the cases of the El Paso Natural Gas Company in which the definition of the term competition was broadened; the Continental Can Company, dealing with the defining of the product market; and the Penn Olin Chemical Company which was concerned with the possible constraints to competition following the formation of a joint venture.

These outstanding actions by the Supreme Court served to inhibit the merging of a number of our leading firms, for example, Humble Oil and Tidewater Oil. In several instances accomplished mergers were rescinded and divestiture followed. Continental Can Company's abandonment of its union with Hazel-Atlas Glass Company and Alcoa's divorce from Rome Cable Corporation which it had rather recently acquired illustrates the practical effect of this change in the legal view on certain mergers.

In most of these and similar cases a major consideration for questioning or preventing merger was the relative share of a specific product market which was involved. The Supreme Court had, in the Philadelphia National Bank case (1963), set 30% as the upper limit beyond which the concentration was considered to be a real threat to competition. Subsequently, in the Continental Can case, the threshold was lowered to 25%. In the Alcoa case the determining factor was the approximately 28.7% of the aluminum cable market which was involved, with no stress being put on Rome Cable Corporation's position in the copper conductor wire market.

These legal constraints on merger until this point seem to exclude most conglomerates since the focus had been almost exclusively on an expanding firm's competitive position within a relatively narrow product line. In 1967 the Supreme Court made a momentous decision in upholding the Federal Trade Commission's challenge of Procter and Gamble's acquisition of Clorox Chemical Company. The Court now ruled that Section 7 of the Clayton Act bars mergers of companies that are not direct competitors but that are in related product lines, in this case, soaps and liquid household bleach.

CONGRESSIONAL ACTION

Although action in the courts through legal suits is one very effective way to get results in curtailing conglomeration an even more fundamental remedy is through legislation. Current indications point to imminent Congressional action. For example, Chairman Mills of the House Ways and Means Committee introduced a bill in February 1969 which would do the following:

1. Limit the tax deduction a corporation could claim for interest paid on debentures used in acquisitions. This limitation would apply only in cases where the debentures' value was 35% or more of the total acquisition price.

2. Prohibit the deferment of much of the income tax now permitted when common stock is converted into debentures. Current practice sanctions tax deferment until the debentures are paid off.

Another meaningful expression of Congressional concern over the effect of the tremendous increase of mergers particularly in big business was made by Congressman Celler, chairman of the House Judiciary Committee. Mr. Celler indicated that his committee's antitrust subcommittee was investigating conglomerate mergers. In addition to his subcommittee's investigation, Congressman Celler stated that at least six other major studies of conglomerates and merger matters were under way in other governmental agencies. One of the reasons for this keen congressional interest in the conglomerate phenomenon is the negative effect on many communities that are losing corporate headquarters when the locally based firms merge with the huge conglomerates that are generally headquartered in New York, Dallas, or Los Angeles; for example, in the last two years, 9 out of the 23 major corporations headquartered in Pittsburgh have moved out of that city.

Congressman Celler also indicated that a very large number of business leaders had come to Congress " 'begging for help with reference to this avalanche of take-overs.' He said he'd never seen such strong support in the business community for new antitrust legislation." [1]

Although Congressman Celler did not predict the specific legislation which could be forthcoming, he did imply that some form of control over the maximum size of large-scale corporations might be enacted. This follows from the recognition that "size in and of itself can be antisocial or so subject to abuse that control is necessary." [2] Congressman Celler also focused on the potential inefficiency and social cost of overdiversification. "No man is genius enough to hold the reins on so many operations. You can't have your behind on 17 horses and drive the team at the same time." [3]

A rather significant suggestion for legal restriction of mergers was

[1] *The Wall Street Journal*, 2 (June 13, 1969).
[2] *Ibid.*
[3] *Ibid.*

made by James J. Ling, probably the best known of all conglomerators. Even after his acquisition of Jones and Laughlin Steel Corporation was challenged by the Justice Department, Mr. Ling stated his sentiments for greater Government control. His proposal was for a 2% merger tax on the value of assets or securities involved in acquisition. Ling estimated that, at the current merger tempo, such a tax would bring $1½ billion into the Treasury.

Although the flow of new tax funds into the Federal coffers would be a real boon, Mr. Ling's suggestion for such a merger tax was not exactly prompted by any balance-the-budget considerations. In his talk at a National Industrial Conference Board seminar in Chicago, Mr. Ling "appears unhappy about the proliferation of unsound mergers, . . . 'Such a tax would not only bring in needed government revenues, but would act as a monetary damper on any uneconomical merger or acquisition,' Ling predicted, saying it would put mergers 'to the most severe economic test of viability and feasibility.' " [4]

ADMINISTRATION ATTITUDE

There is certainly no absolute government attitude toward mergers. Just as the Supreme Court through a long series of legal decisions, and Congress in its enactment of laws have manifested changes in their attitudes, so too other governmental agencies reflect these changes. For example, the Johnson Administration had taken the position that most conglomerate mergers did not violate present antitrust laws. Relatively little was done by the Johnson Administration to prevent or even to slow down the conglomeration tempo. Consequently, as stated by Richard W. McLaren, current Assistant Attorney General, the past administration's permissiveness in these matters "let the merger movement get clear out of hand." Within several months after the inauguration the Nixon Administration gave solid evidence that it was going to disallow some of the very biggest conglomerate mergers. The first to feel the changed government attitude was Ling-Temco-Vought, whose 63% interest in Jones and Laughlin was now questioned. The Justice Department indicated it was going to seek court-ordered divestiture by LTV of the nation's sixth largest steel producer.

This action was predicated on the Nixon Administration's conviction, contrary to that of the Johnson Administration's, that Section 7 of the Clayton Act could and should be used to stop the flood of economic concentration. Consequently, the Justice Department's current thinking

[4] *Business Week,* "Management Briefs" (April 26, 1969).

is that massive business combines do post dangers to competition if only because of the immense financial and market power they wield. The antitrust division lawyers also argued that the conglomerate firms provide too many opportunities for collusive reciprocal trading relationships. Following still another line of reasoning they contended that these mergers do diminish potential competition between the merging partners and even on this basis alone should be outlawed.

LTV's response was immediate. As legal advisor it hired the firm of Arnold and Porter, one of the nation's leading antitrust law firms. This is the law firm of Thurman Arnold, the well-known New Deal trustbuster who once crusaded against big business but who now uses his talents to defend the business interests. This law firm also included Abe Fortas before his elevation to the Supreme Court (and subsequent abdication). LTV also took two-page advertisements in a number of leading newspapers with an open letter to its shareholders (and the public) decrying the Federal attack in what it termed "generalized criticisms often expressed of conglomerates." This advertisement was printed in full on pages 16 and 17 of the March 13, 1969 issue of *The Wall Street Journal.*

The "potential competition" argument in particular poses serious threat to conglomerators. In the LTV suit, which was actually filed in mid-May 1969, the Government contended that through the acquisition of 33 corporations since 1961 LTV had come the country's

—largest seller of sporting goods
—third largest meat packer
—seventh largest commercial airline
—third largest car-rental concern
—eighth largest prime defense contractor
—one of the largest makers of copper wire
—sixth largest steelmaker

In addition LTV is a substantial producer of jet fighter planes, sound equipment, chemicals, electronic controls, and aluminum wire. The suit contended that LTV plans to continue to make acquisitions specifically in aluminum, auto parts, chemicals, drugs, insurance, and a number of other areas. With these and its current activities LTV is a potential competitor of Jones and Laughlin, which in 1967 adopted a formal acquisitions program of its own emphasizing its intent to make acquisitions in aluminum-construction, copper products, machine tools, chemicals, and other fields.

The Justice Department also pointed out that LTV's National Car Rental System (since disposed of) is a large buyer of cars. Allegedly, LTV could use its purchasing power to induce auto makers to buy steel from Jones and Laughlin. This was just one example showing how reciprocity could be effected.

The second major case of this kind was precipitated by the Justice Department's filing an antitrust suit to force International Telephone and Telegraph Corporation to divest itself of Canteen Corporation. In this instance, the suit makes no charge that ITT and Canteen are potential competitors but charges that the combined companies have the power to employ reciprocity. This reciprocity, or the use of a company's economic power to induce vendors or purchasers to give it special treatment, was supposedly in the furnishing of vending and in-plant feeding services. The suit contended that Canteen's competitors in these areas would be foreclosed from doing business at plants owned by ITT and its many subsidiaries. Very likely, the suit further charges, these smaller companies competing with Canteen would "seek to protect themselves" by looking for merger partners like ITT which have large multiplant operations with built-in clients.

In a remarkable parallel action the Justice Department two months later challenged ITT's proposed combination with Hartford Fire Insurance Company, the nation's sixth largest property and liability insurer. If this merger is assumed, as it was agreed to a few months previously by both companies, the new firm would have assets in excess of $6 billion. Although specific grounds for the complaint were not initially stated, it was fairly obvious that the Justice Department was concerned about the very real possibility of reciprocity. In its corporate confederation ITT then had about 75 subsidiaries, including the nation's largest baking company, the second largest car rental firm, a major home building firm, one of the two largest hotel chains, and a leading chemical producer. These and the other ITT corporate components are all major purchasers of property and liability insurance. Consequently, the imminence of reciprocity seemed real and serious.

This Justice Department action against ITT in both the Canteen Corporation and Hartford Fire Insurance Company cases can be interpreted as a stiffening of governmental resistance to certain mergers, particularly to large-scale conglomerations. Actually, early in 1968 ITT, faced with government opposition to its takeover of American Broadcasting Company, scrapped this proposal because of the Federal opposition. Obviously, the future limits of merger permissibility will not be set until quite a few more test cases such as ITT's three recent classic contests are resolved.

The Justice Department is probably the best mirror of an administration's legal attitude. During the Johnson Administration a special antitrust task force headed by Phil C. Neal, Dean of the University of Chicago law school, recommended new laws which would empower the Government to break up companies in oligopolistic industries. The report was kept secret during the Johnson Administration but was released late in May 1969 by Richard McLaren, Nixon's chief trustbuster. The report recommended new laws that would enable the Government to break up companies in industries "where monopoly power is shared by a few very large firms". For example, a "Concentrated Industries Act" would force the reduction in size to no more than 12% of the market share for firms in the so-called oligopolistic industries in which four or fewer firms control 70% or more of an industry and a "Merger Act" would impose severe limitations on certain would-be mergers. *Time* aptly summarizes by stating the following:

Many businessmen believe that the Neal proposals to break up bigness would only reduce U.S. industrial efficiency and competitiveness in world markets. The chances seem remote that any of the recommendations will be written into law. Congress always has trouble agreeing on antitrust-law amendments, and the controversial ideas in the Neal report are political orphans.[5]

FEDERAL TRADE COMMISSION

The Federal Trade Commission is still another possibility for further merger control; for example, in May 1969 the FTC announced a significant step in this direction when it required that 475 of the nation's biggest corporations must file special report forms disclosing to the Government any plans for substantial acquisition or merger. This group of major firms included 265 manufacturing companies, 23 merchandising firms, 74 life insurance companies, 31 property and liability insurance companies, 9 consumer loan companies, and 33 one-bank holding companies. In addition, the FTC served notice that smaller companies planning mergers involving combined assets in excess of $250 million must likewise fill out special forms at least 60 days before the merger.

Furthermore, the FTC is requiring notification within 10 days after acquiring 10% or more of the voting stock of another company with assets of $10 million or more. (This might be termed the 10-10-10 rule) Also, before a firm can acquire 50% or more of the stock of another company 60 days notification is required.

These premerger data would not be made public but would be used by investigative personnel of the FTC and Justice Department's Antitrust Division. These data would ask the names, addresses and principal

[5] *Time,* 80 (May 30, 1969).

business activities of the parties involved, a description of the manner in which the transaction is to be carried out, and copies of all financial reports sent to stockholders during the last three years. The form also asks for a tabulation of recent sales in specific activities such as manufacturing, wholesale and retail trade, finance and insurance, together with questions about plants, past mergers, and product lines. The identification could be quite specific, going as far as individualizing activities down to the definitive four digits of the Census Bureau's standard industrial classification (SIC, which is discussed more fully in Chapter 15).

The Federal Trade Commission also complements the Justice Department in policing activity as in the attempted takeover of Allis-Chalmers Manufacturing Company by White Consolidated Industries. The conglomerator's president. Edward S. Reddig, contended that there was no significant area of overlapping between White and Allis-Chalmers and so merger would not constitute a violation of antitrust laws. The FTC nevertheless without actually taking action against White brought a complaint asking that White voluntarily not take any steps to integrate with Allis-Chalmers. If White should refuse, the FTC indicated its intentions for asking a Federal Court to issue a preliminary injunction to bar "scrambling" of the two companies pending determination of the case.

The complaint is based on charges that both companies are potential competitors; for example, White already has about 10% of the national $2 billion annual electrical appliances market and Allis-Chalmers is a "most likely entrant into this market." Other similar potential competitive areas include paper-making machinery, crawler-tractor, rolling-mill machinery, and other heavy equipment. The FTC also charged that White and Allis-Chalmers, both with annual sales approaching $1 billion and both in the approximately $80 billion machinery building industry would tend toward increased concentration and undue market power.

The Federal Trade Commission has recently attracted attention in its challenge of the "failing company" doctrine. This doctrine rests on a 1930 Supreme Court decision and it is also written into an amendment to the Clayton Act. In substance the 1930 decision reversed a FTC decision against International Shoe Company by holding that an acquisition should be excluded from antitrust law if without such acquisition the acquired firm was in dire danger of failure with consequent substantial injury to stockholders, employees, and the community.

A classic test of this "failing company" doctrine occurred in 1969 when the FTC ordered U. S. Steel Corporation to divest itself of Certified Industries, a ready-mixed concrete producer it acquired in 1964. The FTC conceded that Certified Industries probably would have gone out of business if it had not been taken over by U. S. Steel. However, it was pointed out that just a few years before the acquisition, Certified purchased only about 8% of its cement requirements from U. S. Steel's cement-making subsidiary, Universal Atlas Cement. By 1964 Certified bought 88% of its cement needs from Universal Atlas. Then, too, the FTC contended, the ready-mixed cement market was characterized by many small locally competitive companies. U. S. Steel's absorption of Certified drastically changed the competitive character of the New York metropolitan market. Consequently, the "failing company" doctrine should not be presumed to exclude acquisitions which would lead to restraint of trade. Then, too, the FTC spokesmen argued, the 1930 ruling was made at a time of severe depression and has no value or meaning in today's dynamic economy.

The seriousness of the FTC's intentions of voiding the "failing company" doctrine became suspect when in the summer of 1969 the FTC voted 3-to-2 to permit, tentatively, Occidental Petroleum Corporation's proposal to acquire Maust Coal and Coke Company. One of Occidental's earlier acquisitions was Island Creek Coal Company, the nation's third largest coal producer which accounts for nearly 5% of the nation's output. If the merger were consummated, the combined coal output of the merged firms would be just slightly above 6%. The FTC majority in this 3-to-2 ruling admitted that the merger of the two coal companies could have serious anticompetitive effects. However, the majority voted approval because otherwise Maust probably would enter bankruptcy proceedings "within a matter of several weeks." It was pointed out that Maust has had extreme financial difficulties in recent years and "has not met principal or interest payments on about $20 million of loans. A Maust bankruptcy, the majority continued, could work hardships on employees, creditors, and stockholders as well as the mining communities in which the company operates." [6] It was also stressed that Maust had explored thoroughly its sale to other companies and that Occidental through its subsidiary, Island Creek, was the only interested buyer.

This recent ruling raises serious questions as to the applicability of the "failing company concept." How much information should be made available and what "failing" criteria should be applied are matters that seemingly need redefinition.

SECURITIES AND EXCHANGE COMMISSION

As a rule the Securities and Exchange Commission is not concerned with stopping mergers. The SEC does, however, require certain informa-

---

[6] *The Wall Street Journal*, 32 (June 11, 1969).

tion from firms contemplating merger. Current SEC regulations require that a company registering securities in connection with the proposed acquisition of another company must provide certified financial statements for the firm to be acquired, which cover at least a three-year period. A 1968 law provided that anyone acquiring 10% or more of a company's stock must disclose this fact to the SEC. Additionally, anyone making a cash tender offer for 10% or more of a company's stock must disclose the identity of those planning the offer, the source of their funds, and their purpose in making the offer. A revision of this law would broaden the disclosure rules to apply when 5% or more of a company's stock had been acquired or was being sought through a tender offer. Additional powers would also be given the SEC to guard against fraud and manipulation in takeover attempts.

The SEC has also taken steps to require companies to report separately on those products or services that during the previous two fiscal years contributed at least 10% to total sales and operating revenue. Basic to the SEC's concern is the belief that investors and financial analysts need such specific information if they are to evaluate a firm's performance and worth.

The SEC's more vital role is in policing the securities market particularly to keep firms from making misleading statements; for example, in 1969 Susquehanna Corporation was charged with making false and misleading statements concerning its successful tender for 38% of Pan American Sulphur Company common stock. In documents filed with the SEC, Susquehanna said it did not "plan or propose" to merge Pan Am Sulphur with any other concern or make any other major changes in its business or corporate structure. Yet almost immediately after the successful tender offer, Susquehanna proposed that Pan Am Sulphur acquire American Smelting and Refining Company through an exchange of securities. Pan Am Sulphur's directors said they had not authorized such action. This precipitated the charges that Susquehanna and its president, Herbert F. Korholz, planned to use control of Pan Am Sulphur to force the company to acquire or merge with other companies that would bring "material changes in Pan American's business and/or corporate structure."

Similarly, the SEC serves as a sort of referee in many merger disputes. In the General Time Corporation-Talley Industries merger venture, a group of disgruntled General Time stockholders challenged the proposal through the SEC contending that the merger was unfair. They argued that Talley changed the terms of the merger to its own advantage. The General Time stockholders who approved the merger by only a small margin were supposedly unable to protect their rights, since Talley immediately on getting control appointed its own Talley nominees to the 10-man General Time board of directors. Consequently, "the subsequent merger terms couldn't have been negotiated by the two companies at arms length." [7]

STOCK EXCHANGES

On occasion the New York Stock Exchange has let it be known that it was considering the possible refusal of applications of "one or two" Big Board conglomerates to list securities issued in connection with recent or proposed acquisitions. The concern on one particular occasion was because of an overpreponderance of debt securities to equity securities in a certain concern's corporate makeup.

Early in 1969 the New York Stock Exchange made some pronouncements relative to certain member firms' attempts to protect themselves against takeovers. Among these defensive measures were the following proposals:

1. A requirement that 80% of the shares be voted in favor of merger when the would-be-acquirer owns more than 10% of any class of the company's equity securities. In other cases a two-thirds vote would be required for approval.

2. Creation of a small class of preferred stock placed privately that would have an 80% requirement to permit merger.

3. A proviso that at least two-thirds of the shares be voted for a proposed merger by *both* parties.

These and similar defensive measures were apparently being considered or even being enacted by a growing number of Big Board members who were becoming more and more apprehensive over the threat of being taken over by more aggressive firms.

"Automatic" Sprinkler Corporation of America (which has since changed its name to ATO, Inc.) was one of the first of the major conglomerates to adopt such defensive measures. At its 1969 annual meeting, although disclaiming that it knew of any other firm's desires to acquire "Automatic" Sprinkler, the company nevertheless presented almost insurmountable roadblocks to being captured. The shareholders approved an amendment to the company's articles of incorporation requiring approval of 80% of the voting power of all classes of stock on any merger where the other party owned more than 5% of any class of "Automatic" stock. In addition, they amended the company's regulations

[7] *The Wall Street Journal*, 10 (June 23, 1969).

to prevent removal of a director by shareholder vote if the votes cast *against* his removal would be sufficient to elect him a director under cumulative voting at a regular directors' election. This latter clause would make it very difficult for any merger-prone minority interest holding stock in "Automatic" to oust any incumbent director.

As a concomitant of this and similar merger-fearful firms the New York Stock Exchange ultimately adopted a policy of disapproval of certain of these defensive measures in the conviction that this would tend to discriminate against certain shareholders. The Exchange's disapproval immediately brought forth critical statements from individuals and groups who felt that the Exchange had no right to legislate in matters which belonged with Federal lawmakers and the courts.

PROFESSIONAL ASSOCIATIONS

The 18-man Accounting Principles Board of the American Institute of Public Accountants is one of the most important professional groups to be concerned with legislation for the merger movement. After quite a lengthy depth analysis of some apparent abuses, this group came up with a set of proposals to set stiffer rules in accounting for business mergers. One of the areas of concern was the common practice known as pooling of interests. Under this controversial concept a pooling treats two merged companies as if they were always combined. The two concerns not only combine current results but also restate past results to account for the merger. One of the serious objections to this practice is the facility with which a company with an unsavory record can conceal its bad performance by merging with a profitable firm. Pooling of interests has been likened to a "Bikini bathing suit—this is because what it reveals is interesting, but what it conceals is vital." [8]

In a 1967 study by Pennsylvania State University Professors Copeland and Wojdak of 26 acquiring companies, each of which had at least three acquisitions and with a grand total of 169 poolings, the estimated *unrecorded* goodwill for these transactions was in excess of $1.6 billion.[9] The difference between book value and purchase price averaged almost 2½ times the book value. The net effect of this practice was and is to overstate the earnings of the parent corporations.

In contrast those who favor the purchase method of accounting say

[8] Abraham Briloff, "Distortions Arising from Pooling-of Interests Accounting," *Financial Analysts Journal*, 24, 75 (March 1968).
[9] R. M. Copeland, and I. F. Wojdak, "Goodwill in Merger-Minded Companies," *Financial Analyst Journal*, 25, 57 (Sept.-Oct., 1969).

that an acquiring corporation should show its newly acquired assets (both tangible and identifiable intangible assets) at their fair market value. This would mean that any excess in the price paid over the fair value of the assets must be recorded as goodwill. Current accounting practice gives considerable latitude to a company in the way it handles goodwill. In some cases, it is carried on the books indefinitely, in other instances, it is written off over an arbitrary life span. The new regulations, however, would set a requirement that such "goodwill" as resulted from merger must be written off over not more than 40 years. In addition, this proviso would apply to writing off all intangible assets purchased by the company.

The real concern over the arbitrary use of the pooling-of-interests method focuses on the almost universal practice whereby a "sweetener" is used to attract the stockholders of the merger-desired firm. Many instances of this tactic have been cited in the previous chapters. An excellent example is Xerox Corporation's 1969 acquisition of Scientific Data Systems for Xerox stock valued at $892 million. Scientific Data's book value at that time was only $78.3 million, thus resulting in a goodwill payment of $814 million or nearly 11 times in excess of what the acquired firm was worth according to its book value.

The conventional practice would have been to ignore this massive overpayment hoping it would disappear over time. According to the Accounting Principles Board's proposal of a mandatory maximum 40-year writeoff, Xerox's annual earnings would be reduced by 26 cents a share until the year 2008, assuming no change in the number of shares outstanding. In 1969 this would have meant that Xerox earned only $1.82 per share as contrasted with the $2.08 the company claimed it earned, or a difference of 13%.

Numerous similar profit-pattern distortions result from the pooling-of-interests gimmickry. In 1967 Continental Telephone reported earnings per share of $1.08. However, if all its acquisitions had been reported under the purchase method, earnings would have been more realistically set at $0.02 per share. Similarly, ITT reporting earnings of $2.27 per share that same year would only have been able to report per share earnings of $0.17 under the purchase concept.

The accounting profession, through its Accounting Principles Board, is providing a much-needed surveillance in an area where ethics and equity have too often been relegated to a back seat. Even more such conscientious soul-searching and self-medication by related professions and merger-minded corporations would diminish the need for restrictive governmental actions.

INDUSTRY ITSELF

Policing action taken by the courts, Congress, governmental agencies, and the Stock Exchanges can and probably should be bolstered by industry-initiated controls. This can come from the initiation of forward-looking policies by individual companies or by industry associations. For example, one of the most serious condemnations of conglomerate practices concerned the indiscriminate lumping of sales, net income, and assets of the many subsidiaries into the consolidated conglomerate profit and loss and balance sheet summaries. Several years ago Indian Head, a diversified company, began to break down financial reports to show how each division contributed to the composite report. In addition, Indian Head's very readable 1968 annual report was one of the first to carry detailed economic information about each industry in which the company operates. Rather than being penalized by such unsolicited disclosure, Robert W. Lear, president of the firm, indicated that he believed that the company, its stockholders, and financial analysts were benefited. In particular the significance of diversification is highlighted. Thus as recently as 1964 all of Indian Head's sales and profits were concentrated in one area, specialty textiles. Four years later, only 50% of sales and 43% of operating profit came from textiles. Metal and auto products, first added in 1965, contributed 29% of sales and 22% of profit; glass containers added 20% to sales and 35% to profit. The breakdown also indicated that the firm's entry into a glamour field, information technology, was not doing so well with only about 1% of the total sales and with a loss in operating revenue.

This sort of financial reporting, increasingly more common, facilitates communication between the firm and the public. If more companies could appreciate the value and even the necessity for such up-to-date reporting, there would be less need for government imposed rules and sanctions; for example, the SEC's proposal to force disclosure of contributions to a parent firm by each of its major subsidiaries would not be necessary.

Although individual companies can do much by way of setting precedents that lead to merger constraints, group action is probably more effective. This has been the experience of British industry where takeovers have a longer historical background. Some years ago the British counterpart of Wall Street, known as the City of London, decided to police the merger movement. This forward step was motivated in part by the realization that if industry did not attempt self-policing the British Labor Government would very definitely impose State-policing. The result has been a voluntary control system. An eight-man watchdog committee passes judgment on proposed takeover attempts. The committee is guided by a list of 35 rules that act as merger constraints. For example, Rule 26 provides that merger proposals that involve less than 100% of the offered company are undesirable. Then, too, all bids must first be made to the board of the firm to be acquired. This is in distinct contrast to the American practice where merger proposals so frequently appear in the newspapers without even the second party's knowledge.

These and similar group-initiated merger-policing constraints formally or even informally set by industry itself could be preferable to Government edicts. Since the need for some sort of semblance of order is obvious, if industry, collectively or as individual firms, does not set acceptable constraints, then imposed controls will be set by the sovereign referee—the Federal Government.

15

MERGERS AND INDUSTRIAL TAXONOMY

Taxonomy refers to a classification system in relation to certain general laws or principles. For many centuries it has been customary to classify work and workers according to product lines. Thus we had the butchers, the bakers, the weavers, and the tailors whose lines of endeavor identified individual industries. During the medieval era, this centripetal pull manifested itself in the formation of guilds; that is, associations of persons engaged in the same business or plying the same craft. This industrial classification was so important that during this medieval period, the Guilds were the only countervailing force to the absolutism of the Church and Feudalistic nobility.

Even to the present day differentiation of jobs and industries by product or product-group names continues to be the best business classification technique. However, assuming conglomeration continues at its current rapid pace, many once-familiar industry classifications will have no meaning. Unless, through legal sanction, Federal agencies insist that the vast multiindustry companies report performance data and other pertinent statistics on a divisional or product basis, it will become virtually impossible to get data on once-familiar industries. Within the last few years entire industries have disappeared as meaningful sectors of our business society. A few include coal mining, meatpacking, and moviemaking which were readily identifiable entities five years ago. Even major industries such as steel have been radically revamped by recent mergers. In steelmaking, which is still a readily identifiable industry, the major steel-producing corporations listed in Table 15-1 were the subjects of takeovers or near-takeovers during 1968–1969:

Table 15-1

Fortune 1968 Ranking	Company Losing Autonomy	Controlling Firm
96	Jones and Laughlin	Ling-Temco-Vought
124	Youngstown S and T	Lykes
278	Crucible Steel	Colt Industries
287	Wheeling Steel	Pittsburgh Steel
344	CF and I Steel	Crane and Co.
385	Sharon Steel	NVF Co.
—	Detroit Steel	Cyclops (pending)

These seven producers had sales, before merger, of about $2.8 billion; assets totaled $3.3 billion and their combined workforce was almost 110,000. This group constituted more than one-sixth of the entire iron and steel industry.

A similar change has radically altered the bituminous coal mining industry. Most of the major coal producers have been taken over by firms which previously did not engage in coal mining. As a consequence, today it is almost impossible to identify the industry or to apply analytical tools to measure structure and performance. The biggest coal mining concern, Consolidation Coal Company (itself a horizontal merger of Pittsburgh Coal Company and Consolidation Coal), was taken over in 1966 by Continental Oil Company for $281 million in partial payment plus a promise to pay $460 million from future production. The next largest coal producer, Peabody Coal Company, was acquired by Kennecott Copper Company in a $622 million deal, whereas Island Creek Coal Company merged into Occidental Petroleum. Other leading coal mining firms such as Clinchfield (acquired by Pittston) also succumbed to merger during 1965–1969. The list of other coal producers which lost autonomy includes Old Ben Coal Corporation (acquired by Standard Oil Company, (Ohio), Bear Coal Company (purchased by Atlantic Richfield), Ayrshire Collieries (purchased by Ashland Oil and Refining Company), and Pittsburgh and Midway Coal Company (now a Gulf Subsidiary). In addition, the petroleum producers took title to extensive coal-bearing tracts in anticipation of getting into the coal mining business in the very near future. Humble Oil and Refining Company has bought very large coal acreage in southern Illinois, and Shell Oil Company won exploratory rights to the Crow Indian lands in Montana. Although there still are several thousand small coal mining operators, the 12 or so firms accounting for perhaps one-third of the industry's output are now parts of conglomerate empires.

The same phenomenon is evident in the meatpacking business. Wilson and Company was acquired by Ling-Temco-Vought, and Armour and Company, after a bitter battle between General Host Corporation and Greyhound Corporation, succumbed to the latter conglomerator. Other ownership changes include AMK's acquisition of John Morrell, and Hygrade's capitulation to Beck Industries. Cudahy and Company, although staving off merger overtures from U. S. Smelting and Refining which once owned 18% of Cudahy's voting stock, continues in a somewhat precarious position. Late in 1968 Cudahy, presumably in a gesture to discourage acquisition-minded firms, embarked on its own merger program. Cudahy acquired Allied Kid in a stock swap which had the net effect of reducing U. S. Smelting's minority position.

Even family owned firms such as Oscar Mayer and Company (about 200 members of the Mayer family with stock are in the company) and Rath Packing Company have had serious merger feelers. Rath, in particular, appears to be a natural for takeover since it has shown obvious regression syndrome symptoms, including losses totaling $115 million over the last three years. During the past 14 years Rath slumped in *Fortune*'s listing from 110 to 347 in sales and showed similar negative achievement in every other norm (assets declined from $44 million to $37 million and the workforce shrank from 8300 to 4800.

Even the industry giant, Swift and Company, with sales of about $3 billion, has not been immune to takeover. In particular, Northwest Industries made serious gestures to get control of Swift. Other large conglomeration-prone financial interests, including Norton Simon, Central Securities Corporation, and Henry Crown have likewise accumulated sizable blocks of Swift stock. Early in 1969 Swift made several strategic moves in order to block aggressors. Among these moves was an increase in the authorized common stock from 16 million shares to 30 million shares, and in authorized preferred stock from one million to seven million shares. This move would provide Swift with considerable more flexibility in warding off aggressors.

These are just a few of the more outstanding examples. Almost no industry sector has escaped unscathed. Although the examples are all from manufacturing, there is just as much and, perhaps, even more merger movement in other business areas such as banking, railroads, utilities, insurance, and so on. In the entertainment field by mid-1969, nearly all the independent major movie companies had been taken over by conglomerates. Metro-Goldwyn-Mayer was dominated by a financial group, among whom Edgar Bronfman (Distillers Corporation-Seagrams) was very prominent. Transamerica Corporation acquired United Artists; MCA captured Universal Pictures and Warner Bros.–Seven Arts, Ltd., went through a series of merger gyrations involving Kinney National Service and Commonwealth United Corporation. A lone standout, Twentieth Century–Fox Film Corporation, became the object of a take-over bid late in February 1969. Supposedly friendly interests, in the guise of Darryl F. Zanuck and his Trans-Lux Corporation, came to the rescue and, at least temporarily, kept Fox from being conglomerated. However, this friendly gesture became suspect when it was rumored that Trans-Lux's interest in Fox was being masterminded by McGraw-Hill, the publishing firm, which owns 5% of Trans-Lux's stock.

The virtual disappearance of the once-conventional industry categories has more than a nostalgic or historical meaning. Unless there is some logical differentiation of industrial endeavor, it becomes almost impossible to tabulate performance results and to evaluate productivity and profit relative to specific products. This, for example, has tremendous significance to the discerning investor who seeks a company that has shown dynamism and vision by concentrating on a growing industry. A conglomerate's consolidated profit and loss summary gives no such index. Similarly, depreciation policies, research and development allocations, advertising direction, and all other very vital facets of business enterprise tend to be "leveled" in the massive ecumenical umbrella which envelops the typical conglomerate.

If the conventional industry lines of demarcation disappear, there seems to be a need for some newer and, perhaps, better classification technique. This need is especially essential if conglomerates do become the corporate structure of the future. Assuming this eventuality, it is reasonable to infer that legislation will inevitably force the multiendeavor firms to provide the government and the public with an index of where the corporate action takes place. The Securities and Exchange Commission in September 1968 proposed to amend registration forms so that companies registering securities with the Commission would have to disclose the relative contribution major product lines and services made to that firm's earnings. This regulation and, perhaps, even far more stringent rulings should be expected if diversified companies continue the current practice of lumping sales, earnings, and assets in consolidated reporting.

Late in February 1969 the SEC modified its proposal, still insisting that companies report separately on those products or services that, during the last two years, contributed 10% or more to total sales or operating revenue. In the revision, however, the SEC eliminated the proposed requirement that companies disclose the approximate amount of assets employed in each segment of the business. The rationale for this relaxing in proposed requirements was the contention that it is difficult in many instances to place a realistic value on all assets.

Assuming that some day the SEC or any other empowered government agency does force differential reporting by multiproduct firms, significant changes will be effected in industrial taxonomy. This reclassification will probably result in the abandonment of the present product, trade, or process industry names and the substitution of numerical coding. Some very laudable steps have already been taken to systematize the indexing of the seemingly infinite variety of industrial activities. By far the most sophisticated and most meaningful attempt at this type of categorization is the four-digit coding prepared by the Technical Committee on Standard Industrial Classification under the sponsorship and guidance of the Office of Statistical Standards of the Bureau of the Budget, Executive Office of the President. In this coding the first two digits of the SIC number show the major industrial group in which that company is engaged. The basic ten categories are

01 to 09	agriculture, forestry, fisheries
10 to 14	mining
15 to 17	contract construction
19 to 39	manufacturing
40 to 49	transportation, communication, utilities
50 to 59	wholesale and retail
60 to 67	finance, insurance, real estate
70 to 89	services
91 to 94	government
99	nonclassifiable

These ten categories are then subdivided into major groups; for example, group 60 includes all banking, and group 61 covers credit agencies other than banks. Further subdivision of the major groups leads to rather narrow and very meaningful categorizations. In *Poor's Register*, for example, the numerical division of major groups includes more than 1000 individual industries, designated by four-digit coding.[1] This logical systematizing should aid in the better understanding of mergers and conglomeration. Take, for example, a manufacturer of tobacco products. If the firm restricts its endeavors to manufacturing cigarettes, then the SIC four-digit index assigned to this firm is 2111. The first two digits, 21, relate to the basic division manufacturing and specifically tobacco manufacturing. The third digit, 1, places this operation in the cigarette sec-

[1] *Poor's Register of Corporations, Directors and Executives 1970*, Standard and Poor's Corporation, New York 1970, pp. 1-21.

tor of the industry. The fourth digit further differentiates within that
sector. If this particular manufacturer also makes cigars, then this portion of its endeavors would be classified under SIC 2121; chewing and
smoking tobacco, together with snuff, are numbered SIC 2131, and tobacco stemming and redrying are labeled SIC 2141.

The proper use of this classification index would tell the public, or at
least the analyst, that if a company were indexed as 2111, 2121, 2131,
and 2141, this company would be engaged in four different lines of endeavor, all within the two-digit category 21—tobacco manufacturing. If
this enterprise were to expand vertically backward into the growing of
tobacco, then it would get the additional SIC number, 0114, meaning
that it grows tobacco. The 01 digits apply to agricultural production in
general and the 14 digits indicate tobacco growing.

Assuming that this firm decided to integrate vertically forward into
the selling of its products, the SIC number, 5094, would apply since this
indicates wholesale and retail trade (the first two digits, 50) in tobacco
and its products (the last two digits, 94). The company could also get a
5993 classification number if it entered the cigar store and cigar stand
field. The classification numbers thus far mentioned would apply to expansion in very closely related lines of endeavor. The vertical integration, 0114, 2111, 2121, 2131, 2141, 5094 and 5993, might be supplemented
by horizontal integration which would entail no new SIC numbers, just
use of more of the same.

If, however, this tobacco grower-manufacturer-distributor decided to
acquire grocery stores (5411), confectionery stores (5441), drug stores
(5912), or even liquor stores (5921) as outlets for its tobacco products,
then diversification of a different sort is indicated. If in its agricultural
subsidiary (0114), it decided to practice rotation of crops and consequently grow cotton (0112), vegetables (0123), poultry (0134), or hogs
(0136), then the classification index would show such expanded operations.

If categorization of this sort were properly carried out, mergers and
conglomerations could be better identified as to scope of endeavor. If
weights based on sales, earnings, or assets employed were also used either in absolute or relative terms, then the interested public might once
again be able to differentiate among industrial conglomerates. It must
be admitted, however, that no matter what numerical or mnemonic
technique might be applied, the relative ease in identifying firms as part
of the steel, coal, or chemical industries is a thing of the past.

Although SIC designations are now being used, there is serious need
for more rigid and more universal classification. The following examples
should illustrate this point.

Glen Alden Corporation

In the 1970 edition of *Poor's Register of Corporations, Directors and Executives*, Glen Alden Corporation is identified as being active in consumer products, retail stores, textiles, building materials, and operations of motion picture theaters and is assigned SIC numbers 6711, and 7832. Two years previously this corporate conglomerate was given SIC numbers 1111, 2299, 3111, 4225, and 7831. It would appear from simple inspection that Glen Alden had curtailed its diversification during this two-year period. Actually, the company might have reduced its anthra-

Table 15-2

Schenley Industries, Inc.	B.V.D. Company	Philip Carey Corp.	RKO-Stanley Warner	Opp and Micolas Mills	ILC Indus. and Swift Textiles
2084			2046		
2085					
				2211	2211
	2252				
			2259	2259	
	2321				
	2322				
	2323				
	2329				
	2341		2341		
	2342		2342		
	2384				
	2385				
		2649			
		2661			
			2822		
			2834		
			2891		
		2952			
		3275			
		3292			
		3294			
		3431			
		3662			
					3811

cite mining interests (1111), but it certainly had expended endeavors by gaining a dominant position in Schenley Industries. Table 15-2 shows the SIC coding of Glen Alden's 1970 subsidiaries' activities.

Even though this listing is more complete than the SIC 6711 and 7832 coding shown for the parent company, there are serious shortcomings. Although a simple list of SIC numbers might be useful in a few cases, it would generally be inadequate.

The next step in the better utilization of SIC codes would entail weighting; for example, W. R. Grace and Company's conglomerated ventures are listed in Table 15-3.

Table 15-3

SIC Code	Activity	Approximate Sales Percent
2042	Animal feeds	?
2071	Candy, etc.	13
2818	Ind. organic chemicals	
2819	Ind. inorganic chemicals	66
2879	Agricultural chemicals	
3079	Misc. plastics	?
4511	Air transport	?
?	Export-import	4
?	Steamship	7
?	Other	10
		100

This is an excellent beginning toward a more rational portrayal of diversified endeavor. W. R. Grace and other firms which provide comparable breakdowns should be commended. By contrast Gulf and Western Industries, a much diversified firm, is given 1970 SIC designations of only 5013, 7813, and 7814, with no real index of individual division contribution toward the parent company's performance. Actually, a partial analysis involving four Gulf and Western recently merged components (E. W. Bliss, Brown and Company, Consolidated Cigar, and Universal American) indicates that Gulf and Western should also show SIC numbers 0114, 1999, 2121, 2432, 2611, 2621, 2647, 2649, 2818, 2891, 3321, 3323, 3441, 3461, 3499, 3522, 3531, 3536, 3537, 3541, 3545, 3548, 3559, 3562, 3585, 3622, 3644, 3662, 3679, and 3729, in addition to the officially designated 5013, 7813, and 7814. In this case there is also an obvious lack of data as to divisional or product-line contribution.

One of the very best examples of the SIC categorization, as shown in *Poor's*, is Singer and Company. In 1966 this corporation differentiated its major divisions and used 24 different SIC numbers, ranging from 2511 to 7391. In 1969 Singer had expanded its listing to 61 SIC designations, ranging from 2284 to 8999. Although the expanded range does indicate diversification, the increase in total SIC numbers reported (from 24 to 61) over the three-year span also testifies to better analysis. In 1966, 19 out of the 24 categories were in the 3500 to 3700 range; in 1969 43 out of the 61 categories were in this range.

The SIC taxonomy could ultimately be used for at least two-dimensional classification of diversified business activity. The category designation could be shown horizontally as a "span of endeavor"; for example, this is how three leading chemical manufacturing firms can be viewed:

Monsanto   2821 ——— 3079
                                      (5 SIC numbers)

Du Pont   2813 ————— 3079
                                      (15 SIC numbers)

Union Carbide   1062 ————————— 8911
                                      (42 SIC numbers)

This simple comparison clearly shows the far greater span of endeavor characterizing Union Carbide as compared with DuPont and especially as compared with Monsanto. If we assume the accuracy of the SIC designations, Monsanto is obviously sticking to its "chemical last," and Union Carbide is, in effect, a conglomerator.

The second dimension, the respective weight associated with each of the specific SIC numbered activities, can be viewed vertically.

Monsanto Company

Million   SIC Numbers, Hypothetically Weighted
Dollars   2821   3079

50
100
200
300
400
500

In Monsanto's instance the relatively few SIC designations facilitates analysis. Plugging in the second dimension, sales per SIC category, provides a comparison norm with meaningful control possibilities. For example, let us assume Monsanto evidenced interest in merging with another chemical producer that had a sales volume of $400 million in the product category SIC 2821. Questions then might be raised as to the propriety or legality of this "constraint-in-competition" union, since Monsanto's position in SIC 2821 would now be increased significantly.

Thus graphic presentation, if set forth to scale, would also show that Monsanto's activities are restricted to a relatively narrow band on the business spectrum from SIC 2821 to SIC 3079. The range of only 258 numbers, although it is not a precise measure of diversification, does provide an index of product mix. Union Carbide's range of 7849 numbers in sharp contrast does tell us that this firm's endeavors are spread over a much wider business spectrum.

Graphically depicting this two-dimensional taxonomy according to corporate relative diversification becomes quite difficult with conglomerates. Figure 15-1 is a first attempt at diagramming Textron's product mix. The current issue of *Poor's Register of Corporations, Directors and Executives*, 1970, shows Textron with 17 SIC designations ranging from

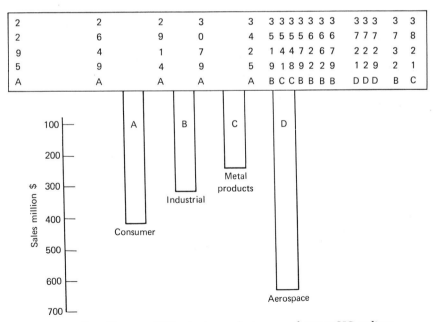

Figure 15-1 Textron, 1969 sales by product group, showing SIC codings.

2295 to 3821, a range of 1526. Once again it must be emphasized that the range itself is not an absolute or accurate index of diversification or of conglomeration, but it does show a relative corporate activity over the total business spectrum. In this instance, Textron might be viewed as less of a conglomerate than Union Carbide, if the range alone were the criterion. The same inference would be made if Textron were compared with Gulf and Western whose activities extend from SIC 0114 to SIC 7814, or a range of 7700.

Any meaningful index of relative diversification must include a set of weights related to the specific SIC-numbered areas of activity. This weighting encounters obstacles, because most corporate accounting procedures do not reveal this information to the public or even to the professional investors. Corporations such as Textron and Monsanto deserve much credit for at least presenting these data broken down into related groups. Thus in Figure 15-1 the five SIC activities marked A are lumped in the Consumer products group. Similarly, the other three groupings, Industrial products with 6 SIC numbers, Metal products with 3 SIC numbers, and Aerospace with 3 SIC numbers, provide a means for generalized graphic comparisons.

Assuming that Federal regulations would mandate corporate reporting along SIC category lines, it would be a relatively simple matter to determine the extent or degree of specific SIC categories. A relatively simple computer program, on a two-dimensional basis (span of endeavor and volume of activity), could be structured for analysis purposes. The financial analyst, and even many of the more sophisticated investors, could then get a better viewing of a diversified corporation's endeavors and performance. This might be helpful for rational investment purposes. From a regulatory point of view such a two-dimensional portrayal might have value for determining competitiveness within specific product lines.

At least one other area in which a SIC-type taxonomy could prove beneficial is in the analysis of individuals as conglomerators. The much overused adage, "Don't put all your eggs in one basket," as applied to the financial field has obvious meaning and application. However, in our steadily more complicated industrial society, this "spreading around of eggs" can have tremendous implications. The Mellon family might be considered the epitome of this type of diversification. In two excellent articles on the Mellons, *Fortune*[2] tells of the widely dispersed and very significant holdings of the Mellons.

---

[2] *Fortune*, "The Mellons of Pittsburgh," by Charles J. V. Murphy, October 1967 and November 1967.

Comparing the Mellon family's "span of endeavor" with that of most conglomerators evokes a fairly obvious inference (see Table 15-4): there is little, if any, real difference between the Mellon empire and most of the more loosely knit, semiautonomous conglomerates. The binding force is financial, reinforced by mutual or interlocking directorates; for example, until recently, Mr. Richard King Mellon was on the board of at least four of the firms (Mellon Bank, Gulf, Alcoa, and General Motors).

Table 15-4   Mellon Equity Position: Percent Ownership and Company SIC Codes

25%	30%	20%	20%	$200MM	20%	$20MM
Gulf	Alcoa	Koppers	Carborundum	Mellon Nat. Bank	Etc.	GM
			1099			
1311						
		1621				
		2491				
		2815				
		2818				
	2819					
		2833				
2911						
		2951				
		3079				
			3229			
			3291			
			3297			
		3312				
	3334					
	3352					
	3357					
		3554				3585
						3632
		3564				3639
						3711
		3566				3722
						3729
			3679			3741
		3722			6211	
					6322	
				6025	6332	

A number of other interlocking directorships tie all the Mellon-influenced corporations into what might figuratively be called the Mellon empire. As with so many of our conglomerates, the Mellons likewise take virtually no active role in the operational aspects of any of their varied interest but let this phase of the business reside in the hands of hired managers.

The point being stressed here is that the concept of conglomeration when practiced by individuals or families attracts less attention, yet in its financial and managerial implications it is almost identical with corporate conglomeration. The roster of individual or family conglomerators might include names such as Howard Hughes (with at least a score of SIC numbers covering his manifold interests), the Rockefeller family (likewise with a multiplicity of endeavors), Norton Simon, and hundreds of lesser known enterprisers. This is certainly not meant as criticism—it is axiomatic that diversification in an individual's investment portfolio is a mark of good business judgment; but if it is good common sense for individuals to diversify their investments, then perhaps it is equally defensible for corporations to do the same. Although this chapter is not intended as a defense of diversification-conglomeration, the discussion does focus on the need for an improved classification device so that the extent and intensity of diversified endeavor can be better understood by the general public.

SUMMARY

The dramatic change currently taking place because of extensive diversification confounds industry identification and nomenclature. No longer is "a rose, is a rose, is a rose" but rather "meatpacking, is coal mining, is brewing, is steel making, and so on." A few years ago an informed investor purchasing stock in a particular company knew fairly well what he was investing in. Similarly, managers knew specifically what they were to manage and what they were to produce. Likewise, employment by a given firm generally meant work of a specific kind, rather easily identified by job titles. A prospective employee who might have had an aversion or an allergy to a particular product or job could readily recognize what he should avoid. Today the merger mishmash has erased many lines of demarcation among jobs, product lines, executive functions, and even business organizations.

Assuming further conglomerate momentum it seems inevitable that industry, government, and the concerned public will become conditioned to a new and more meaningful classification of business endeavor. In addition to group, family, or "zaibatsu" names, an increasing possibility is that we might adopt the equivalent of a corporate zip code system.

16

THE CORPORATE NAME GAME

As a conservative estimate there will be approximately 1000 name changes this year among our nation's top 100,000 corporations. This 1% name-change rate is nearly three times that of the comparable rate 20 years ago. There are undoubtedly a great variety of reasons for this accelerated corporate name changing.

Recently Xerox corporation announced that one of its subsidiaries, Scientific Data Systems, whose name was commonly abbreviated to SDS, was changing its name to Xerox Data Systems so that it would now be referred to as XDS. The presumed need to change names in this case seems obvious—to avoid confusion with the better-known SDS, the campus-disrupting Students for a Democratic Society.

In an increasing number of instances our rapidly advancing technologies leave some firms with rather archaic names. It seems reasonable and even mandatory that such outmoded names be modernized. Then, too, increasing stress on diversification resulting in 5000-plus mergers per year necessitates corporate name revamping. "Automatic" Sprinkler's directors recently voted to change its name to A-T-O (the letters are the Company's New York Stock Exchange ticker symbol) because the firm, once primarily concerned with fire protection systems, had expanded into multiproduct venture. National Dairy Products Corporation also decided to take a new name, Kraftco Corporation, because, as stated by the firm's chairman, Gordon Edwards, "We have been more than national for a long time and many of our processed packaged convenience food products make us more than a dairy company."

In a few instances, as in the tobacco industry, public opinion, real or presumed, has lead to the erasure of the word "tobacco" from most of that industry's leaders' names. Other reasons for name changing seem to stem from a corporate inferiority complex, the result of extended misera-

186

ble performance. Hopefully a new name might lead to a more propitious future.

Considering the increased incidence of corporate name changing, it is important to attempt to learn if such drastic action is worthwhile. It seems obvious that this course of action is both confusing and costly. After years of associating a particular firm's name with product excellence, or its lack, the public, the employees, and the customers must abruptly make mental adjustments. Even after several years of usage, it probably takes most old-time acquaintances of the United States Rubber Company just a few extra seconds to associate the name Uniroyal with this firm. The name-changing process is also costly. Stationery and similar forms must be altered and advertisements must be placed in the communications media. Xerox subsidiary's disassociation with SDS (to XDS) resulted in an expensive advertising campaign with among others a two-page advertisement in *Business Week* and a full-page one in *The Wall Street Journal* rationalizing the name change. One should ask how much of the previous years' investments in enhancing the corporate name and image will be salvaged and transferred to the new identity. This raises an important question: Is corporate name changing worth the confusion and the cost? Since so many intangibles, imponderables, and nonquantifiable variables are involved, attempting even a semblance of a cost-benefit analysis can be a most difficult and perhaps even an impossible task. Consequently, the study that follows does not attempt to measure the "worth" of any specific change in corporate name.

WHAT'S IN A CORPORATE NAME—BACKGROUND

It is interesting to note that in the several centuries during which corporations have been recognized as legal entities, the corporate name-giving process has been significantly influenced by social and political forces. The earliest known corporate prototype, a joint stock company, had the title of "The mysterie and companie of the Merchants adventurers for the discoverie of regions, dominions, islands and places unknown." This first corporation, organized in 1553, was soon after its inception commonly referred to as The Russia Company.[1] The roster of early quasicorporations included many unusual but vividly described business promotions. There was a "Company for purchasing perpetual advowsons, rights of patronage and next presentations, and for improv-

---

[1] E. V. Morgan and W. A. Thomas, *The Stock Exchange*, Elek Books, Great James Street, London, 1962, p. 12.

ing glebe and church lands, and for repairing and rebuilding parsonage and vicarage houses." [2]

This descriptive mouthful is equally matched by "A Society to insure all masters and mistresses whatever loss they may sustain by theft from any servant that is ticketed and registered with this society." Obviously these wordy titles were more in the nature of statements of objectives rather than simple company names. Consequently, it is logical that corporate names soon gravitated to more simple terms of corporate function such as "The Governor and Company for making Iron with Pit Coal," and "The Governor and Company for Making Hollow Sword Blades in the North of England."

Three hundred years ago one of the most important of our earliest corporate firms was called "The Governor and Company of Adventurers Trading into Hudson's Bay." The name identified the corporation, its purpose, its leadership, and its geographic environment. However, with the passage of time and the inexorable pressure of social and political forces, corporate name giving has undergone several periods of modification. Even 200 years ago names such as "The Philadelphia Contributionship for the Insurance of Houses from Loss by Fire," founded in 1752 by Benjamin Franklin, were in style. Today one would be more apt to refer to this venerable insurer as The Contributionship or perhaps even as PCI. Similarly, the "Governor and Company of Adventurers Trading into Hudson's Bay" is now called Hudson's Bay Company and is known to its customers as the "Bay." There is nothing so strange about changing patterns in corporate name-giving. Similar modifications can be observed in the custom of christening, baptizing, or otherwise assigning a specific name to every new-born citizen. The process is likewise observable in the Americanization of "old-country" family names where hundreds of thousands of hard-to-pronounce and alien-sounding names have been and continue to be homogenized into the American name pattern.

Even first names have, in the last century, reflected changing tastes and preferences. The once fairly commonplace Faiths and Prudences, Joshuas and Eliases have been out of style for several generations. More recently the Marys and the Margarets, the Josephs and the Johns have diminished in favor. Similarly, corporate names seem to be subject to fads in name selection. There is at least one big difference—a citizen's life span is measured in decades; a corporation's life span, although theoretically infinite, might reasonably be measured in terms of centuries.

During the period 1880–1920, a time characterized by the formation

[2] *Ibid.*, p. 34.

of both the trusts and the modern large-scale public corporation, there was a distinct propensity to give every corporation a dual name. One portion of the name referred to a specific industry: steel, tobacco, automobile, and so on. This was the product line or family name. This familial designation helped the discerning investor to make decisions. He knew, for example, that a given product-line family such as steel meant certain inherited characteristics: cyclical fluctuations, intensive use of labor, a one-to-one, or even less, relationship between sales volume and dollar investment. On the contrary, a company in the meatpacking family would tend to have a much higher volume of sales to investment, a steadier demand pattern, and other "inherited" characteristics.

In addition to the generic, family, or industry name, nearly every company had the equivalent of a first or Christian name. As with people there was, and continues to be, considerable variety in these first names. The great majority probably could be categorized as follows:

1. *Entrepreneurial.* Whether out of deference, homage, or mild egomania, at least half and probably as much as two-thirds of all our major corporations were initially named after the founder of the enterprise. Many venerable corporations still bear the names of these outstanding architects of our business system, of which a few are Ford, Chrysler, Du Pont, Westinghouse, Goodyear, Boeing, Weyerhaeuser. In *Fortune*'s current listing of the top 500 American industrial firms, at least 254 bear the name of the company's founding father.[3] A growing confusion, however, in this category is due to the merger mania that has led to an increased duality in the merged firm's name as, for example, McDonnell Douglas, Lear Siegler, and less recently Sperry Rand, Olin Mathieson, Procter and Gamble, or Jones and Laughlin. The confusion was heightened when, for example, Ling-Temco-Vought, in absorbing Wilson and Company, had to decide whether to add Wilson (which then accounted for about one-half of its sales) to the corporate name and expand the alphabetical title from LTV to LTVW, or just to skip the renaming.

2. *Geographic.* The list of geographic corporate first names is quite extensive. Among the more frequently used are Pacific, Western, Eastern, Pittsburgh, and Southern. An element of local or regional dedication, and even of patriotism, is evident in such terms. In the past the geographic designation also served to identify the company's production or marketing concentration. For example, out of our top 20 air transport companies all but two still have names tied to a geographic designation such as Northwestern, American, or Eastern.

[3] "The Fortune Directory, The 500 Largest U. S. Industrial Corporations," *Time, Inc.*, 1968.

3. *Chauvinistic.* Corporate names in this category stress the patriotic motif, although the geographic factor can also be discerned. Among the most popular was, and still is, the term *American*. Thirty years ago nearly 2.5% of all corporations listed in *Moody's Industrials* [4] used the designation, American. Even today despite a somewhat decreased popularity, at least 1.4% of similarly listed firms bear this name.

Other chauvinistic or superpatriotic designations are United States, National, Canadian, Union, Republic, and Federal. These six names, plus American, still account for more than 3% of *Moody's Industrials*. This, however, is a rather sharp drop in the use of these seven chauvinistic names from the 7% of listings 30 years ago.

4. *Ecumenical.* Names in this group imply universality, stability, and dependability. Among the most frequently used ecumenical names are General, United, Universal, Standard, Allied, Consolidated, Continental, and International. These eight names accounted for about 5.1% of all *Moody's Industrials'* listings three decades ago but now represent only about 3.5% of comparable listings.

Looked at analogously, the chauvinistic and ecumenical categories are the corporate Faiths, Prudences, Joshuas, and Eliases. They have an aura of morality and solid substance. They inspired (and still do) a degree of confidence and acceptance that other-named firms often find elusive even after indulging in huge advertising and image-building expenditures. Despite the relative decline in these two categories, it must not be assumed that they are to disappear within the next generation or two. Among the 50 largest corporations in this country, 23 still have chauvinistic or ecumenical "first names." Out of *Fortune's* top 500 at least 91 firms are in these categories, of which a few are: American Telephone and Telegraph, General Motors, Standard Oil Company (New Jersey), International Business Machines, General Electric, United States Steel, Republic Steel, and National Steel.

CURRENT TRENDS OR FADS

With the more recent upsurge in conglomerates there seems to be a tendency away from the first of the historical categories, that is, naming the company after the entrepreneur or founding family. Nevertheless there are some notable exceptions such as the recent reorganization and renaming of Hunt Foods and Industries to Norton Simon. (An even more interesting, though not so prominent a renaming occurred in the merger of two Big Board members, Thomson and McKinnon, with Au-

---

[4] *Moody's Investors Service—Industrials.*

chincloss, Parker and Redpath. The new firm's name is Thomson and McKinnon Auchincloss). Likewise, chauvinistic terminology is "out" and so are the older versions of ecumenism. Although geographic designations continue to be in vogue, they are being slightly deemphasized. Today, the "in" name patterns for new, reorganized, or retitled firms seem to be the following:

1. Scientific. This is a rather wide category comprising firms with functional or product-process designations. There are the "family" terms such as electronics, geophysics, engineering, instruments, or research. Representative companies include Packard Bell Electronics, Geophysical Service, Visi-Trol Engineering, and Texas Instruments. The latest *Poor's Register* [5] lists 111 firms with the *first* name as some modification of electric (electra, electro, electrical, or electronic). Including companies with the term electric as the second or family portion of the name (General Electric, Westinghouse Electric) and including Utilities would increase this category's number by several hundred.

In addition, there is a growing number of firms with other versions of technological and space-age sounding names (Geodesics, Control Data, Sealed Power, Victor Comptometer and the prestigious Communications Satellite Corporation).

There seems to be no visible horizon for innovative terminology in this category as science accomplishes ever greater and further breakthroughs. It is conceivable that within our lifetime there will be companies with names as intriguing as Heart Replacement Service, Smog Distillates Corporation, Laser Liquidaters, or Moonmaid Modeling Associates.

2. Polyglottic. This category is another rather new and very interesting one that includes a wide variety of esoteric sounding titles such as Uniroyal, Teledyne, Visi-Trol, Memorex, Tektronix, Compudyne, Computex, and the lamentable Westec. This group strives for a sort of mnemonic mystique which presumably follows from the superscientific implications in the juncture of specially selected syllables. If these firms can match the imagination shown in selecting their names with innovation and efficiency in their long-run performance, they might well become the firms of the future.

3. Syncopated. Presumably, as communication in printed form by radio and on television intensifies, it becomes necessary for accuracy and economy to shorten some company names. It is only natural to synco-

---

[5] *Poor's Register of Corporations, Directors and Executives, 1970,* Standard and Poor's Corporation, New York, 1970.

pate E. I. du Pont de Nemours and Company into Du Pont. More recently West Virginia Pulp and Paper Company was renamed Westvaco.
Similarly, Pepsi Cola Company has been transformed into Pepsico and
names such as Westclox, Valspar, Tenneco, Genesco, and Melpar come
up more and more frequently in business discussion. In addition, there
is a confounding array of Vasco, Vatco, Varo, Vanco, Volco, Varco,
Wilco, Welco, Wesco, Watsco, Walco, and Walcon. (These are only a
few examples from the v's and w's.) While apparently corporate name
syncopation saves on printer's ink and eardrum resonance, this practice,
if continued can lead to a Babel in Business.

   4. *Alphabetic.* An astounding 1.5% of *Poor's* 31,000 corporation listings currently are nameless, legally possessing only a short string of un-
pronounceable letters of the alphabet. (There is even a Corporation S, a
subsidiary of Recognition Equipment.)
   A few of the better known firms are ACF, AMK, ABEX, AVCO,
CF&I, FMC, LTV, SCM, TRW, and ITEK. A rough check of *Poor's* [6]
shows the following incidence by letter of the alphabet of corporations
which use alphabetic names:

A	57	H	13	O	8	V	7
B	28	I	27	P	16	W	8
C	32	J	14	Q	0	X	3
D	23	K	21	R	24	Y	0
E	14	L	17	S	22	Z	1
F	16	M	35	T	13		
G	21	N	10	U	13	Total	443

   If industrial firms alone were considered, the incidence of alphabetical
corporate names as listed in *Poor's Register* would be estimated at about
2½ or 3% of all firms.
   In addition to these officially registered alphabeticized firms, a steadily growing number of conventionally named companies are referred to
colloquially by convenient abbreviations. For example, Radio Corporation of America becomes RCA; American Telephone and Telegraph is
familiarly known as AT&T; International Business Machines is recognized worldwide as IBM. This group also includes, among others, firms
such as ITT, ALCOA, ARMCO, A&P, S&H, GM, and ALCAN. The alphabetic fad will very likely accelerate as the investing public gets more
acquainted with the succinct, but effective, stock market references to
corporations by their ticker symbols.

---

[6] *Ibid.*

There is nothing wrong in truncating or abbreviating a name if identity is preserved. We have used Joe, Bill, Bob, and Dick as short versions of men's names for several generations. If, however, the public, and particularly the investing segment, gets lost in this alphabetical maze, then syncopation serves no good purpose.

5. Neoecumenical. The "neo" prefix is included here to show that other groupistic or universal classifications have been previously used, as was described earlier. The most frequently used term in this "neo" category is Industries. In this group we have Schenley, Kaiser, Mohasco, Burlington, Monogram, Dresser, Spartans, Gulf and Western, White Consolidated, Allegheny Ludlum, Litton—all Industries. In several instances, in addition to the "neo" anonymity, a dual universality is achieved by juncture with the alphabetical (MSL Industries and U. S. Industries). In a few cases such as Electro Scientific Industries the stress is on the technological.

A less commonly used neoecumenical designation is Associates (Varian, Microwave, Electronic), where participation and group decision making seem to be implied. There is also an increased use in terms such as Zenith, Systems, and World. An interesting juncture of the neoecumenical, the syncopated and the polyglottic, is found in Pan Geo Atlas Corporation. Surprisingly, there has been no great rush to revive use of terms such as amalgamated or consolidated. Neither has the term *confederated* come into vogue, yet it quite fittingly describes the alignment of firms within many of the very loosely joined conglomerates that have recently emerged.

6. Elliptic. A number of well-established older companies have modernized their names by the very simple expedient of dropping the restrictive second portion, the product line designation from their titles. Thus Singer Sewing Machine Company became Singer; Bigelow Sanford Carpet Company was shortened to Bigelow, Sanford; Signal Oil and Gas Company has been renamed Signal Companies. In the once well-defined tobacco industry, only one firm, Brown and Williamson Tobacco Company, now retains the term tobacco in its name. Liggett & Meyers changed its name in 1968, Reynolds dropped the designation tobacco in 1969, and American Tobacco Company has been renamed American Brands. These changes are similar to the Americanization of old country names by our new citizens when they dropped Mac-, Mc-, -ini, -ski, -onis, -stein, -dorf, and the like from their ancestral names. In this corporate instance modernizing removes the stigma of one-line endeavor and creates an aura of ecumenism.

COMPARISON: PAST AND PRESENT NAME FADS

The classification of corporate names into the four categories of old-fashioned Faith-and-Prudence-type names and into the six categories of "in" or space-age names is certainly not definitive. It does, however, emphasize the fact that a corporation, like an individual, *needs* a name and attaches real meaning and value to that name. All this comes back to the importance of *identity* in companies and in men. And here is the "rub."

As the alphabetic, elliptic, polyglottic, and similar meaningless new names become universal, the public will undoubtedly have real problems of differentiation. The present trend toward developing a better informed public will certainly not be accelerated if, for example, all 2500 Big Board listings will be legally and universally referred to by their stock ticker symbols. Although this practice is efficient and desirable in the sphere of professional investment, it is fortunate that no comprehensive examination on ticker symbol identification is required of prospective stockbrokers. If it were, an abyssmally low score would necessarily have to be set as a passing grade considering, for example, just one incidental segment of alphabetical permutations now in use as stock market ticker symbols: A, AA, AB, ABA, ABC, ABE, ABG, ABJ, ABK, ABL, ABN, ABR, ABT, ABW, ABX. The 26 letters of the alphabet, using only up to three-letter combinations, would permit more than 17,000 stock market ticker symbol listings. Using five-letter ticker symbols could result in 12,000,000 corporate codings—and complete confusion. Although mathematically possible, such an extreme eventuality can be envisaged only when computers conquer all.

However, even the most sophisticated computer would suffer a complete nervous transistor breakdown if another incipient corporate name fad were ever to become popular. This potential name fad is using numbers as a corporate name; for example, 721 Corporation (Bonwit Teller) and 795 Corporation (Pierre Hotel Corporation) are pioneers in this regard. The combination of numbers, together with terms such as Corp., Co., Inc., Industries, Associates, and similar designations, could expand the numerical naming possibilities into infinity. Commenting facetiously, if higher numbers meant greater image value, it is conceivable that we could then have firms with names such as The Quadrillion Corporation which could also be syncopated to the 10^{15} Corporation.

The fad-impact on corporate names is succinctly shown in Table 16-1 which covers a 40 year range from 1930–1970. During this interval the incidence of new corporate names has changed markedly. In the earlier

Table 16-1   Incidence of New Corporate Names (Estimated)

	Category	Percentage Year Incorporated	
		1930	1970
1.	Entrepreneurial	55	20
2.	Geographic	13	8
3.	Chauvinistic	11	2
4.	Ecumenical	8	4
5.	Etc.ᵃ	13	5
6.	Scientific	0	20
7.	Polyglottic	0	14
8.	Syncopated	0	10
9.	Alphabetic	0	9
10.	Neoecumenical	0	5
11.	Elliptic	0	3
		100	100

ᵃThe 1930, Etc. category includes the relatively few firms with names from the last six categories.

period about seven out of every eight new or renamed corporations selected a name from one of the first four categories (entrepreneurial, geographic, chauvinistic, ecumenical). More than half of these firms bore the entrepreneur's name. In the succeeding four decades the popularity decline of these four types of old-fashioned names is evident, since at present approximately only one firm in three follows the previous practice. In marked contrast nearly two out of three new or renamed firms select the sophisticated, glamorized or "jazzed-up" names of the last six categories (scientific, polyglottic, syncopated, alphabetic, neoecumenical, elliptic). All indications point to a continuation of these trends with even further declines in the entrepreneurial group. Geographical appellations could plateau or even increase if rising nationalism abroad results in deemphasizing the broader all-encompassing version of internationalism and stressing nationalistic joint ventures instead (Arabian-American Oil Company, British-American Tobacco Company). This same exaggerated nationalism will undoubtedly bring forth a large number of foreign firms with chauvinistic names; in the United States, however, the possibility is less imminent of reviving this patriotic naming of new firms.

CONGLOMERATES AND CORPORATE NAMES

The new name fad seems to be accelerated by the conglomerates' need for identity through other than product, process, geography, or entrepreneur connotations. A name with broad, all-encompassing implications seems to be imperative for the new multipurpose firms. In the image which the newer conglomerates' names are intended to create there is a great measure of what figuratively might be termed the "factotum effect." In this analogy the "factotum effect" connotes a jack-of-all-trades, a handyman's handyman. In the classic *Largo al factotum*, Figaro, the epitome of factotums, boasts of his manifold attributes—he'll sing or dance, trim your hair, or leech your blood. Or if you seek an amorous escapade, Figaro's your boy for contact purposes. Similarly, the factotum conglomerate is a business jack-of-all-trades; for example, Gulf and Western Industries will provide you with sugar, beef, or oranges (South Puerto Rico Sugar Company), and after an epicurean repast you can have your cigar (Consolidated Cigar). Then for relaxation there is television (the set itself is Chromatron Color Tube), the station (Famous Players Canadian Corporation), and the reception (pay TV, in this instance, International Telemeter). The television program is likewise provided (Paramount Pictures). This is just a very tiny part of the many goods and services this single corporate factotum can offer one. In detailing its attributes one would have to get acquainted with the variety of endeavors engaged in by G and W's steadily increasing member firms such as Universal American, E. W. Bliss, New Jersey Zinc, E. S. Youse, Brown Company, Associates Investment Company, in addition to the previously mentioned and other subsidiaries. In effect, the extent of activities encompassed by a growing number of the newer conglomerates ranges from man's cradle-to-crypt needs. Obviously it becomes quite a challenge to select or invent a corporate name which can express adequately this factotum corporate aspiration.

DOES THE "RIGHT" NAME HELP PERFORMANCE?

Although a corporate name, per se, certainly does not make or break a company, the feeling persists, and even seems to have become chronic, that specific names can help or hinder corporate image building. Presumably, the Faith and Prudence corporate-naming fads of the past were motivated by a deepseated hope that a "good" name would enhance performance prospects. Similarly, today's stress on scientific, polyglottic, syncopated, alphabetic, neoecumenical, and elliptic names definitely stems from the corporate sentiment (or perhaps superstition) that a proper and "in" name will help performance, whereas old-fashioned and "square" names will be detrimental.

Even though this sentiment seems to be commonplace, the hypothesis should be tested. The remaining few paragraphs are dedicated to such an analysis, seeking to find what impact if any, the corporate name game has on corporate life. In this instance the test is for continuity, durability, or the simple ability to survive. In other words, good performers will tend to retain their autonomy and identity, whereas poor performers will disappear from the competitive scene either by liquidation or merger. Then, too, many a weak performer will strive to change its "luck" by modifying its corporate name. (A year after Westec Corporation was brought out of bankruptcy proceedings (Chapter 11), its directors proposed changing the corporate name to an even more scientific-sounding name, Tech-Sym Corporation).

The data source in this test is *Moody's Investors Service—Industrials,* both the annual roster of industrial corporations and that of firms which have been removed from listing in the recent past. In 1938 *Moody's* listed approximately 13,000 companies of which 1350 (or

Table 16-2   Data on Thirteen Most Commonly Used Corporate First Names, 1929–1968

	Moody Listings		Attritions, 1929–1968				
	1938	1968	Total	Name Change	Liquidation	Merger	Index (%)
American	295	191	227	56	112	59	93
National	168	147	138	45	48	45	82
Canadian	139	146	103	23	38	42	72
General	133	126	89	22	45	22	68
International	100	101	62	19	24	19	62
United	91	81	95	20	44	31	110
Standard	71	65	60	13	28	18	88
United States	68	54	60	15	19	26	98
Western	40	54	51	21	10	20	108
Consolidated	81	54	84	25	31	28	125
Continental	53	44	30	5	17	8	62
Union	77	39	48	12	21	15	83
Universal	34	34	29	11	10	8	85
Total	1,350	1,136	1,076	287	448	341	86

source: *Moody's Investors Service—Industrials*

10.4%) made use of 13 ecumenical or chauvinistic names as shown in Table 16-2. By far the leading preference was for the name *American*, then used by 295 firms and presently used by 191 companies.

Table 16-2, column 1, shows the number of *Moody*-listed firms which in 1938 used the 13 most common generic terms in their corporate names. Column 2 shows the current incidence of these preferred names. Column 3 indicates the 40 year (1929–1968) attrition for each of these names. The next three columns break total attrition down into name changes (column 4), liquidations (column 5), and mergers (column 6). The last column (7) is an approximation at an attrition index; for example, the 295 firms using the name *American* decreased to only 191 in 1968. During the 40-year span a total of 227 *Moody*-listed companies with the designation *American* ceased to exist, resulting in an attrition index of 93%. In this instance about half the corporate attrition was the result of liquidation, whereas the remainder was almost equally shared by mergers and name changes. Note that the highest relative declines were for the names *Consolidated* (125%) and *United*(110%), whereas *Continental* (62%) and *International* (62%) were most stable.

In the entire *Moody Industrial* listing, 1076 of these 13 preferred-name firms disappeared during the 40-year period for an attrition rate of 86%. Out of this group of 1076 corporations, which lost their identity during the 40-year period, 287 were name changes, whereas 448 were liquidations and 341 were absorbed by mergers.

Table 16-3   Total **Moody** *Delistings, 1929–1968*

Period	Total	Attritions, 1929–1968			Index (%)
		Name Change	Liquidation	Merger	
1959–1968	2470	872	206	1392	
1949–1958	1617	432	266	919	
1939–1948	1555	361	437	757	
1929–1938	1679	294	706	679	
	7321	1959	1615	3747	55

By contrast, as shown in Table 16-3, the attrition index for the *entire Moody* listings during this period was approximately 55%. If these data were further refined to exclude the 13-name categories, the index for the total *Moody* listing drops even lower to about 52%. This is in contrast to the 86% attrition index for the 13-name sample. On the basis of this evidence it does seem that the 13 ecumenical and chauvinistic name categories fell far below the remainder of the American industrial corporate world in performance. This inference is substantiated in Table 16-4.

There is practically no difference in the proportions of delistings for both all *Moody's Industrials* and the 13-preferred-name group on the basis of name changes, but the difference in liquidation ratios seems quite significant. It would take much more than chance to account for the 41.6% liquidation rate characterizing the 13-preferred-name group as contrasted with only 22.1% for all *Moody's Industrials*. Since liquidation is the ultimate in corporate defeat and degradation, it must be assumed that the once-high-image names (chauvinistic and ecumenical) provided no sanctuary or success guarantee. Actually, it might be implied that many fly-by-night and fast-buck firms, together with other inferiority-complexed and weak-structured firms, sought the unattainable by means of "in" appellations.

Table 16-4 Moody's *Industrials Delistings, 1929–1968*

	Percentage of Delistings		
	Name Change	Liquidation	Merger
Total *Moody's Industrials*	26.7	22.1	51.2
13-Name Sample	26.6	41.6	31.7

Of course, this type of analysis has its weak spots. It deals in composites and averages. It does not differentiate the firm structured on solid substance from the firm with flimsy fabric. Nevertheless from this cursory analysis it does seem legitimate to conclude that in the recent past adoption of an "in"-type or mystique-connoting name has not guaranteed long-run success to the image-sensitive firm. On the contrary, it appears that an inordinate number of anemic companies have in the past tried to disguise their lack of robustness by latching on to an aristocratic, patriotic, or grandiose name. The inexorable forces of business competition did not respect the prestige appellations in the past and there is no reason to believe that the newer firms, including many conglomerates seeking image, acceptance, and success through high-sounding or mystique-syllabled names, will get better treatment. It will be interesting, two or three decades hence, to see which, if any, of the currently popular corporate designations (scientific, polyglottic, syncopated, alphabetic, neoecumenical, and elliptic) will have done better than average as to survival and, presumably, as to performance. Meanwhile we might speculate as to what new directions the corporate name game will take.

17

THE ONE-BANK HOLDING
COMPANY

The phrase, "the business of banking," first coined in 1838 now appears more vague than ever. Legislation has periodically been passed in an attempt to clarify this "business of banking" in which 13,488 banks now engage. The Bank Holding Act of 1956, for example, prohibits holding companies that own more than one bank from entering business unrelated to banking. Ownership is defined as having more than 25% of a bank's common stock. When a holding company does own 25% or more of the stock of two or more banks, it must register with the Federal Reserve Board and it comes under FRB supervision. The 1956 Act, incidentally, was an attempt to plug a big loophole in the initial Glass-Steagall Act of the 1930's which sought reforms deemed imperative after the 1929 financial crash.

Although holding companies with two or more banks are regulated, holding companies that own only one bank are exempted. This exemption was included because the lawmakers recognized that in many small communities family holding companies in addition to owning the bank also engaged in a great variety of other business ventures. To outlaw these small, local, one-bank holding companies was deemed unfair and harmful to the community.

In the last few years many of our largest banks have taken advantage of this legal loophole and have reorganized their corporate structures. The usual practice is to have the bank's management create a holding company and to transfer ownership of the bank to that holding company. However, management of both the holding company and the bank remains the same. This permits the holding companies to enter into a variety of nonbanking activities, principally in the insurance and financing spheres but even moving into transportation, agriculture, mining, and retail sales. These moves have aroused concern in many quarters. William McChesney Martin, Jr., former chairman of the Federal Reserve Board, has been widely quoted on the danger of mixing banking and other business: "This is a real can of worms. It can affect the whole capitalistic system in the United States. The line between banking and commerce should not be erased." [1]

Representative Wright Patman of Texas, chairman of the House Banking Committee, called for amendments to the Bank Holding Company Act of 1956 stating, "The rapid movement of commercial banks into nonbanking activities through loopholes in the holding company act threatens to change the entire character of the nation's economy." [2]

The situation was brought into sharp focus when the major banks, including 34 of the top hundred, moved in this direction. Nationwide attention was focused on the problem when First National City Bank of New York (the country's third largest bank), Bank of America (the nation's number one bank), and Wells Fargo (eleventh largest) announced that they were setting up one-bank holding companies. Within a three-year period the commercial deposits of one-bank holding companies soared from $15.1 billion in 1965 to $108.2 billion in 1968. The number of one-bank holding companies increased in this period from 550 to 783. As recently as 1955 there were only 117 one-bank holding companies with deposits of only $11.6 billion. Thus in the interval there has been a sevenfold increase in number and ninefold increase in size.

The rapid rise in one-bank holding companies and their attempts at intrusion into business ventures other than banking precipitated strong public and legislative reaction. Strongest of the opponents was Congressman Wright Patman. He introduced legislation which would put a big crimp in the one-bank holding company fad. Among the more severe of his proposed restrictions were the following:

1. Allowing the Federal Reserve Board to determine on the basis of substantial evidence that a holding company had "actual control" of a bank even though it owned less than the 25% permissible under the Bank Holding Company Act.

2. The exemption permitting partnerships to control one or more banks without registering as bank holding companies would be removed.

3. Including within the regulated group cases where one bank through its trust department holdings controls another bank and where

[1] *Business Week,* 28 (February 15, 1969).
[2] *Ibid.*

two or more persons or banks "acting in concert" own more than 25% of a bank.

4. A prohibition on banks requiring a customer to purchase other bank services or to do business with affiliates of the bank.

5. Extension of the divestiture requirements of the 1956 Act wherein one-bank holding companies whose affiliates were deemed by the FRB to be insufficiently related must be divested within five years.

6. Interlocking directorates would be forbidden. A House Banking Committee study showed that 48 commercial banks in 10 metropolitan areas had 572 interlocks among their officers and directors and those of other financial institutions.

Congressman Patman's rather rigid restrictions would be tempered considerably if other legislation were adopted instead. In particular, the Treasury Department has proposed less severe legislation; for example, the Treasury Department would permit one-bank holding companies to enter unrelated fields, even manufacturing, on proof that the community would be benefited. It would also permit "congeneric activities" such as equipment leasing, computer service, factoring, mortgage brokering, mutual funds, and warehousing.

The Treasury Department's position is assumed to be influenced by the fact that at least four top Treasury officials left banking to enter this area. David M. Kennedy, Secretary, was formerly board chairman of Continental Illinois National Bank and Trust Company. Robert P. Mayo, Nixon's budget director, was a vice-president at Continental Illinois. Undersecretary Charles E. Walker is former executive vice-president of the American Bankers Association. Undersecretary for Monetary Affairs, Paul Volcker, had served as a vice-president of Chase Manhattan Bank. It is interesting to note that one-bank holding permits were granted to both Continental Illinois and Chase Manhattan.

There is considerable suspicion that any legislation supported in particular by the Treasury Department would simply be a ruse. Although keeping the banks out of commerce and industry, it would presumably permit them to enter other lucrative financially related businesses. There is also a feeling that legislation curbing commercial and industrial activities in one-bank holding companies would simply be a maneuver by the banks to keep the more energetic conglomerates from invading banking. In the last two years more than 20 banks, with deposits of almost $3 billion, have succumbed to conglomerates.

Among the arguments precipitating legislation against one-bank holding companies is the belief that bank acquisitions of other enterprises can give banks competitive advantages not based on economic efficiency. Reciprocity and coercive tie-ins of separate products such as loans and insurance would be among these unfair advantages. Then, too, there is the danger that, particularly during periods of tight money, the banks might give favorable loan treatment to borrowers who do business with a bank's affiliate. This form of business persuasion might result even without coercion when clients would seek to ingratiate themselves in the hope of improving their chances to obtain credit on more favorable terms from the banks. The banks presumably would have an unfair advantage since they have exclusive access to money in its cheapest form—demand deposits. Industrial competitors, in particular, would have considerable difficulty since they must pay double or more than the rate paid by commercial banks for such funds.

The fear of massive economic power being concentrated in 40 or 50 major one-bank holding companies has some factual support. Under federal law a bank may make secured loans up to 10% of its capital and surplus to a single affiliate and 20% to all affiliates together. The top 50 commercial banks with 1969 combined capitalization in excess of $14 billion could thus employ $2.8 billion in their own nonbanking pursuits. This diversion of funds from current uses would have a significant impact on our economy. In Congressman Patman's view this would be a tremendous step toward a cartelized economy. Even a bank president, Ernest J. Barber of Dade National Bank, "concedes that 'there would be a definite conflict of interest . . . if we tried to get into such unrelated fields as manufacturing.' " [3]

Another reason for stiffer and clearer legislation is the fear that one-bank holding companies would put the bank's depositors in jeopardy. The counterargument states that under the one-bank holding company structure only the holding company's stockholders assume any risks. The depositors in the bank are, so it is said, adequately protected by existing legislation. Yet many skeptics maintain this protection would be illusory if the holding company's nonbanking components did actually get into serious difficulty. It is conceivable that the bank, directly or indirectly, would make massive attempts at saving its sinking subsidiaries. The bank's depositors, by no stretch of the imagination, could be assumed to be safely ensconced nonparticipants to the bank's holding company's plight.

On the positive side proponents contend that there are some very significant values in the bank holding company concept; for example, in this arrangement a sort of financial supermarket is set up in which a variety of financial services can be had at one place. This would be a distinct

---

[3] *Fortune*, 56 (November, 1968).

service to the public. The entrance of big banks into new areas, geographical and service, would also stimulate competition and give many citizens now subject to near-monopolies a greater choice at more reasonable costs. In particular, uncompetitive and unprofitable banks would have a tougher time. Assuming legislation affecting one-bank holding companies permitted bank acquisitions by industrial conglomerates, some of these less profitable banks might be taken over by conglomerates. This could be a positive factor since injection of new funds and of more dynamic management could resurrect these ailing banks.

A limiting factor is the uncertainty of public reaction, particularly as expressed in restrictive legislation. For example, First National City Corporation called off its planned merger with Chubb Corporation, a major insurance concern, after the Justice Department indicated it would file suit to prevent the acquisition. Chubb Corporation was itself a holding company for several insurance companies. Both firms had a fairly long previous association, leading to the suspicion that this was an insider deal. For several years George S. Moore, First National's chairman, and Percy Chubb II, chairman of Chubb Corporation, served on each others' boards. Since major banks tend to have an extremely large number of such direct interlocks plus an even greater number of indirect interlocking relationships, a feeling existed in some quarters that legitimatizing such mergers could lead to charges of collusion.

In this instance, both firms tried to avoid some of the interlocking stigma by obtaining resignations from their boards of eight individuals who were already on other bank or insurance company boards. The following left the First National board:

Gordon M. Metcalf, chairman of Sears, Roebuck and Company, which owns Allstate Insurance Company;
Gordon Grand, president of Olin Mathieson Chemical Corporation, who is also a director of Prudential Life Insurance;
George P. Jenkins, chairman of the financial committee of Metropolitan Life Insurance;
Percy Chubb II, chairman of Chubb Corporation.

The following resignations occurred on Chubb Corporation's board:

George S. Moore, chairman of First National;
L. A. Lapham, vice-chairman of Bankers' Trust Company;
Thomas Rodd, executive vice-chairman of Morgan Guaranty Trust Company.

This venture, the first by one of our nation's biggest banks to enter a nonbanking field by means of the one-bank holding scheme, would have had a value of $376 million, represented by nearly 2 million shares of First National City Corporation common stock, together with 4.7 million shares of convertible preferred stock.

The Justice Department also investigated proposed acquisitions of Associated Mortgage Companies by Pennsylvania Corporation, the holding company for First Pennsylvania Banking and Trust Company. Previously, during a Justice Department investigation of First National Bank in Dallas' plan to acquire Lomas and Nettleton Financial Corporation, the proposal was dropped.

Although the movement of banks into the holding company pattern has increased numerically, the actual entrance of banks into unrelated activities is still just a trickle. Conversely, conglomerates have been more aggressive by actually acquiring banks and integrating them into the conglomerate corporate framework. "In the past year and a half about twenty banks with deposits of close to $2.4 billion have succumbed to tenders from nonbank corporations." [4] Some very reputable industrial firms such as C.I.T. Financial Corporation, Signal Companies, Gulf and Western Industries, and D. H. Baldwin and Company include banks within their corporate families. Actually, some portions of the financial function (but not banking itself) have been carried on by industrial firms for several years. In particular, the automobile industry and the farm equipment industry have through subsidiaries such as General Motors Acceptance Corporation been financing customers' purchases for many years. The current movement, however, is more extensive since it encompasses the banking activities proper.

It is still too soon to determine how a multiactivity financial firm such as the Phoenix-based holding company, Arizona Bancorporation (banking, life insurance, real estate, and manufacturing), will fit into the conglomerate Signal Cos. Similarly, it is premature to judge Greatamerica's role in the Ling-Temco-Vought conglomerate empire. LTV acquired Greatamerica, a holding company controlling Braniff International, National Car Rental Systems, a California bank, and three insurance companies. Another recent example was Control Data Corporation's acquisition of the country's second largest independent finance company, Commercial Credit Company. By this one significant action Control Data, with assets of only $350 million, acquired Commercial Credit's more than $3 billion assets. As stated by William C. Norris, president of Control Data Corporation, in a letter to the company's shareholders, ". . . we believe an affiliation with a large financial service company

[4] *Fortune*, "The Case for the One-Bank Holding Company," by Sanford Rose, 164 (May 15, 1969).

having the capital resources of Commercial Credit should greatly help Control Data to capitalize to an even greater extent on its present leading position in very large computers, and to assist us as well in such areas as peripheral equipment and new applications of computers. Commercial Credit will furnish Control Data with financial support in its rapidly growing leasing business, its time-sharing business, its expanding United States and foreign network of data centers and its professional service business, in addition to manpower to be added by Commercial Credit." [5]

There are, however, publicly expressed fears that combinations of this kind can become major power centers dominating our economy. Secretary of the Treasury, David Kennedy, commenting on this phenomenon has stated that "Unless the government moves quickly to forestall such tie-ups, 'we would find ourselves in a structure dominated by some fifty to seventy-five huge centers of economic and financial power—each of which would consist of a corporate conglomerate controlling a large bank or a multibillion-bank controlling a large nonfinancial conglomerate.'" [6]

The previously described attempt in Chapter 13 by Leasco Data Processing Equipment Corporation to take over the nation's sixth largest bank, Chemical Bank New York Trust Company, chilled the financial community with the very real prospect of a small-scale conglomerate taking over a huge bank. Chemical Bank, at the time, had assets of about $9 billion, whereas Leasco only a year earlier had assets of only several million dollars. (In the meantime Leasco had engineered a successful takeover of Reliance Insurance whose assets approached $700 million.) In this instance Chemical Bank, presumably aided by the banking community, beat off this brash attempt. But the posssibility of future conglomerate penetration into the staid financial field of banking could now be viewed as a very real threat.

CONGLOMERATES IN FINANCE COMPANIES

The conglomerate move into banking is paralleled by attempted acquisition of finance and insurance companies. Xerox Corporation's proposal to acquire C.I.T. Financial Corporation, the nation's second largest finance company, with interests also in banking and consumer goods, is a classic example. Xerox would have exchanged 5,190,000 shares of its stock worth about $1.5 billion for the common stock of C.I.T. In turn,

[5] *The Wall Street Journal*, 19 (June 28, 1968).
[6] *Fortune*, "The Case for the One-Bank Holding Company," Sanford Rose, 163 (May 15, 1969).

Xerox's assets would have vaulted from $800 million to $4.2 billion, presumably permitting a massive expansion program. Xerox was planning to expand in copying, education, health, and computer peripheral equipment, and had to pay for tremendous investments in research and engineering. A juncture with a finance firm with very sizable funds seemed logical.

Xerox, in order to expedite the acquisition, provided the usual conglomeration sweetener—a significant premium in the price offered over the current market price per share. C.I.T. stock had been trading at about $45 a share. Xerox now offered nearly $70 per share for a premium of 55%. In this and comparable instances, the merger proposal was complicated by prevailing price-earnings ratios. Xerox stock was selling at a price-earnings multiplier of 55, whereas C.I.T. stock was priced at only 15 times earnings.

As expected C.I.T. stock spurted upward immediately with almost a 14 point advance in the two days following the merger announcement. In sharp contrast Xerox stock slumped nearly 21 points, reflecting a common stock devaluation in its 22 million shares of nearly a half billion dollars. This unfavorable view so dramatically expressed by the investing community was a real surprise to the intended merger participants. It did appear that such a union would have eased Xerox's growing pains by providing easy access to large sums of much needed money. C.I.T. handled such huge sums, ranging up to $2 billion at any given time. However, financial experts were skeptical about Xerox's ability to continue its excellent earnings' growth pattern if it were saddled with the less dynamic C.I.T.

Although the Xerox-C.I.T. merger attempt was abandoned, it must be stressed that negative market pressures rather than legal interference halted this union. Actually, the previously mentioned accomplished acquisitions by Signal Cos., LTV, and Control Data seem to indicate that there is far less opposition in this area than with one-bank holding companies.

INSURANCE COMPANIES

One Wall Street analyst commented that " 'Insurance companies have changed more in the past year than in the 100 years before that.' Old line industry giants, once symbols of resistance to change, have become holding companies so that they can diversify into an ever-widening range of noninsurance areas." [7] Much of this new momentum comes from

[7] *Business Week*, 114 (March 15, 1969).

the realization, particularly by life insurance companies, that progressively larger portions of the public's savings dollar now goes into other than life insurance. Twenty years ago nearly half of all savings went into life insurance, but at present only about one-seventh is so invested. Life insurance company assets have grown by 250% in the last 20 years, and mutual fund assets have shot up by 1400%. In recognition of this disparity numerous insurance companies, including stalwarts such as Travelers, John Hancock, Mutual of Omaha, Connecticut General, Fidelity Mutual, and General American, have moved into the mutual fund field by either acquiring existing funds or starting their own new funds.

This entrance of life insurance companies into mutual funds is being stimulated by the establishment of holding companies. Most states bar insurance companies from making noninsurance acquisitions. However, as with the one-bank holding company, the many positive features of the holding company concept in insurance likewise proves to be irresistible. Among the big advantages of such a corporate structure for large insurance companies are the following:

1. They can put excess funds to more productive use.
2. They can issue debentures and preferred stock which insurance companies cannot do.
3. They get tax and accounting advantages.

Howard C. Reeder, CNA's chairman and president, described the holding company in the insurance field with a word of his own invention—synerance. Reeder said that a synerance is an insurance company that for synergistic reasons is acquiring other but closely allied companies that will make it a stronger insurance company. James J. Ling, chairman of Ling-Temco-Vought, has referred to them as "conglomerate merchant banks."

Conglomerate action in the life insurance field is more than paralleled in the fire and casualty fields. Among the more notable recent junctures or attempted junctures were City Investing Companies' acquisition of Home Insurance Company, one of the biggest fire and casualty companies. Gulf and Western Industries acquired a majority interest in Providence Washington Insurance Company and National General Corporation purchased a large block of Great American Holding Corporation stock.

Probably the most controversial merger proposal involving a conglomerate and an insurance company was International Telephone and Telegraph's attempt to acquire Hartford Fire Insurance Company. The deal, if consummated, would have been the nation's largest merger. ITT, which already had 6% of Hartford Fire stock, proposed to purchase the rest for $1.45 billion in a new convertible preferred stock. This massive merger was opposed by the Justice Department which contended that there was serious danger of reciprocity arrangements.

SUMMARY

The ever-widening conglomerate periphery, first in manufacturing, then into service industries, and now into banking and insurance, can only have positive economic connotations. In our free enterprise system it is axiomatic that resources, particularly financial, entrepreneurial, and managerial, will gravitate toward those business components that yield the greatest return. As a rule a greater or lesser return on investment is the consequence of changes in productivity and efficiency. In turn these changes follow the introduction of new and better techniques. In this instance, it does appear that the concept of conglomeration as applied through holding companies is a distinct "technique" improvement. The discovery and application of a new technique in business, such as the holding company in banking and insurance, will invariably lead to misunderstandings and misapplications. This calls for reviewing by regulatory bodies, redefining and restructuring the rules of the game.

18

THE RESURRECTED RAILROADS

Railroading provides us with an excellent example of the typical industrial growth cycle. The inception period, which included discovery and the first crude attempts at application, covered the period from the late sixteenth century to about 1800. Then came the era of rapid growth, covering the entire nineteenth century. This was followed by the maturity phase (1900–1925) with relatively little growth, and then came the senescence period (1925–1970) when, except for a decade or more during World War II, railroads experienced a noticeable and perturbing decline. What the future will be in railroading is a matter of crystal-ball prophesizing.

Typical of all industrial rapid growth periods, there was relative ease of entrance into railroading during the post-Civil War period until the turn of the century. However, there was also a comparable catharsis. In the last quarter of the nineteenth century, 685 railroads, as listed in *Moody's Transportation Manual*,[1] were subjected to the brutal legal process of receivership and foreclosure. During this period receiverships and foreclosures averaged almost 28 per year. The magnitude of this cleansing operation is evident in the trackage involved. These 685 railroads, subject to receivership and foreclosure in the 1876–1900 period, had 114,000 miles of track, five times the length of today's Penn Central's 22,000 miles.

The harsh therapy of receivership and foreclosure eventually began to be mitigated so that in the next quarter century (1901–1925) only 260 railroads were subjected to this treatment. The rate in the current decade approaches zero, indicating both an economic and philosophical aversion to the severity of receivership and foreclosure. As contrasted

[1] *Moody's Transportation Manual*, a82-a85 (September 1968).

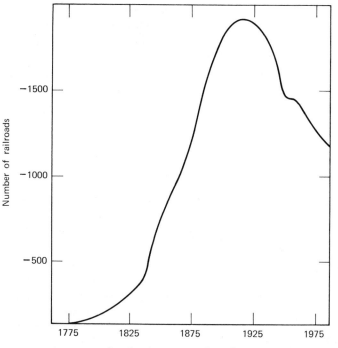

Figure 18-1   Railroad industry growth cycle, 1775–1975.

with the 1876–1900 large-scale cleansing (685 foreclosures involving
114,000 miles of railroad), there have been only 23 such receiverships
and foreclosures involving a mere 4121 miles of railroads in the past
quarter century. This change in attitude is evident in Table 18-1.

However, the data in Table 18-1 must not be misconstrued to mean
that status quo prevails. There is an equally manifest catharsis, but it

*Table 18-1   Railroad Receiverships and
Liquidations, 1876–1970* [a]

Period	Number	Average per Year
1876–1900	685	27.4
1901–1925	260	10.4
1926–1950	144	5.7
1951–1970	12	0.6

[a] Data from *Moody's Transportation
Manual,* a82–a85 (September 1968).

lacks the sting of receivership and foreclosure. *Moody's Transportation Manual* lists all transportation companies, including railroads, which have disappeared as autonomous entities since 1925.[2] In this interval more than 1000 railroads have lost their identity. Although only 156 of these suffered the ignominy of receivership and foreclosure, another 330 or so are labeled by *Moody's* as dissolved, abandoned, ordered to cease, discontinued operations, no recent information, or even sold as scrap. This was an ignoble fate for any railroad company terminated in this fashion.

Far less degrading were the approximately 520 mergers, acquisitions, purchases, sales to, and similar orderly and not completely penniless transactions. It was pointed out in Chapter 3 that foreclosures, liquidations, and similar heavy-handed terminations of business have gone out of style in manufacturing industry. Merger is the modern way to dispose of a poor performer. This merger phenomenon is facilitated by tax loss carryback provisos in our Federal Internal Revenue taxing policy and by other economic considerations. From an industrial philosophy point of view there are very significant managerial and social implications. A merged firm is not a dead firm. Although there generally is some firing of top executives and directors, most of the manpower and physical facilities continue to be employed. Consequently, large numbers of workers and huge aggregates of capital are not tossed on the scrap heap but are continued in use, at least for some additional time. Although this continued use through merger sometimes means a functional degradation, a reduction to a lower order of work, nevertheless it seems preferable to the permanent layoff and scrapping associated with liquidation and abandonment.

This theme, developed more fully in Chapter 3, is equally applicable to the railroad industry. Obviously as consolidation progresses this phenomenon will have less meaning since there recently has not been, and in the near future very likely will not be, any further expansion in the number of railroads. This is a direct consequence of poor performance and the very evident regression syndrome symptoms.

If the regression syndrome were the sole propelling force inducing merger, then our railroad companies should be the best prospects for merger. Ample evidence shows that railroads in general have not kept up with the dynamic progress made by our economy in the last several decades. The 1956 *Fortune* listing of the top 50 transportation companies included 37 railroads. In sharp contrast the 1970 *Fortune* list included only 19 railroads. In 1956 all top 10 transportation companies

[2] *Ibid.*, pp. xxxii-XLiii.

were railroads, but in 1969 they included only 5 of the top 10. The competitive ineffectiveness of railroads, despite their local and regional marketing monopolies, is evident in both passenger service and in freight carrying. The airlines which just 14 years ago placed only 7 firms in the top 50 transportation companies, now have 15 in this category. Trucking firms now have 12 in the top 50, whereas 14 years ago not a single trucker was important enough for this list.

The relatively poor performance of railroads and the consequent manifestation of regression syndrome symptoms are evident even in the biggest firms. The components of Penn Central, the merged Pennsylvania Railroad and New York Central, had only a 12% gain in operating revenue and a 13% gain in assets over the past 14 years. These gains are considerably less than the inflationary markup of the last 14 years. In sharp contrast the leading industrial firms had far more impressive records. Standard Oil (New Jersey) increased sales by 124% and assets by 133% ; General Motors increased sales by 84% and assets by 110% in the same period. Equally significant were changes in other performance norms. In number of employees, for example, although Standard Oil (New Jersey) kept a relatively constant labor force and General Motors expanded by 20%, the combined Penn-NYC labor forces declined from 195,000 to 113,000, a loss of 42% .

These and other factors show that even the biggest and best known railroads have evidenced chronic symptoms of the regression syndrome. Seeking out the causes for this poor performance could be a most frustrating experience. However, it has been stated and underscored (in this study) that chronic business sluggishness invariably follows from unimaginative, lackadaisical, and incompetent top management. This conclusion seems to be verified in the railroad's directorate structure and performance. Railroad boards of directors, almost from their inception, have been populated by the conventional outside directors. Table 18-2 provides a tabulation of the directorate composition of a sample of 40 large railroads. It is obvious that even in 1925, officer directors constituted only about one-fourth of the typical railroad board. Currently, this ratio has declined to just a little better than one in six.

This lack of "insiders" has not received adequate attention. In the far more dynamic industrial sector, officers and former officers serving as directors make up nearly 60% of the typical board. By inference the railroads' outside directors, like the industrial outside directors, serve minimal purposes. They lack a comprehension of crucial problems, have other areas of incompetency, and give too little time to the railroads since they serve other firms in more stimulating and demanding capacities. Fortunately, in the industrial sector, most boards, even those with heavy

*Table 18-2 Board of Directors Composition
in Forty Leading Railroads*

	1925	1950	1970[a]
Officers	136	110	84
Outsiders	374	472	394
Percent officers	26.6	18.9	17.6
Average board			
officers	3.4	2.8	2.5
outsiders	9.4	14.8	11.6

[a] The original 40 railroads have been reduced to
34 by bankruptcy and merger.

outsider representation, have some officer-director representation in addition to the chairman and the president. In sharp contrast the typical railroad board of directors has only the equivalent of one-half an officer in addition to the chairman and president.

The malstructure of the board of directors is shown further in the propensity of railroad boards to give outside directors indefinite tenure. In 1969 about 37% of the outside directors had served on that railroad's board for more than 20 years. As a consequence of such long tenure the median age of railroad boards of directors tends to be much higher than that in manufacturing industry; for example, the Chicago, Rock Island and Pacific's board has 7 members out of 13 outside directors who have each served more than 20 years. The board's median age is about 69 years, with only four directors under 60 years of age. Similarly, Central of Georgia has 10 of its 16 outside directors with 20 or more years of service on the board. The median age of this board is likewise about 69, with only five directors under age 60. These and quite a few identical situations seem to indicate a case of leadership entrenchment. There is no parallel situation in our society except, perhaps, the Supreme Court where such life tenure is bestowed regardless of performance records.

This static state at the directorate level has also had pronounced effects at the executive and managerial levels. Until quite recently there had been virtually no hiring from without—college recruitment programs were so incidental they were scarcely noticed. Management development programs were conspicuous by their absence. Hirings of researchers, and particularly those with earned doctorates, were minimal. The education level of railroad managers and executives was far below their counterparts in industry. Expenditures on research and development were microscopic. The net result of this inertia was a static industry.

Optimistically, an improved future seems in sight both in management and in technology. The initiation of high-speed modern trains, such as the 320-mile Tokaido line between Tokyo and Osaka in 1965, and comparable progress in many European countries seem to indicate the advent of the much needed technological changes. Penn Central's Metroliner which went into service early in 1969 between Washington and New York is the first real indication of such improvement to come in this country. The tremendous cost for such massive modernization is the big deterrent. In the Metroliner experiment a sizable subsidy was made by the Federal Government as part of a study of the effect of high-speed ground transportation on intercity ground travel systems. In mid-1970 the Senate, by a onesided 78-3 vote, passed a bill that would establish a government-backed corporation to operate the nation's ailing intercity passenger trains. The bill would provide for a profit-making corporation to take over much of the country's passenger service. The corporation with a board of directors of 15, eight named by the President of the United States, three by common stockholders which would be individual railroads, and four by the public holding preferred stock, would function much like Comsat which operates a communications satellite system. Even with Federal subsidies, however, the twenty-first century railroads will need corporations with tremendous assets and with far more imaginative and venturesome managers.

Merger and specifically conglomeration offer the logical course of action. It should be pointed out that railroads have previously participated in joint ventures. The classic example is Railway Express Agency, which is owned by 57 railroads. This was not, however, a typical merger situation and it antedated the present movement by many years. Within the preceding decade the urge-to-merge, so rampant in the industrial sector, seems very likely to be imitated by the railroads. Amazingly, the Interstate Commerce Commission and other Federal and State regulatory agencies seem to be setting up a minimum of roadblocks to slow this movement. The merger of Pennsylvania Railroad and New York Central Railroad, discussed subsequently, is a classic example. In addition, there has been merger action in other quarters. Among the more notable is the formation of Burlington Northern through merger of Great Northern, Northern Pacific, Chicago, Burlington and Quincy, and Spokane, Portland and Seattle railroads. This union of four railroads with nearly 27,-000 miles of railroad, vast timber and mineral resources, and total assets in excess of $3 billion was truly an accomplishment. The urge to merge in this instance was certainly not a rash action—as far back as 1893 Great Northern attempted to get control of Northern Pacific but was effectively blocked for 77 years by adverse rulings of the Supreme Court.

In February 1970 the Supreme Court gave unanimous approval, thus reversing its previous stand.

In addition to the union of railroads with other railroads, the merger movement has also led to the formation of holding companies by railroads for the express purpose of entering nonrelated business activities. This phenomenon will be discussed in greater detail. In many instances, railroads have abandoned their prime endeavor and have sold out their railroad facilities. With the proceeds the former railroad managements have then moved into conglomeration. Finally, a number of conglomerates have sought, for various reasons, to take over a number of railroads.

The remainder of this chapter will deal with these four quite different manifestations: horizontal mergers of several railroads, conversion of the railroad into a holding company for conglomeration purposes, invasion of railroading by industrial conglomerates, and abdication of railroading and an outright move into conglomeration.

PENN CENTRAL COMPANY: A HORIZONTAL MERGER?

The deal to merge two of the nation's biggest railroads, Pennsylvania Railroad and New York Central Railroad, was first proposed seriously in 1958. After a decade of uncertainty, maneuvering, and even two trips to the Supreme Court, the merger was finally consummated. With its current $2 billion-plus in operating revenue and its nearly $7 billion in assets, this is the nation's biggest transportation company. In a sense the merging of the two biggest companies in the same industry is rather atypical. It seems highly unlikely that any comparable merger would have been tolerated by Federal antitrusters in any other industry, but, in this case, it was felt that the union was imperative for survival.

The juncture of these two entities, previously structured and conditioned for intensive competition, into a harmonious and efficient single unit was a massive task. By contrast in mergers involving a giant and a much smaller acquisition, the dominant component invariably sets the pattern and the smaller firm quickly adapts. In this union of equals, neither of these two giant railroads could act as the undisputed leader. As a consequence, the speed factor and incisiveness in decision making were affected; for example, in striving for improved efficiency, particularly through abandonment of redundant facilities and excess personnel, accomplishment was too often a wish rather than a reality. Much of the projected cost savings was conditioned by labor-union restrictions. "Many railroad officials outside the Penn Central are bitterly critical of what Saunders (PC chairman) gave up to the labor unions in return for ending their opposition to the merger. . . . The Penn Central guaranteed that 'none of the present employees of either railroad shall be deprived of employment or placed in a worse position with respect to compensation, rules, working conditions, fringe benefits, or rights and privileges.' " [3]

Although this guarantee of employment is laudable, it could defeat the purpose of merger by severely restricting necessary labor-saving improvements. Railroads have been notorious for their featherbedding. In 1963 there seemed to be solid prospects for real productivity improvement when the railroads won their long battle against make-work restrictions. Railroads were conceded the right to reduce some train and yard crews by one man and gradually to ease 90% of freight and yard diesel firemen out of their jobs. The 20-year decline (1949–1969) in total railroad employment from 1,300,000 to 590,000 likewise seemed to indicate productivity improvement. On the negative side, however, after a brief drop, labor cost as a percentage of operating revenues rose again so that 54 cents of each revenue dollar is now spent on labor. This is the highest such expenditure in recent railroading history.

Perhaps in recognition of railroading's dilemma, even the biggest railroads are anxious to diversify. Although Penn Central began as an horizontal merger, the corporation soon made conglomeration gestures. Its first serious attempt at unrelated diversification was a plan to acquire Kayser-Roth Corporation, a major apparel concern. Had the plan gone through this would have been a $230 million transaction. After several months of deliberation, the deal fell through.

In mid-1969 Penn Central announced that, assuming Interstate Commerce Commission and Internal Revenue Service approval, it would redo its corporate structure. A new holding company, Penn Central Company, would be set up to control the company's 186 subsidiaries, including Penn Central Transportation Company, the railroad-operating component. The new holding company would presumably facilitate diversification. "Chairman Stuart T. Saunders says flatly that it 'has turned on a massive diversification program in order to supplement its earning power. Almost all of our consolidated net income last year came from our investments in pipelines, hotels, industrial parks, air rights, commercial real estate and other nonrailroad properties.' " [4]

In 1969 when the company reported a loss of $121.6 million the firm's nonrailroad investment subsidiaries earned nearly $60 million. Meanwhile the railroad itself lost $182.3 million on $1.7 billion in operating revenues. (In the first half of 1970 Penn Central's transportation subsi-

[3] *Business Week*, "The Big Merger Begins to Click," 104 (May 4, 1969).
[4] *Business Week*, "Penn Central Tries a Wider Track," 132 (May 10, 1969).

diary lost $142 million.) Among the most profitable of the subsidiaries were the real estate and pipeline units which were purchased largely from the $65 million the Pennsylvania Railroad received from the sale of its Long Island Railroad. As a condition of the Penn Central merger, the ICC demanded that the company divest itself by 1974 of about $150 million worth of Norfolk and Western Railway stock. With such favorable results from the initial ventures into unrelated activities, it seemed highly likely that most, if not all, the $150 million realized from the Norfolk and Western divestiture would be similarly invested. Penn Central's chairman had stated publicly that the company does not intend to subsidize rail service out of nonrail earnings. "We cannot continue to cannibalize our nest egg to finance the railroad. That must be made to stand on its own feet." [5]

As subsequent Penn Central events have shown, there certainly was no magic in this merger. The expectations of synergy never materialized. The "green" (for the color of its box cars) New York Central team seemed to be treated as an acquisition rather than a full-fledged merger partner of the dominant Pennsy "red team." Alfred E. Perlman, who became New York Central's chief executive officer in 1954 and reconstituted that near-bankrupt Vanderbilt possession, is quoted as being less than enthusiastic over the merger. "This wasn't a merger—it was a takeover," Mr. Perlman conceded to friends after the two roads joined.[6] This attitude was reflected in the flight of many top executives from the newly merged railroad. "And if they didn't quit, they were often relegated to positions where they didn't get responsibility commensurate with ability, knowledgable observers say." [7] Mr. Perlman himself was shunted into an out-of-the-way corporate corner as vice-chairman.

Penn Central's common stock in synergistic expectation, zoomed above $86 per share soon after the merger. Then, as merger miracles failed to appear, the price steadily slumped and on that fateful June 8, 1970, when the $7-billion-asset holding company petitioned for bankruptcy, the stock slid to a pathetic 5⅞ per share. On the basis of the 23.1 million shares then outstanding, this drop represented a paper loss of nearly two billion dollars the biggest such single company loss in recent stockmarket history.

On the managerial scene the bankruptcy resulted in the immediate firing of three of the four officer-directors. Only Paul A. Gorman, the recently hired (from Western Electric) president was retained. In the next month nine of the company's 19 outside directors resigned, almost

[5] Ibid.
[6] The Wall Street Journal, 17 (June 12, 1970).
[7] Ibid.

all because they feared conflict-of-interest charges. These were directors with intimate banking ties (Penn Central's board had a total of 17 different directorate contacts with major banks) and these banks could have been involved in refinancing attempts. It is a pathetic commentary on this particular board of directors that with so many finance experts "to manage and control" the corporation it nevertheless fell into such a financial mess.

Subsequently there was considerable handwashing by some of the outside directors who claimed they were not informed of the facts. Some of the outside directors felt they had been "hoodwinked" by management and maintained that the first information they had about the rapidly deteriorating cash situation came from that fateful prospectus issued in conjunction with the $100-million, 25-year, 10½ per cent debenture offering which precipitated the bankruptcy. The prospectus revealed not only to the public but even to the directors (so the directors claimed) the corporation's extremely tight cash position. The directors "really didn't know what was going on," said one well-informed railroad analyst. "One or two of them might have done their homework but they didn't have the power to sway Saunders. The rest didn't even know what questions to ask." [8]

The subsequent condemnation of the Penn Central board of directors was widespread. "One disgruntled conductor at Penn Central's Philadelphia Suburban station said he thought 'there'd be a heckuva lot more spirit if they cleaned out all those bums at the top.' " [9] The need for drastic reformation of this and similarly structured boards seems apparent. Penn Central's board members averaged 65 years in age. Daniel E. Taylor, one of the directors who resigned after the fiasco, did so because he was approaching the company's mandatory retirement age of 70. "Mr. Taylor could not attend every directors meeting. Because of his aversion to flying, he usually came to Philadelphia on a private Penn Central railroad car." [10]

But the age of its directors was not the only obstacle to effective performance and successful merger. Friction among members of the two components increased with each month. The inability of the two railroad teams to resolve their differences and to work in harmony highlights the critical issue in all mergers. No union of entities can be successful unless the parties subordinate their differences and pitch in enthusiastically toward the common goal. Otherwise merger can be successful, as was stressed in Chapter 9, only by following Machiavellian

[8] *Business Week*, 19 (June 13, 1970).
[9] *The Wall Street Journal*, 3 (June 24, 1970).
[10] *The Wall Street Journal*, 9 (July 10, 1970).

tactics. If the executives and key managers of the acquired firm cannot be integrated without serious friction, there is only one alternative— they must be fired.

ILLINOIS CENTRAL INDUSTRIES

One of the pioneers among railroads in the conglomeration trend was Illinois Central Railroad, which in 1962 incorporated a holding company, Illinois Central Industries, which then became the railroad's parent. Soon after the holding company purchased Chandeysson Electric Company, a small producer of heavy electrical equipment.

This bold diversification move seemed justifiable and even mandatory. In the previous 12 years Illinois Central had actually stood still: its 1955 and 1966 operating revenues were almost identical at about $295 million. Assets had increased only 17% to $807 million; net income had declined 10% to $23 million, and the labor force had shriveled by 35% to 21,523. Regression syndrome symptoms were obvious in these and related data.

Diversification at the new Illinois Central progressed very slowly. In 1968 Waukeshan Foundry Company a manufacturer of precision castings and corrosion-resistant pumps, was purchased with stock valued at about $10 million. The really big move took place a few months later when Abex Corporation was acquired in an exchange of stock valued at around $160 million. Abex likewise was a good example of the regression syndrome with slumps in *Fortune*'s ranking between 1956 and 1967 as follows: sales from 234 to 289; assets from 237 to 317, and net income from 260 to 321. Typically, other aggressive conglomerators had sensed Abex's vulnerability with North American Rockwell making a serious public bid. This was only one of about 15 acquisition feelers for Abex in the preceding year. In an attempt at image improvement Abex had even changed its name from American Brake Shoe Company.

Acquisition of Abex's $300 million annual sales in fluid-power controls, friction controls, and wear controls for the railroad, automotive, aircraft, construction, mining, rubber, and machinery industries was a distinct step into conglomeration. The exchange of 0.72 share of a new Illinois Central Industries convertible second preferred stock, worth about $56 per share, for each Abex common share, indicated about a 100% premium over the then-current Abex stock quote of $28. In this payment of a huge premium for control, Illinois Central was definitely behaving like a conglomerate. Also, by adding seven Abex representatives to its board of directors, Illinois Central manifested the "confederation" characteristics so evident in the typical conglomerate takeover of a major acquisition.

NORTHWEST INDUSTRIES: A NEW CONGLOMERATE

Late in 1968 Loew's Theatres took over Lorillard Corporation and almost concurrently began to acquire large blocks of stock in B. F. Goodrich Company, the nation's fourth largest rubber company. Within several months Loew's had acquired 358,450 shares or about 3% of Goodrich's outstanding common stock. Since Loew's had become a very acquisitive conglomerate, there was much speculation as to a possible takeover of Goodrich. Then in a surprise move, Northwest Industries, a rather recently put-together conglomerate, proposed a billion-dollar tender offer for Goodrich stock. The first Goodrich officials heard of this proposal was in the newspapers. Goodrich's chairman, J. Ward Keener, reacted strongly saying Northwest acted in a reckless manner.

This bold maneuver is remarkable in that a former railroad, the Chicago and North Western Railway, could make such a brash proposal. Less than a year earlier (1967), Ben Heineman, the railroad's president, had set up a holding company, Northwest Industries, as the railroad's parent. In an aggressive diversification move Northwest acquired Philadelphia and Reading Corporation, a former railroad company which had abandoned its railroading and had become a $350 million nonrailroading conglomerate. Its products included underwear, steel fabrications, lighting components, and boots. Another acquisition was Velsicol Chemical Company, a maker of insecticides, herbicides, caustic soda, chlorine, and other chemicals.

Northwest Industries also tried to capture Home Insurance Company but failed. It made an abortive attempt to acquire Essex Wire Corporation but also failed. Subsequently, in a dramatic move Northwest attempted to take over the nation's biggest meatpacker, Swift and Company, but was again repulsed.

The Goodrich takeover attempt is an excellent example of a talented and aggressive conglomerator using all means at his disposal to take over a reluctant and equally talented management. Not only Heineman and Northwest Industries but the entire financial community was taken by surprise at Goodrich's determined defense. Chairman Ward Keener, a one-time economics professor, conducted what probably will go down in the financial chronicles as the classic corporate counteroffensive against an unwanted advance by a superaggressive conglomerator. Among the strategic defenses were the following:

1. A petition to the U. S. District Court at New York accusing Northwest Industries, its chairman, Ben W. Heineman, Loew's Theatres, and Loew's chairman, Laurence A. Tisch, with violating Federal Securities laws. It was pointed out that Tisch was a director and a member of Northwest Industries' executive committee and that both he and Heineman were working together to acquire Goodrich shares. This presumably could be in violation of the Securities and Exchange Act of 1934. As an interesting sidelight, although not part of the suit, it should be pointed out that Goldman, Sachs and Company served as investment banker to both Northwest Industries and B. F. Goodrich, and John Weinberg, a Goldman, Sachs partner, was a member of the Goodrich board holding the boardroom seat previously occupied by Sidney Weinberg, his father, and also a Goldman, Sachs partner.

2. Goodrich engineered the issuing of 700,000 shares of its stock to Gulf Oil Corporation for that firm's half interest in Goodrich-Gulf Chemicals. By this move Goodrich's management put a very sizable block of stock in "friendly hands."

3. At the annual meeting Goodrich's management won stockholder approval for a staggered system of electing directors and for cumulative voting, thus ensuring representation by current management for at least three or four years, even if Northwest Industries did succeed in its tender offer.

4. Goodrich purchased for 55,415 shares of its common stock the privately owned Motor Truck Freight Company. By this action Goodrich became involved in the transportation industry which presumably would involve the Interstate Commerce Commission if Northwest Industries persisted in its takeover attempts. This could mean lengthy hearings and protracted litigation. Also, issuance of the stock for this purchase served to dilute further Northwest's ownership which by this time was about 16% of Goodrich's outstanding common.

5. Goodrich hired White and Case, the legal firm that had masterminded American Broadcasting's successful defense against Howard Hughes. It also used three top public relations firms including Hill and Knowlton. Among the many attempts at influencing public opinion was a full-page advertisement published in a number of leading newspapers including The Wall Street Journal, reprinting an article from the April 15, 1969 issue of Forbes. This advertisement stressed that Heineman, as a corporate general, failed to follow the three basic strategems adhered to by all great military leaders: take the enemy by surprise, do not underestimate him, and know well the terrain on which you must march and fight. Forbes points out that Heineman did fulfill the first prescription by his "sneak attack," but he grossly underestimated Goodrich man-

agement's capabilities and its tenacity. "Heineman, an articulate, intelligent man, has a major fault: arrogance. He assumed that Goodrich management, out there in Akron, Ohio, wouldn't be a match for him." (Likewise) "Heineman attacked not out of strength but out of weakness. He badly needed a victory. (But) he neglected to study the terrain. He failed to allow for the fact that legal, political and public opinion was beginning to harden against takeovers." [11]

Regardless of the outcome of this "blitzkreig," the significant point is that many, if not most, mergers of this sort come about because the aggressor is bold and confident and the aggressed is timid and yielding. This does prove that the neoentrepreneur conglomerators and their cohorts, the macromanagers, are a different breed. They have not yet become soft and pliant through long tenure in sinecure spots. Nor have they become bureaucratic robots, cogs in a supposedly immutable and immortal corporation.

On the other hand, the Goodrich reaction to Northwest Industries might indicate that most present managements can be converted and transformed into the new-breed macromanagers. However, in this transformation it is absolutely imperative that some meaningful therapy be administered to counteract the regression syndrome symptoms. These symptoms were very evident in B. F. Goodrich, which between 1955 and 1969 had slipped in *Fortune*'s ratings as follows: sales, from 38 to 90; assets, from 50 to 86; and net income, from 37 to 148. Winning the battle in this instance is not enough—the victorious Goodrich management must gear to win the war.

KANSAS CITY SOUTHERN INDUSTRIES

The move by industrial firms or conglomerates to take over railroads is a distinct rarity. The poor performance records, stringent regulations by State and Federal agencies, entrenched and retrogressive unions, and an apparent lack of anything worth acquiring seem to provide railroads with sanctuary. However, the recent bid by Lee National Corporation for Kansas City Southern Industries might indicate a changing attitude. Kansas City Southern operates the Kansas City Southern Railway and the Louisiana and Arkansas Railway and it has interests in mutual fund management and in radio and television stations. Lee Industries itself was a very small enterprise, formerly known as Lee Rubber and Tire Corporation. It had rather recently gotten out of the rubber industry and now owned six shopping centers and department store properties.

[11] *Forbes*, "The Last Great Battle?," 48 (April 15, 1969).

In this instance, Kansas City Southern stockholders reacted immediately and decisively in rejecting the upstart by overwhelmingly approving a series of measures to make takeover by outside firms, including Lee National, more difficult. Among these measures was a raising from 60 to 70% of the stock required to authorize a sale, lease, or exchange of all assets. Election of directors on a staggered basis was also approved as was an increase in authorized common shares from 4 to 7 million, together with 2 million shares of preferred. These countermoves are enumerated since alone or together they form the most commonly used defense by managements against unwanted acquisition attempts.

MSL INDUSTRIES, INC.

In 1960 Minneapolis and St. Louis Railroad Company sold its railroad assets, changed its name to MSL Industries, and set out on a broad-based industrial development program. In the next few years the new company acquired 21 major companies, including fasteners and metal fabrications, plastic products, steel tubing, aerospace and engineering products, motors and energy systems, and nonwoven textile products. Sales spurted from an initial $15 million in 1961 to $118 million in 1968.

In the acquisition process MSL absorbed only three publicly owned firms; the remainder were independent firms managed by their owners. Without exception the managements of each of these companies became a part of the MSL organization and continued to run the business of the component it formerly owned or headed. Seven of the key managers have been added to the board of directors.

Although the personal abilities of the independent entrepreneurs are used to advantage, there is a distinct trend toward centralization through confederation. Each operating division is a profit center, but marketing and manufacturing services have been coordinated for effective common use. Each component is assured of the best available services from a steadily developing professional group of "conglomerated" managers. Additionally, the company now selects operating executives on a corporate-wide basis. MSL's eightfold growth in an eight-year period could serve as an example for other small railroads to follow. In an era of the macro- and the mega- in railroading, with at least three of our major railroads each covering more than 20,000 line miles, it seems hopeless for the small railroad to survive. MSL could be the prototype for many similar railroad transformations. As a caution it should be emphasized that such a resurrection is probably impossible without massive management redoing.

EVALUATION

The MSL example, in particular, focuses on the absolute need for macromanagers in any successful conglomerate endeavor. Railroads taking this route are even more in need of these new managers as a consequence of past neglect in management development. Then, too, industrial enterprise is an alien field for most railroaders. Consequently, to facilitate rejuvenation through conglomeration or by any other means, serious attention must be given to increasing the number and improving the caliber of the new managers.

On the positive side, railroads and ex-railroads do have some advantages for multiindustry endeavor. Prime among these is the inevitable need for more and better mass surface transportation as population expansion and pollution problems place limits on competing transport means. Even more significant is the great potential of railroads' land resources. Penn Central, for example, is one of the largest real estate companies in the country. Its complex of office buildings on Manhattan's Park Avenue, built on "air rights" in the Grand Central Terminal area, bring in a rental income approaching $20 million annually. It also has a quarter interest in Madison Square Garden Center, on and around Manhattan's old Pennsylvania Station.

Among other notable Penn Central properties are Gateway Center (Chicago), Penn Center (Philadelphia), and National Visitors Center (Washington). The company's Arvida, Great Southwest and Macco real estate divisions have recently embarked on large-scale developments.

Penn Central, although the biggest, is certainly not the only participant in this new activity. Illinois Central has developed a 1000-acre site outside New Orleans as an industrial park and proposes a similar project near Memphis. The Norfolk and Western has embarked on a $100 million residential and commercial development near Kansas City. A number of other railroads are moving in this direction, maximizing use of their off-track land holdings. Some of these holdings are rather extensive, with Union Pacific's 900,000 acres being the prime factor in the reorganization of that railroad into Union Pacific Corporation, a holding company with three divisions: transportation, land, and natural resources. Union Pacific has invested an additional $80 million in purchasing nearly 17,000 acres in urban areas for residential and industrial developments. It also opened up a new copper mine in Southwest Colorado, is developing an uranium deposit, and is building a soda ash-producing facility. Its ventures into oil and gas exploration are even on a grander scale.

CONCLUSION

While diversification offers sound prospects, it could also mean further contraction in railroading. The ICC, disturbed at Northwest Industries' large-scale conglomeration, questioned that firm's president, Ben Heineman, about the prospects that his railroad-turned-conglomerate would continue to invest in a marginal rail operation. "Heineman admitted that a determined management could starve a property, but he observed that doing so would be foolish because the railroad would end up in bankruptcy, 'and one would lose one's total investment.'" [12]

A short time after making this statement Heineman seriously considered a proposal by a group of its employees, North Western Employees Transportation Corporation for sale of its railroad facilities. The employees group would pay $30 million and assume $340 million in long-term debt of which most was secured by locomotives, cars, and other equipment. This maneuver would give the holding company, Northwest Industries, a tax credit of about $225 million. It would also mean the abdication by that company of its historic role in railroading. Pessimism on this score becomes even greater when other major railroads attempt similar abandonment. In mid-1970 Katy Industries proposed leasing or outright sale of its deficit-ridden subsidiary, the Missouri-Kansas-Texas Railroad, to the newly conglomerated Burlington Northern.

The future of our railroads rests to a great degree on the caliber and intentions of its managers. If like the raiders of two decades ago they will prefer profits through liquidation rather than profits through operation, then prospects are bleak. If, however, they can use diversification through conglomeration as a rejuvenator, then some railroads, perhaps in a scarcely recognizable form, will undoubtedly continue to compete in our enterprise system.

[12] *Fortune*, "The Railroads are Running Scared," by Gilbert Burck, 123 (June 1969).

19

CONGLOMERATE LABOR UNIONS

Consolidation, amalgamation, or confederation are not foreign phrases in the labor movement. On the international plane the World Federation of Trade Unions (WFTU) was organized in 1945. Because of its allegedly communist domination, the competing International Confederation of Free Trade Unions (ICFTC) was established in 1949. Both these unions emphasize confederation. In our own country the first trade union, the Federal Society of Journeymen Cordwainers, was founded in Philadelphia in 1794. Large-scale amalgamation began with the Knights of Labor (1869–1900) and the far more successful American Federation of Labor (1886). The AFL, as its name indicates, is a loosely knit confederation of independent unions, stressing economic improvement rather than political involvement. The Congress of Industrial Organizations (CIO), founded in 1939, also states its all-encompassing cooperative aspirations in its very name. A Congress is an assembly or conference constituting a legislative body. Some of the individual unions, such as Amalgamated Clothing Workers, Amalgamated Meat Cutters, and Butcher Workmen, have confederation very conspicuously stated in their titles. Then several dozen unions have the term *United* (Mine Workers, Auto Workers, Packinghouse Workers, etc.) prominent in the title. If we add the words Brotherhood (Railroad Trainmen, Teamsters) and International (Electrical Workers, Chemical Workers), then at least three-fourths of all unions, by their very names, imply consolidation, amalgamation, or confederation.

The need for still more union in unions is becoming obvious as industry expands its scale of enterprise through both internal growth and particularly through conglomeration. Labor leaders have long recognized that union fragmentation means weak bargaining power. Yet for many years segments of the labor movement have been entrenched in the manner of feudal fiefdoms. A labor leader, once ensconced in his power center, is just as intractable as any Persian satrap or Chinese warlord.

The AFL was a distinct move toward a pooling of interests. Its limited success, together with its obvious imperfections, led to establishing an even more ambitious amalgamation, the CIO. This was largely in response to the labor movement's changing characteristics and needs, gestated by significant changes in expanding American industry. The consequences of "dual unionism," long an anathema in labor movements throughout the world, led to a juncture, a conglomeration of the AFL-CIO in 1955. Although the results were partially positive, this super-union or labor conglomerate failed to merge all unions into a single entity. John L. Lewis' United Mine Workers, once the AFL mainstay and then the vital force in organizing the CIO, subsequently reaffiliated with the AFL, and later again disassociated. The UMW then remained independent refusing to join the conglomerate AFL-CIO. The biggest component, the Brotherhood of Teamsters, with nearly two million members, was spun-off in 1957 because of corruption charges. Both its president, James Hoffa, and former president, David Beck, were judged guilty and given lengthy prison terms. Also in 1968 Walter Reuther led his million-and-a-half United Auto Workers out of the AFL-CIO conglomerate he had helped put together.

Just a month after his AFL-CIO disaffiliation, Reuther announced the formation of a new labor conglomerate, the Alliance for Labor Action (ALA). According to initial organizational plans, the ALA would widen considerably the unionization horizons. Not only would it seek to take in all present unions but it would seek to organize the 60 million or more employed but unorganized Americans (compared with approximately 20 million unionized workers). Farm workers, white-collar workers, service workers, government employees, and other largely unorganized workers would be primary objectives.

Just as important as the widening membership perimeter is the greatly expanded scope of social welfare aspirations. The proposed ALA would be the following:

—A real-estate developer, planning, designing, and building low-cost urban housing for slum dwellers, retired union members and others, using advanced building technology.

—A private antipoverty program sponsoring job-training centers and slum neighborhood service centers that would take an ombudsman's role in helping the poor with legal, medical, and financial problems.

—A ghetto-mobilizing "new politics" machine, organizing, registering, and "educating" black and other minority voters to increase pressure on city hall, school boards, landlords, and merchants.

—A new well-financed organizing force, aiming to spread unionism to low-wage industries and to unorganized regions, such as the South.

—A new bargaining-table combine backed by a huge strike fund, eager to match muscles and wits with corporate conglomerates.[1]

This manifesto is certainly in keeping with Walter Reuther's long-time fight for social progress. It is also in step with prevailing sentiments in regard to hoped-for improvements in the social sphere. Very significantly, it is in stride with the rampant giantism in government, education, religion, and industry. In some respects this could be viewed as a very necessary move to set up a countervailing force to balance the might and muscle of the conglomerate corporation.

In addition to the power-balancing feature of the AFL-CIO and the ALA, there are some very practical operating considerations. Even after the formation of the AFL-CIO conglomerate, some of our major corporations continued to experience serious collective bargaining difficulties in dealing with a myriad of small but vociferous unions. For example, General Electric has about 80 unions representing 130,000 workers (out of a total workforce of 400,000) at 150 locations scattered around this country. Railroad managements must deal with a total of 24 unions. Even in a relatively simple situation such as Campbell Soup's five major canneries, four unions (United Packinghouse Workers, Amalgamated Meat Cutters, International Association of Machinists, and International Brotherhood of Teamsters) have exclusive bargaining rights in one or other of the canneries. Similarly, almost every major corporation has to deal with several or even many unions. This confused collective bargaining condition continues to disturb both management and labor.

Recently a group of eight unions, representing most of General Electric's organized employees, tried to engage in joint talks with the company. When this failed, the dominant union, the International Union of Electrical Workers, proposed a series of GE-IUE bargaining sessions. This proposal, however, came to an end when the company discovered that the IUE bargaining panel included representatives from all the seven other unions. The IUE claimed these non-IUE members were actually representing the IUE by looking after their own individual union's interests. This was obviously a step by the unions toward collective company-wide negotiations.

Subsequently the National Labor Relations Board ruled that the IUE bargaining panel, including the other union representatives, was exactly what the IUE claimed: a group of its own representatives. After getting

---

[1] *Wall Street Journal,* "Union Conglomerate," by James P. Gannon and Laurence G. O'Donnell, 1 (May 14, 1969).

a court order, the union compelled GE to bargain and a settlement (practically identical with what GE had initially proposed) was reached.

This NLRB ruling casts a new perspective on collective bargaining. The NLRB had itself defined the scope of most of GE's unions, certifying them as the specific bargaining agents for local units voted into being by the unions themselves. The question, then, is, should the definition, scope, and function of collective bargaining units be redefined in the light of swift-moving changes on the corporate scene? Perhaps, as William N. Chernish, in his book, *Coalition Bargaining*,[2] points out, expediency mandates a new union approach. He defines coalition bargaining as the joining together of a number of local unions having different international affiliations for the purpose of bargaining with a company or an industry as a single unit.

The concept of multiunit bargaining is certainly not new. Numerous industries, such as coal mining, have long had negotiations and labor contracts on an industry-wide basis. In coal mining the phrase "No contract-no work," became axiomatic, binding the entire industry. During the 1940's and 1950's the practice was adopted by a number of the newer unions. In some instances, such as in the automobile and steel industries, tactical considerations favored concerted union pressure against only one or a few of those firms most likely to capitulate. In these instances the total strength of the union, together with the almost total support of other unions refusing to cross the picket line, was aimed at individualized opponents. Even in this selective-striking there was still a manifestation of union solidarity.

Less than 10 years ago some unions began to sense the inadequacy of both industry-wide bargaining and the strategic selection of one or two firms to be hit. The newer approach was the concept of "coordinated bargaining" or "coalition bargaining," the objective of which is to present a solid union bargaining front by combining all the unions dealing with an employer or an industry into a single coordinated negotiating team.

Coalition bargaining, although it is a step short of conglomeration, will very likely lead to union consolidation. In a little more than a year the number of AFL-CIO affiliates shrank from 141 to 122, largely through merger. The United Steel Workers absorbed the emaciated Mine, Mill and Smelter Workers and almost immediately precipitated a half-year shutdown of the nation's copper mines and other copper-processing facilities. The sentiment among labor leaders was that in the

[2] William N. Chernish, *Coalition Bargaining*, University of Pennsylvania Press, Philadelphia, 1969.

past the small, underfinanced but independent Mine, Mill and Smelter Workers union had deliberately settled for inferior contracts in previous collective-bargaining sessions with just one aim—to survive.

After 10 years of negotiation, the United Packinghouse Workers and the Amalgamated Meat Cutters and Butcher Workers finally merged into a 465,000-member union. The Laborers International Union (formerly the Hod Carriers) absorbed the tiny Journeymen, Stone Cutters Association, a 120-year-old union with only 3000 members. The Laborers International Union, now a half-million strong also discussed amalgamation with a number of other unions, including the United Brick and Clay Workers (21,000 members), the United Stone and Allied Products Workers (12,000 members), the Granite Cutters International (2000 members), and the United Cement, Lime and Gypsum Workers (30,000 members). All these unions were in allied fields and in previous years had often engaged in jurisdictional disputes and other internecine activities.

Despite the pros and cons for union merger there are many obstacles to a wholesale amalgamation. As previously stated, when the AFL and CIO accomplished their seemingly impossible dream, there was serious talk of consolidating the 140-plus unions into a streamlined two or three dozen. The failure to do so has been a disappointment to many labor idealists, among them George Meany, president of AFL-CIO, who has stated he has "tried to get the boys together but the boys have been too strong-minded. Under AFL-CIO policy, no affiliate can be pushed into a merger." [3]

Much of this strong mindedness can be attributed to traditional rivalries, personal animosities, and the reluctance to reduce staff and executive jobs. However, there also are philosophical and ideological differences that create merger obstacles. The disparate juncture of industrial CIO unions with the trade-oriented AFL was in itself a blending of oil and water, as subsequent ideological disputes have proved. Among the congenital differences, for example, was the Samuel Gompers-William Green-George Meany brand of unionism as contrasted with Walter Reuther's stress on social action. Then, too, the CIO components give rank-and-file members considerable power in all phases of union decision making, whereas the AFL unions tend to put more reliance on decisions made by their elected officials. Structurally, AFL unions have been described as being "horizontal" and CIO unions are "vertical." There are also some seemingly unreconcilable economic considerations such as the equating of fringe benefits and particularly retirement benefits. When the United Steel Workers absorbed the much smaller Mine, Mill

[3] *Business Week*, "The Urge to Merge Hits Unions Again," 64 (April 20, 1968).

and Smelter Workers, many of the steelworkers objected vocally at the USW's following annual convention. Critics accused the USW's officials of wasting union funds in "buying" the MMSW union.

Assuming that outright merger is just as painful, or even impossible, for ideologically different unions as it is for incompatible corporations or individuals, then the logical route seems to be the previously mentioned coordinated bargaining or coalition bargaining. By this means individual differences and even idiosyncracies can continue without impeding the necessary collective action. Here the unions have all the benefits of marriage without actually going through the ceremony.

It cannot be determined at this time whether this coalition approach would ultimately result in outright merger or simply in the establishment of coordinated bargaining alliances of autonomous unions. Nevertheless some counterpart of the corporate conglomerate will probably evolve. Very likely the new super unions will not be patterned after the eclectic, hodge-podge former District 50, United Mine Workers, which was John L. Lewis' answer to the ecumenical AFL-CIO. More likely the new super unions will be structured along very broad product or service lines. As President Ralph Helstein of the United Packinghouse Workers has stated, " 'My idea is that there shouldn't be more than ten or fifteen unions in the United States. There should be one transportation union, a metal trades union, a food-and-drink union, and so on.' " [4]

The formation of the United Transportation Union, by a merging of four of the biggest unions in railroading, might be the first of such new super unions. Early in 1969 spokesmen for the four unions, Brotherhood of Railway Trainmen (125,000 members), Brotherhood of Locomotive Firemen and Engineers (40,000 members), Switchmens Union (10,000 members), and the Order of Railway Conductors and Brakemen (15,000 members) agreed to amalgamate. This new union would cover about 75% of all railroad operating personnel not including such workers as porters or ticket agents. A referendum of the members indicated the rank-and-file support for merger when 97,728 voted in favor with only 15,067 opposed.

Although very distinct steps are being taken to amalgamate in some sectors of the labor movement, the really big question remains unanswered: How can unions contend with corporate conglomerates? At the 1969 Miami Beach meeting of the AFL-CIO, President Meany said, "Some people are talking about 'labor conglomerates,' as an answer to union problems in dealing with such business combines." [5] The AFL-CIO

---

[4] *Dun's Review*, "The Super-Unions?," by Murray Seeger, 79 (October 1968).
[5] *Eugene Register Guard*, 4A (February 25, 1969).

executive-council asked for a congressional investigation of conglomerates, stressing that it is extremely difficult for craft or industrially structured unions to deal with multi-industry conglomerates. This difficulty is shown in the following diagram.

Union profile on one conglomerate

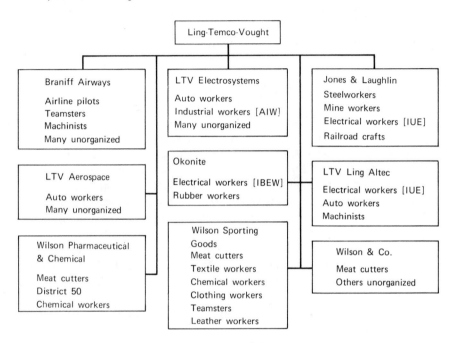

Data: Ling-Temco-Vought and Research Dept.,
Amalgamated Meat Cutters

W-12 *Source:* Business Week, "Do mergers need a union label," p. 86 (May 17, 1969).

Ling-Temco-Vought, just before its really big conglomerate surge, dealt with six major unions. The acquisition of Braniff Airways added two more; six were added through the acquisition of Wilson and Company, and at least another three big unions had to be considered after 63% of Jones and Laughlin stock was purchased. Although on one hand the multiplicity of unions can create collective bargaining nightmares for management, the negative results for the union can be catastrophic. The confederation of so many diverse industries within a single corporate entity makes the previously very effective industry-wide and selective-company strike-threat techniques far less effective. It is highly unlikely that any strike called by, say, the Meat Cutters against the Wilson and Company component could cripple the entire LTV conglomerate. Shutting down all of Wilson and Company's meat-processing facilities could be 100% effective against that subsidiary and its entire line of products, but the conglomerate's other components, engaged in unrelated product lines, would presumably be unaffected. Obviously, LTV would be hurt but not crippled even by an extended strike in its Wilson and Company subsidiary. Consequently, coordinated bargaining, coalition bargaining, or outright conglomeration seems to be imperative.

SUMMARY

The labor movement's historic stress on solidarity can certainly be interpreted as a form of conglomeration. The periodic attempts among American trade unions to coalesce into a single national union supports this inference. "Dual" unionism is, and probably always will be, an anathema to diehard unionists. Although the Utopian appeal of brotherhood and kinship of all workers has lost much of its emotional fire, economic and political considerations continue to provide a commonality of purpose.

"Workers of the world, Unite!," although now seldom heard as a battle cry, is very much a moving force. Now, however, the motivation for the workers of the world to unite is not so much to break the chains of bondage but rather to grab a bigger chunk of "the action." Despite courageous attempts by individual union leaders to stress the primacy of social reform as *the* ideal of all unionism, the immediacy of material gain seems to subordinate the Utopian dream. As a consequence, graft and power ploys, splinter groups and schisms, internecine conflict, and outright rebellion continue to prevent the long hoped for unity.

In the labor movement's inability to attain its ecumenical ideal we seem to have an excellent example of the centripetal-centrifugal dichotomy discussed in a previous chapter. There are certainly advantages in size which seem to necessitate consolidation and confederation of all unions into one huge conglomerate. This is the centripetal force.

Conversely, there is the centrifugal force, equally real and equally powerful. Where it initiates is a matter of conjecture—perhaps in the animal instincts in man. Nevertheless it results in spin-offs and disunion. What too often begins as a peaceful Utopian clasping of hands in union solidarity so easily degenerates into wrist-wrestling, fisticuffs, and bruised knuckles.

20

MERGERS ABROAD

Reference was made in Chapter 3 to the universality of the current trend toward corporate merger and especially toward conglomeration. It was pointed out that British and Japanese industries, in particular, are very definitely merger prone and have been for some time. Although until recently by far the vast majority of foreign mergers have been of the vertical or horizontal type, there is now an increasing manifestation of unrelated firms being conglomerated into huge combines. In Japan a number of the Japanese zaibatsu might be said to have anticipated the American version of conglomeration. The old zaibatsu corporate structure and the reasons leading to the building of these large-scale industrial ventures do, however, differentiate them from the conglomerates of the current era. Similarly, the present British merger movement is more than just a case of like absorbing like in a natural expansion process.

The prime reason for merger and conglomeration abroad seems to be the realization that ability to compete internationally is distinctly correlated with scale of enterprise. Sir Donald Stokes, architect of the merged British Leyland Motor Corporation, has stated "A company cannot survive in the international world without size, without marketing and service outlets, and without the advantages of scale for research and development." [1] Foreign firms must get bigger if they are to be successful international competitors. In many cases, scale of enterprise in most other countries, if limited to a single product line, would still mean small-scale endeavor when compared with the American corporate mammoths or with such multinational firms as Unilever or Royal Dutch /Shell. Consequently, there is presently no better way for foreign firms to

[1] *Fortune*, 43 (September 15, 1968).

grow than through the combination of many smaller firms making unrelated products into a confederation. Another term for this phenomenon is conglomeration.

This recognition of the economies associated with large-scale operation is not restricted to manufacturing. Recently the Common Market's executive body proposed a multibillion dollar scheme to encourage farm mergers. The proposal would serve to cut the number of Common Market farms from 11 million to only 5 million by 1980. About two-thirds of the area's farms would be merged into units eight to twelve times their current size. At present two-thirds of Common Market farms are less than 25 acres, whereas under the proposal the smallest subsidized farm would have to be between 200 and 300 acres. This anomaly, outright support of Bigness by Government, runs counter to the American experience where farm subsidy programs have been severely criticized for benefiting the large, prosperous farms. In this case, the Common Market officials believe that eliminating small inefficient farms is essential.

Although large-scale enterprise is mandated by international competitive pressures, a strong secondary conglomeration propellent is the regression syndrome, discussed in previous chapters. This is particularly the case in older, family-run companies. Until recently, most foreign firms, even the biggest, have been owned and run by descendants of the founder-entrepreneur. In too many instances local and national competition has been so insignificant that these feudal enterprises had virtual monopolies. The growth of international markets and the evolution of the multinational corporation now threatens this corporate entrenchment. Multinational firms must prove themselves competitively. Although government favoritism by way of subsidies, tax concessions, reciprocity, labor-cost underwriting, quotas, and similar aids can still make a significant difference, the long-run emphasis is on efficiency. In far too many instances here and abroad this vital efficiency or productivity improvement is seriously impeded by perpetuation of mediocre managements and apathetic owners. A catharsis is imperative. In the United States this essential catharsis has been provided through conglomeration or often just the threat of being taken over.

Great Britain

The need for corporate catharsis, through merger, conglomeration, or some other form of violent upheaval, is probably even more evident in British firms than in American enterprise. The British textile industry is a classic example. For more than half a century Britain's ancient textile industry, particularly the cotton production component (initiated in the mid-eighteenth century), was on the competitive downgrade. The once-flourishing export market had virtually disappeared and there was serious doubt that Great Britain could continue any longer manufacturing cotton textiles.

In a spirit of concern the British government took positive action in 1959 by offering, among other things, subsidies to companies that wanted to abandon obsolete equipment or even to go out of business. Within two years about 420 mills were shut down and in the ensuing decade another 400 to 500 mills gave up. More than half the nation's spinning capacity and close to half its weaving facilities were scrapped.

Despite this major attempt to improve the industry the fundamental problems remained. There were simply too many small producers and a distinct lack of imagination and innovation. " 'Before the scrapping we were producing unwanted goods on old machines,' says one textile executive, 'after it, we were producing unwanted goods on new machines.' " [2]

The big improvement came only when the major synthetic fiber producers gave stimulus to large-scale merger, particularly along vertical lines. The wider use of synthetics, together with the benefits of larger-scale endeavor, gave the industry a new momentum. For example, Courtaulds, Ltd., began a large-scale acquisitions program and now operates over 200 plants and accounts for over one-third of Britain's spinning capacity. The important feature of this merging was a greatly increased efficiency. The bigger scale of operations means smaller inventories of raw materials and finished goods because the merged firm now has more control over materials sources and a greater awareness of market demands. The company can also concentrate certain production facilities in specific plants and schedule longer runs.

Basic to these productivity improvements was the management factor. Courtaulds moved directly into the management of the companies it acquired. The old-line managements of the acquired small family-owned mills were almost all replaced with new professional managers. "Says George A. Samule, head of Courtaulds Northern Textiles Division: 'The old management would have been a problem even with new equipment.' " [3] In many of the acquired mills virtually all the top executives have been fired and almost all the members of the boards of directors have been eased out.

Probably the most drastic management-merger transformation seems to have taken place at Viyella International, Ltd., a "federation" of over 90 companies put together by merger-minded Joe Hyman. Although certain services are supplied to Viyella's members from headquarters, each

[2] *Business Week*, 52 (January 15, 1966).
[3] *Ibid.*, p. 54.

division and every plant runs its own affairs with a large measure of local autonomy. There is considerable shifting around of men and machines in the elusive attempt to find the most efficient combination. Most markedly, "Depending on whom you talk to, Hyman is either a hero or a villain in the textile revolution (in Britain). Says a former managing director of a company acquired by Viyella: 'Hyman has a reputation as a ruthless man because he pays people big salaries and expects them to produce. If they don't, they're out. He thinks more in American terms and this is the American way of doing things. The difficulty is, people don't think that way here'." [4] By the end of 1969 Joe Hyman had meshed more than 200 Lancashire plants and mills into his profitable textile federation. Sales in excess of $170 million accounted for about 17% of British brand-name shirts together with a substantial share of exports. Despite his remarkable success and recognition by many Britons as the kind of enterpriser that Great Britain desperately needed to rejuvenate its decrepit old industries, he was summarily fired late in December 1969 as Viyella's chairman and chief executive officer.

This axing of the corporate founder and its largest stockholder led to considerable speculation. In this case even though Viyella's performance had slipped somewhat, it certainly had not slumped. The consensus seemed to indicate that a retrenchment was in order. "Hyman always pursued an expansive growth policy. Some of his moves have been questionable . . . [but] 'Joe Hyman is not the kind of man to compromise on such matters,' says a British management consultant in London. He has firm views about long-term strategy, and he is used to getting his way —or nothing.' Pushed to the brink, the other eight directors voted him out." [5] Within six months after this ousting of Hyman, Viyella's initiating force, the once-acquisitive conglomerator was itself the subject of takeover. Imperial Chemical Industries Ltd., (ICI) Britain's largest chemical company proposed to acquire Viyella and a second textile manufacturer, Carrington and Dewhurst, Ltd. Although the British government through its Monopolies Commission had in December 1969 issued a "standstill" decree calling a halt to further mergers and acquisitions in the textile industry, the Government sanctioned ICI's proposal. But, even if consummated, Imperial Chemical's takeovers would be limited by law to only a 35% stake in each of the two textile firms and ICI could name only one director to the new company's board. In this instance there would seem to be some corroboration of the previously expressed sentiment that American-style merger is not completely acceptable abroad.

[4] *Ibid.*, p. 54.
[5] *Business Week*, 23 (December 20, 1969).

However, contrary to the sentiment that managers and citizens in other lands "don't think that way here," there is a distinct trend in every industrial nation to consolidate small firms into bigger entities. In some cases this merger incentive is even Government initiated. Early in 1968 the Leyland Motor-British Motor Holding merger was facilitated by a $60 million loan from the British Government's Industrial Reorganization Corporation. In the summer of 1969 the British Government's Industrial Reorganization Corporation went so far as to engineer a merger involving three British bearing makers: Ransome and Marles, Hoffmann, and Pollard. The new company will have 35% of the British market as compared with 27% for Skefco, the British subsidiary of Sweden's SKF, 20% for Timken, and 10% for Fafnir, the latter two being American owned. Among the reasons for the Government-instigated merger was the desire to improve efficiency in this vital industry. Even more important was the British Government's feeling that merger was inevitable, particularly since Skefco had within the last year tried to gain control over two of the smaller bearing makers.

The British experience with nationalized industries is an even better example of industrial concentration with centralized control. The coal industry's takeover by the Government is a classic example. Even more significant is the steel industry's nationalization, first in 1951 and a second time in 1967. In the first attempt the Labor Government took over all 92 of the country's iron and steel companies, giving the owners almost $600 million as compensation. A return of the Conservatives to power resulted in a handing back of the industry to private hands.

The 1967 nationalization was restricted to the 14 biggest companies producing about 90% of Britain's iron and steel. This time the compensation for the takeover was $1.4 billion in government bonds. About 250 smaller firms, most of the specialty steel fabricators, were permitted to remain in private hands. The nationalized iron and steel sector, with plants valued at $4 billion, sales approaching $3 billion, and with 270,-000 employees, is one of the biggest mergers outside the United States.

This realization by major governments that large-scale enterprise is absolutely essential for survival of domestic industries, and even more so for competition on the international plane, will undoubtedly have further merger ramifications. Every foreign-based firm with multinational aspirations will, of necessity, be forced either to set up foreign subsidiaries or acquire already established firms in these other countries. The latter course is faster and surer.

In mid-summer 1969 British Petroleum Co., Ltd., announced the intentions of acquiring Standard Oil Company (Ohio). The British petroleum producer (about half owned by the British Government) with the world's largest crude oil reserves had up to recently been the only international petroleum company without an entry into the United States market. Its first move in this direction was the purchase from Atlantic Richfield Company of the former Sinclair Oil Corporation's retail, refining, and pipeline properties which Atlantic Richfield had recently acquired.

In the Sohio proposal, a rather involved plan was set forth whereby BP would first get a 25% interest in Sohio. Contingent on BP's success in the development of its major oil strike on the Alaskan North Slope's Prudhoe Bay, this stock interest could be expanded to 54% of Sohio's common stock. This juncture of Sohio's $750 million sales and British Petroleum's $5 billion sales would make this one of the biggest of all mergers. In this instance, the direction of merger was both vertical and horizontal. The only semblance of conglomeration was in the chemical, motel, and restaurant businesses which Sohio had undertaken as a means toward diversification. Presumably, with the backing of BP's tremendous resources, this Sohio diversification attempt would be intensified.

The examples of British industry's merger momentum are increasing rapidly. There are even some cases of conglomeration. Recently Rank Organization, Ltd., made an offer of $103 million for the assets of De la Rue, Ltd., a plastics, heating appliance, scientific instruments, and printing concern. Another equally intriguing conglomerate merger would take place if Unilever, Ltd., succeeded in acquiring Allied Breweries, Ltd., one of Britain's biggest brewing companies. Allied Breweries, which itself had been extremely active in taking over smaller breweries, has 8300 pubs, 1800 beer and liquor stores, 70 hotels, and 11 breweries. In this latter instance, a merger with Unilever would facilitate Allied Breweries' attempts at worldwide distribution of its products. Both attempts at large-scale conglomeration were tentatively set aside until the British Monopolies Commission could review the legality of the proposals. This was the first time the commission was asked to rule on mergers that were not strictly vertical or horizontal in character.

Japan

Combines and near-monopolies have long characterized Japanese industry. The zaibatsu, the family-held trusts which have long dominated Japanese business, have become classic examples of oligopolistic enterprise working in close consort with the military and the Government. Although most of the zaibatsu are single-industry companies, three of the largest, Mitsubishi, Mitsui, and Sumitomo, were conglomerates long before conglomeration became the rage in American enterprise. Mitsubishi, for example, is the world's biggest shipbuilder. It also makes automobiles, petrochemicals, machinery, aircraft, cameras, microscopes, and even beer and butter. The Mitsubishi conglomerate includes a major bank, a trust company, a land investment company, and Japan's two largest insurance companies.

Without emulating the American version of conglomeration the new zaibatsu have developed some very similar corporate philosophies and policies. At Mitsubishi, for example, there are 25 major corporate components plus hundreds of smaller subsidiaries and affiliates. There are even many joint ventures with foreign firms, particularly American including Caterpillar Mitsubishi, Mitsubishi Reynolds Aluminum, Mitsubishi York, and a number of other easily recognizable two-nation enterprises. The entire organization is meshed and intertwined in a complex of directorate interlocking and in intricate financial interrelationships.

Cooperation within the group is close, and individual units have relatively little freedom of operation.

Chief guidance is provided by the presidents of Mitsubishi Heavy Industries, Mitsubishi Trading and the Mitsubishi Bank. Heads of the 25 main companies meet monthly to coordinate group activities, discuss over-all goals and plot strategy. In addition, directors of these companies get together twice yearly at special seminars. The same general pattern holds of Mitsui, Sumitomo and the rest of Japan's six major zaibatsu.[6]

The Japanese Government, in contrast to the attitude of the United States Government, not only approves but even encourages the formation of cartels, combines, and conglomerates. In theory holding companies are illegal. General Douglas MacArthur, during the United States occupation of Japan, dismembered the zaibatsu and imposed stringent controls to prevent their restructuring. The Japanese even have a Fair Trade Commission, set up during the United States occupation, to regulate, among other business actions, mergers and similar business combinations. Despite the Japanese FTC, mergers have become considerably more frequent, reaching a rate of almost 1500 a year. This trend is remarkable considering the legal hindrances and also the fact that Japanese industry is already quite concentrated. Fewer than 1% of Japan's manufacturers employ one-third of the labor force and account for one-half of all production.

A real test of Japanese legal restraints on merger occurred in mid-1969 when Yawata Iron and Steel Company and Fuji Iron and Steel Company announced plans to combine. The new firm would actually

[6] *U.S. News and World Report*, "The Conglomerate Way of Life in Japan," 93 (June 2, 1969).

be merging for the second time. The first union was in the 1930's when Japan's military-dominated government forced the two steel producers to combine into Shin Nippon Seitetsu K.K., or New Japan Steel Corporation. This union was dissolved during the American occupation. In the present merger Nippon Steel or the rebuilt New Japan Steel Corporation would have an output of nearly 32 million tons, more than one-third of Japanese total output. The company would also be the world's second biggest steel producer, ranking next to U. S. Steel Corporation.

The Japanese Fair Trade Commission took immediate steps to stop this merger, pointing out that the new firm would account for about 64% of tin plate and cans, 54% of foundry pig iron, all of Japan's railroad rails, and a very high percentage of steel sheet. Despite the FTC objections there seemed to be considerable favorable sentiment not only among businessmen but also among government officials and parliamentarians; for example, the Ministry of International Trade and Industry declared itself in favor of the merger. In April 1970 the Japanese Government approved the formation of the new merged firm, Nippon Steel Corporation.

The Fuji-Yawata union, proponents argue, is absolutely necessary if Japan is to continue to compete on the international scene. The almost cutthroat competition among Japan's 756 steel companies has created competitive problems in Japan and has even unsettled world prices. The Fuji-Yawata merger, a distinct move toward giantism in the Japanese steel industry, would not be out of step with world trends. As previously stated Great Britain's nationalization of its 14 biggest steel firms into the British Steel Corporation is indicative. Furthermore, nearly all of Germany's steel companies are flirting with merger proposals. In France three of that nation's largest steel companies merged into a single firm early in 1969.

Another serious international consideration is the fear many Japanese bankers and industrialists have of foreign firms getting a freer hand to invest in Japan. In that event larger-scale of operations would become absolutely necessary just to survive in the domestic market. Advocates of Japanese industry concentration even proposed that the entire automobile industry should be centered about the two largest firms, Toyota Motor Company and Nissan Motor Company, in order to compete more effectively with the United State's "Big Three" automakers.

An unexpected furor broke out when Mitsubishi Heavy Industries reached an agreement with Chrysler Corporation to assemble Valiant cars in Japan and to import Mitsubishi Colt sedans into the United States. In this instance, although both firms are giants, they do not rank at the top in their respective auto industries: Chrysler is third among the United States "Big Three" and Mitsubishi is a small fourth among Japan's five automakers. A joint venture might consequently assist the relative "little guys."

This fear of a greater investment impact by American firms in Japan was intensified when, at the time of the Fuji-Yawata debate, Walter Kidde and Company announced that it had made an application to purchase a 40% interest in a Japanese textile machinery builder, Yamamoto Kikai Seisakusho. Although a number of American corporations have financial interests in Japan, this was the first move by an unmitigated American conglomerate to make such a move.

From a Japanese point of view there is considerable logic in this propensity in Japanese Government, not merely to tolerate but even to encourage business concentration. The net effect is greater efficiency, improved productivity, and a distinct competitive advantage in international trade. One of the secrets of the Japanese success is the ability (of those involved) to subordinate individualism to rigid group action. Not only is this groupistic control significant in individual zaibatsu-firms, it is equally evident in controls imposed by industrial associations. These groups of peers frequently use an iron fist approach, setting, for example, "voluntary quotas" on exports of textiles or steel to the United States.

The result is one of the world's most tightly managed economies. The Japanese Government not only referees the economic contest but actually participates in a very active manner in planning and controlling. With this neozaibatsu example opponents of American corporate conglomeration probably have good reason to fear that continued conglomeration in American industry will result in comparable concentration.

Germany

Conglomeration in German industry is very significantly being affected by a chance financial factor: the ability of German banks to buy and sell common stock. As a result the really big conglomerators are the commercial banks and, in particular, the Big Three: Deutsche, Dresdener, and Commerzbank. These three commercial banks have more than half of the $22 billion in deposits in all German commercial banks and have assets in excess of $16 billion. The three banks have an impressive industrial ownership interest with more than a 25% interest in the following:

10 breweries, 5 construction companies, 4 department stores,
4 shipping firms, 4 machinery makers, 2 public utilities,

2 porcelain makers, 2 hotel chains and 1 automobile manufacturer. This impressive list would be significantly elongated if the less-than-25% holdings were included.

With such huge holdings, bank directors show up frequently on the boards of industrial companies—thus adding further to the influence banks have on the German economy. No one epitomized this more than handsome, extroverted Josef Abs, chairman of the managing board of the Deutsche Bank . . . at the peak of his influence he was a member of 24 corporate boards, including Daimler-Benz and Deutsche Shell.[7]

This practice has led to serious charges of conflict of interest since the banks buy and sell for their own accounts as well as for their customers. Unlike United States' banks which cannot own stock in other companies, the German banks, as has been stressed, can and do have considerable stock holdings. In addition, German banks perform a presumed service by providing a "share depot" where customers can deposit their shares for voting purposes. The banks then exercise these "depot voting rights" together with voting the shares they own outright.

German tax laws also encourage banks to expand their industrial holdings since the tax rate on dividends is 51% when the ownership interest is less than 25% in a given company, but the tax rate drops to 15% when the ownership interest is above 25%.

The German merger-conglomeration movement is almost certain to be chiefly a banker's game because only the banks can be stock exchange members. As a result, nearly all workers in the stock exchanges are bank employees. "One complaint is that the banks let investors see only a small portion of the total German stock market. Some 600 companies have stock registered for trading: the exchanges, though, report daily on trading of 35 selected issues. Furthermore banks trade with each other outside market hours. Customers can even ask that transactions on the floor be kept secret." [8]

In a sense the German banks provide the same concentrating force for the German economy that the Japanese family trusts and the British Labor Party provide for their economies. The rationale for industrial concentration, together with diversification, seems to result from international competitive pressures. The German coal industry is one example. Steps have been taken to merge all German coal mines of the lower Rhine and Ruhr basin into a single holding company controlling seven subsidiary joint stock companies. These in turn would operate the mines whose former owners would be paid the equivalent of $825 million. The

[7] *Business Week*, 98 (May 24, 1969).
[8] *Ibid.*, p. 98.

pressure for merger in the coal industry was a consequence of the competition of lower-priced United States coal and the increased use of oil. Despite heavy taxes on oil and import restrictions on United States coal, the West German mines continued to decline in output from a 1956 peak of 151 million tons to a current production of only 112 million tons. Employment in the mines slumped even more significantly, dropping from 553,000 coal miners in 1956 to only 150,000 at present. Presumably, a merging of the smaller mines into a huge combine would help overcome the current $5 price differential between a ton of United States produced coal and a ton of West German coal.

An even better example of the international urge to merge is evident in the auto industry. The Japanese situation has already been described. In Great Britain, British Motors Corporation first acquired Jaguar Cars, Ltd., and then merged with Leyland Motor Corporation to form a giant combine that now produces more than a million vehicles. In France, S. A. Andre Citroen was first an acquisition-minded automaker but was subsequently itself the subject of attempted acquisition when Fiat, S. P. A. of Turin, Italy, acquired an indirect minority interest in Citroen.

In Germany Volkswagenwerk A.G. gave evidence it intended to acquire NSU Motorenwerke A.G. whose automobile output was in the 135,000-unit range. A few years earlier Volkswagen had purchased from Germany's second largest automaker, Daimler-Benz A.G., a controlling interest in Auto Union, a Daimler-Benz subsidiary. All indications point to a continued concentration in the auto industry with the ultimate development, through merger, of a German General Motors.

An interesting sidelight of the NSU takeover attempt was the open hostility manifested by a large number of the heretofore silent small stockholders. At the 1969 annual meeting irate stockholders hissed and hooted down a banker trying to cajole them into supporting a takeover by Volkswagen. Considering the dominant role German commercial banks have played in Germany's industrial endeavor, including mergers, this first serious outburst against the acknowledged business leaders could signal a new attitude of Germany's small investors toward corporate control.

France

In the last decade some 160,000 French companies have disappeared, some in liquidation and bankruptcy but by far the great majority through merger. Most of these companies were very small and their demise caused little concern on the national or international scenes. One of the first disturbing actions was General Electric's involvement in the ailing French computer maker, Compagnie des Machines Bull. Then more recently the relative calm was disturbed by an attempted takeover of a venerable large-scale glassmaker, Compagnie de Saint-Gobain, by an upstart fledgling, Boussois-Souchon-Neuvesel. Saint-Gobain is one of the world's oldest corporations, having been founded in 1665 by Louis XIV. By contrast BSN was less than three years old, having itself been put together by merger. Saint-Gobain was also considerably bigger; its approximately $1 billion sales volume was more than four times as large as that of BSN. Although Saint-Gobain is primarily a glassmaker, it is fairly diversified with interests in oil, chemicals, paper, and nuclear engineering.

The unique feature of this attempted takeover was its similarity to the typical American conglomerate acquisition. No cash was involved. The BSN offer was in the form of convertible debentures (the first time used in France) with an offer valued at about $46 per share. Previously, Saint-Gobain shares had been selling at $28.50. This 60% incentive-bonus is very much in the American conglomerate pattern. The tender offer was for 3.36 million shares or about 30% of Saint-Gobain's outstanding common shares. Again there is a similarity insofar as effective control would be based on far less than majority ownership.

In American fashion the aggressor firm sought and had the backing of several important financiers, notably Lazard Freres, Banque de Paris et des Pays Bas, and the Neuflize Schlumberger group. An even more significant similarity was the pretext for takeover namely, the supposed antiquated approach of Saint-Gobain's top management. The average age of Saint-Gobain's directors was 70 and its executives were much older on the average than American executives. As a countermove Saint-Gobain announced a top management shakeup with three younger men moving into key operating jobs and with the planned replacement of its 64-year-old chairman by 52-year-old Edmond Pirlot. No significant changes were, however, made in the board of directors.

Although this single episode certainly does not constitute a trend, it is important to note that even the most venerable, large-scale, publicly owned (200,000 stockholders) foreign corporation cannot be assumed to be beyond reach of merger-conglomeration.

In France, perhaps more so than in most other nations, there is a fierce nationalistic resistance to intrusion by foreign firms into French industry by merger or by any other way. General Electric experienced some of this sentiment in its Compagnie des Machines Bull venture. More recently Westinghouse Electric Corporation was frustrated in its attempt to buy control of Societe Jeumont-Schneider, France's number two heavy electrical equipment producer, from its Belgian and French owners. The French government in a countermove engineered a get together of Jeumont-Schneider with Societe Alsthom, a smaller electrical equipment producer, in a cartel-like agreement. Both firms would be under the management control of Compagnie Generale d'Electricite (CGE) which would concentrate on electrical equipment and leave electronics to another recently merged firm, Thomson-Brandt.

The French Government-initiated cartel proposal is worth noting since it might indicate a resurgent economic nationalism, thereby slowing down multinational conglomeration. It had been assumed that Westinghouse had in mind not only the acquisition of Jeumont (French) but also of the Belgian Empain group which, in addition to controlling Jeumont, also owns Les Ateliers de Constructions Electriques de Charleroi, the number one Belgian electrical firm. It was also rumored that Westinghouse planned eventually to expand this union into a dominant European electrical group including the Spanish firm, Senelesa, and one or two Westinghouse Italian subsidiaries.

Muscovite Merger

Probably the greatest compliment to the effectiveness of merger and conglomeration was the Soviet Union's focus on this phenomenon in the preparation of its most recent five year plan, this one for the period 1971–1975. This most recent five-year plan, the eighth since Stalin started the fad in 1928, has a new twist. One of the prime targets as stated by Dmitri Tzarev, a high ranking Russian economist, "envisions a revolutionary new type of business organization for this Communist state. It is called a conglomerate." [9]

The Russian proponents of this daring new type of economic organization contend that by joining small diverse and generally inefficient production units under a "mother" enterprise, the sluggish Russian economy can once again get moving in high gear. According to Mr. Tzarev, although Russia's large-scale operations continue to show gains in productivity, it is the medium-sized and particularly the small-scale enterprises which are slumping. "The solution, he says, lies in the scheme to form conglomerates." [10]

As in the United States the logic supporting this statement is the belief that combining the small units into the "mother" enterprise will provide better management, improved engineering, research stimulation, more meaningful financial and accounting controls, and efficiencies in other functions. They cite an example of a large Moscow automobile plant which previously was served by a cluster of suppliers producing

[9] *The Wall Street Journal*, 1 (April 17, 1970).
[10] *Ibid.*

frames, trim, carburetors, and so on. When nine of these small plants were merged into the "mother" company, productivity improvements were almost immediately noticed.

As is rather obvious the Russian reference to conglomeration is actually a case of vertical integration rather than of conglomeration. Nevertheless it is worth noting that the Russian economy, rigidly run by the State Planning Committee, or Gosplan, recognizes the effectiveness of merger. In this planned economy, if Gosplan concludes that mergers are good for Russia, a wholesale move in this direction is certainly feasible. Since Gosplan runs everything economic in the USSR, there would be no need for stockholder approval, complicated stock swaps, use of frilly financial obligations such as subordinated convertible debentures or similar capitalistic gimmickry. Also, P/E ratios, pooling-of-interest, raiding, regression syndromes, stockholder derivative suits, proxy fights, and similar merger-related concepts would have no meaning in Muscovite merger. Significantly, the merger-caused catharsis in personnel, blue collar, office help, managers, executives, and even directors would probably have less significance in Russian mergers.

On the positive side the similarities are basically those associated with the economies of large-scale endeavor, both in scale of plant and in scale of organization. It seems to be a Gosplan 1971–1975 aspiration in its newest five-year plan to put more of an onus on managers of large-scale production units. "Enterprise managers have become accustomed to letting the Kremlin do their thinking. The reform demands that management do the thinking instead of the Kremlin." [11] It could be that in this seeming merger movement the Russians after a half-century of rigidly centralized bureaucratic Gosplan planning and control now see the economic light. Through a "way-out" communist conglomerate version, ultimate control by means of financial restraints would still rest with the superconglomerate, Gosplan. However, the theoretical decentralization integral to meaningful conglomeration would now be vested in the operating components.

The impact of this current USSR merger-conglomeration innovation still needs implementation and evaluation. It could be just another Marxian dialectic cover-over for communistic inefficiency. It might also be a real attempt at adaptation of a useful capitalistic concept. How it affects communistic theory is a matter of conjecture. There is even a possibility that by incorporating this capitalistic gimmickry into the communistic Gosplan mechanism, the Soviets themselves might be playing an economic version of Russian Roulette.

[11] *Ibid.*

Other Countries

The merger movement is manifest in every industrial nation. In addition to the six nations just discussed, there has been an increasing corporate concentration in Italy, Holland, Sweden, Switzerland, and even in Communist Yugoslavia. In Yugoslavia, one of the most interesting experiments in socialist conglomeration is Energoinvest. Even the company's name has a ring of space-age zip and superscience. Although private ownership of industry is just as taboo in Yugoslavia as it is in any Communist state, Energoinvest, founded in 1951, has already gobbled up more than 30 smaller Yugoslav enterprises. Beginning with the building of heat and power plants, the company expanded, first vertically and then in conglomerate style, into a variety of endeavors. With its new 200,000-ton alumina plant, Energoinvest promises to become a major European aluminum producer utilizing cheap water power from the Bosnian mountains as well as bauxite from the same province.

Figure 20-1 provides a partial list of corporate get-togethers in 1968. More recently the merger tempo has even been accelerated and subsequent annual listings of foreign mergers will likely be twice as long as that in Figure 20-1.

Figure 20-1 1968's top corporate get-togethers in Europe. *Business Week*, p. 54 (November 23, 1968).

Companies	Country	Products	Form of Relationship
General Electric [Britain], English Electric, Assoc. Elect. Industries	Britain	Electrical goods	Merger
British Motor, Leyland Motor	Britain	Autos	Merger
Int'l Computers & Tabulators, English Electric Computers	Britain	Computers	Pooling of certain computer interests
Rio Tinto Zinc, Borax	Britain	Chemicals	Merger
Schweppes, Typhoo Tea	Britain	Beverages	Merger
August Thyssen, Huettenwerke Oberhausen	Germany	Steel	Merger

Figure 20-1 *(Continued)*

Companies	Country	Products	Form of Relationship
BASF, Wintershall	Germany	Chemicals, oil	Takeover
Siemens, AEG	Germany	Electrical goods	Pooling of power Generating equipment
Bayer, Huels	Germany	Chemicals	Stock purchase
Thomson Brandt, Claret, CSF	France	Electrical goods	Merger
Fiat, Citroen	Italy-France	Autos	Purchase of shares; formation of joint company
Hoechst, Roussel-Uclaf	Germany-France	Drugs	Purchase of shares; marketing cooperation
Pennaroya, Preussag	France-Germany	Metals, fuels, transport	Coordination of activities in lead and zinc
Demag, Richier	Germany-France	Construction machinery	Cooperation on sales, research
Royal Salt, Zwanenberg Organon	Holland	Chemicals	Merger
Verolme, NDSM	Holland	Ships	Takeover
Heineken, Amstel	Holland	Beer	Merger
Grangesberg, Stora Kopparberg	Sweden	Steel	Coordination of facilities; formation of joint export company
Electrolux, 6 small companies	Sweden	Appliances	Takeover
Messerschmidt, Boelkow	Germany	Aircraft	Merger
BASF, Nordmark	Germany	Drugs	Takeover
ASEA, Kone, Thrige-Titan	Sweden-Norway-Finland-Denmark	Elevators	Exchange of stock; coordination of manufacturing, marketing
Brown Boveri, Sulzer Bros.	Switzerland	Turbines	Formation of joint subsidiary

European mergers, as seen in Figure 20-1, are not always restricted by national boundaries. About one-fifth of the listed mergers involve companies from more than a single nation. Early in this study the Fiat-Citroen venture and British Petroleum's acquisition of Standard Oil Company (Ohio) were discussed in more detail. Other consummated or attempted multinational mergers include the following:

1. A joint company formed by British Nuclear Power Group, Ltd., Germany's Gutehoffnungshuette Sterkrade A.G., Italy's Snan Progetti S.p.A., and Belgium's Belgonucleaire S.A. The joint company would produce and market nuclear high-temperature gas reactors.

2. Farbwerke Hoechst A.G., one of Germany's three largest chemical producers, acquired a 22% interest in Roussel-Uclaf S.A., France's second largest pharmaceutical company.

3. Compagnie Francaise des Petroles, France's state-owned oil company, has been very interested in getting a part interest in Gelsenkirchener Bergwerks A.G., West Germany's largest independent oil and coal company.

4. More recently Holland's Fokker and West Germany's Vereinigte Flugtechnische Werke (VFW) announced they were forming a new holding company, VFW-Fokker, to be headquartered in Dusseldorf, Germany. In addition to the Dutch and German partners, two United States firms, Northrop Corporation and United Aircraft Corporation, also have ownership interests of 20% and 12%, respectively.

These are just a few of the more publicized cases. Despite the growing incidence, development of huge multinational firms by conventional merger has run into many snags. Too frequently neighboring states are reluctant to permit takeovers of their own firms by a more aggressive neighbor. There are no international or even Common Market company charters, and national laws vary to such a degree that mergers are sometimes impractical. For example, when the Agfa-Gevaert merger of West German and Belgian photographic interests took place in 1964, the two companies found they had to maintain two corporate headquarters, one in Leverkusen, West Germany, and the other in Mortsel, Belgium. The union has serious problems stemming from the 65% German corporate tax on gross profits as compared with Belgium's 40% tax. These and numerous other difficulties, many of them initiating in the European's deepseated distrust of his neighbors, present seemingly unsurmountable hurdles. Albert Beken, a Belgian director of Agfa-Gevaert, is quoted:

Our Belgian participants in this merger will tend to defend the Belgian point of view at the highest levels and the Germans theirs. Don't ever forget that

Belgians for many, many years have deeply mistrusted Germans. Many of our board members, executives, shareholders and workers lost heavily during the past two wars. This is a psychological factor that posed problems at the beginning of this merger, and it continues today.

A complete merger, given the psychological factors cited by Bekens—was out of the question. Agfa-Gevaert's solution was a "corporate condominium" of two holding companies each owning 50 per cent of the operations in both countries.[12]

For reasons of this sort some authorities have predicted that the majority of European corporate mergers will be made inside national boundaries. However, there are strong counterviews to the effect that a more flexible grouping, a sort of confederation of companies, is needed. Out of this an European form of the conglomerate will gradually emerge to maximize multinational business endeavor.

Some Negative Experiences. Although the Belgian-German joint venture in Agfa-Gevaert has been cited as a tentatively successful experience, there seems to be an increasing number of muddled mergers when national boundaries are crossed.

General Electric's chronic problem with its Machines Bull's investment is a well-known example of the difficulties multination acquisitions and mergers can encounter. More recently Celanese Corporation charged off $135 million in a single year (1968) in eliminating unprofitable foreign units. Among these was Columbia Cellulose Company, based in Canada, and Siace, a Sicilian wood-products company. Siace, in particular, accounted for most of the loss. Mr. John W. Brooks, Celanese president, said, "Celanese was unable to make Siace, acquired in March 1965, a 'commercial operation.' He added: 'We had never been able to put technically qualified management in Siace. If we go into another foreign operation like Siace, we would be sure we had a strong domestic base in the U. S. to provide good management potential overseas.'"[13]

At approximately the same time three other American corporations, Ratheon, Rheem Manufacturing, and Union Carbide, had equally plaguing experiences with joint ventures in Sicily. Ratheon-Elsi filed a voluntary petition for bankruptcy; Rheem Safim shipped its welded pipe plant off to Africa for sale; and Union Carbide sold its interest in Celen S.p.A. to its partner, Montecatini-Edison.

In all four cases the problems facing international joint ventures, conventional or conglomerate, were highlighted. One authority stressed that American firms doing business in Italy must face the problem of whether

[12] *Business Week,* "Agfa-Gevaert, Model Merger?", 63 (July 5, 1969).
[13] *The Wall Street Journal* (February 20, 1969).

to accept the conventional business morality of Italy or to follow "back-home morality." For example, taxation in Italy is a thing to be avoided by any means and if an American firm pays up in typical American fashion, it is at a competitive disadvantage. Hugo Winternitz, managing director of Standard Oil Company's (New Jersey) Sicilian subsidiary, Rasiom S.p.A., emphasizes "that one of the principal requirements for success in Sicily is a staff made up as much as possible with people who know the country, preferably Italians. 'You have to know the cultural history of the region and you have to know the laws.' . . . 'one thing about Sicily is that you can't fire anyone. It is hard here for him to find another job. You have to offer bonuses and other inducements for people to leave.'" [14] Earlier, when Ratheon-Elsi tried to trim operating expenses by laying off 250 workers, the Italian government retaliated by seizing the factory and putting Palermo's mayor in charge.

These recent difficulties point out the significance of people problems in any joint venture involving firms of two or more nations. Although most negative illustrations up to the present involve an American corporation as one of the parties, equally serious difficulties can be anticipated when other countries increase their investments abroad. This raises serious doubts as to the future of multinational conglomeration. As long as the macromerger or even the conglomerate functions within one country's confines, the difficulties encountered tend to be more readily solvable. When the merger is of multinational proportions, numerous additional constraints, political, psychological, cultural, and even religious, are injected. For effective consummation multinational merger, and particularly conglomeration, will undoubtedly demand a new breed of supermanagers.

SUMMARY

Some obvious "people problems" will affect mergers abroad, both those restricted to a single country and those of multinational proportions. At the very corporate apex there is the question of who is to exercise ultimate control. Even in a one-country merger resulting in a national monopoly, who should be seated on the board? Will family trusts, as in Japan's zaibatsu, or bankers, as in Germany's case, or government officials and union leaders, as in Great Britain's Labor Party-sponsored merger-through-nationalization provide the corporate directors? In a multinational merger the allocation becomes even more acute since po-

14 *The Wall Street Journal*, 32 (March 11, 1969).

litical sensitivities are involved. Will Unilever and Royal Dutch/Shell be the prototypes or is some newer pattern yet to be evolved? (Unilever, 50% owned by Unilever N.V. of Rotterdam and 50% owned by Unilever, Ltd., of London, was established in 1928. The Royal Dutch/Shell Group, 60% controlled by Royal Dutch Petroleum of The Hague and 40% by "Shell" Transportation and Trading Co., Ltd., of London, is considerably older, having been established in 1906.)

Kindred problems must be faced at the managerial and the worker levels. As is evident in the Sicilian fiascos, workforce considerations can become a matter of national policy; for example, fringe benefits for workers are higher in Germany while wages are higher in Belgium. So there is union pressure to get the best of both worlds. Consequently, multinational mergers and even mergers within one nation's limits must be considered in terms of labor-force ramifications.

It is in the managerial category, however, that mergers have the greatest people impact. In government-sponsored merger, the possibility is that the managers will eventually become civil servants of the state. One out of every ten employed persons in Great Britain works for a nationalized industry. Government-owned enterprises account for more than one-tenth of all industrial production in France, one-fifth in Austria, nearly one-quarter in Italy. What effect will bureaucratization have on managerial competitiveness, innovation, and efficiency? Also, when mergers cross national boundaries, what can be done about the previously stressed political, social, language, or religious constraints? "In the Agfa-Gevaert joint venture parallel administrations run the enterprise. Not only does the firm maintain two headquarters, but there are dual heads, one Belgium the other German, for each of the nine common councils (organization, personnel, economy, construction, product development, research, advertising, sales, and manufacturing.) At board meetings there are two cochairmen, one Belgian the other German, and all reports must be translated into both languages." [15]

Assuming that the multinational merger and particularly the multinational conglomerate becomes the corporation of the future, it is obvious that new attributes will be needed by the supermanagers. What these attributes will be and how they are to be developed must wait until it becomes more clear whether merger and conglomeration will be used as a tool of restrictive nationalistic policy or whether it will become part of a Common-Market-type of multinational cooperation.

[15] *Business Week*, "Agfa-Gevaert, Model Merger?", 63 (July 5, 1969).

21

THE CORPORATE CONFEDERATE
STATES

SCALE OF ENTERPRISE AND SUCCESS

Conglomeration, merger, and other terms such as confederation, amalgamation, alliance, union, and consolidation all connote a striving for larger scale of operation—a desire to get big and even bigger. Yet there is a widely accepted myth to the effect that Americans are always on the side of the little guy especially if he is the underdog. Consequently, all Americans are assumed to be congenitally against bigness in business. That this is a myth should be obvious in our penchant not only for bigness in business but for big government, big universities, big unions, big cities, big buildings, and even big cars, and big swimming pools. Nevertheless the little-guy myth persists—perhaps in nostalgic wistfulness—in a subconscious yearning for the rugged individualism of the Daniel Boone frontiersman and the Bonanza Ben Cartwright homesteader. This nostalgia, although conducive to sentimental songs and maudlin prose, can be disastrous in economic matters. It is counterpart to the Latin *machismo,* evidenced by the poverty-stricken Latin American peasant with an overabundant family but with impoverished economic means. There may be no question as to his masculinity but there can be doubts as to his rationality. Similarly, there is no question as to the value of individual enterprise, but obsession with the absolute need for small-scale individual enterprise can be costly and regressive. The optimal scale of enterprise, whether in business, government, education, or urban development, is much more a matter of relative efficiencies rather than ideologies. Although we stress the inviolability of competition, for example, we shudder to think of the consequences if the more than 1500 companies which once made automobiles were still in business. On the average, even with our present 10,000,000 annual automobile output, this would mean an annual output of only about 6500 cars per manufacturer. Although this might be the epitome of individualism and competition, car prices would obviously be prohibitive. Autos would still be status symbols and within the means of few Americans. Technology would be limping along and management development would still be a generation away.

Similarly, in every industrial endeavor, from the making of abrasives to zinc smelting, excessive numbers of competitors means small-scale output and disproportionately higher prices. Even in agriculture we have witnessed a tremendous consolidation involving millions of small farms. Consider the consequences of a hypothetical Federal mandate insisting on small-scale farming. In 1900 one farmer on the average produced enough product to feed seven people; in 1970 each farmer feeds an average of about 40 people. This tremendous spurt in farm productivity would have been impossible without the consolidation of small farms. At the turn of the century the typical farm consisted of about 150 acres, whereas today it has more than 350 acres. Assuming that farming still took the effort of 40% of our available labor force (as it did in 1900 instead of the current 5%), we would obviously have lacked the resources to accomplish our massive technological strides. There is no comparison on a productivity basis among the large-scale ranch, the plantation, and especially today's large-scale mechanized farm, with the sharecropper's patch, be it bean, corn, or cotton. Farm merger, although invariably along horizontal integration lines, is nevertheless amalgamation, merger, and bigness.

The story is the same in all sectors of our society. In the sphere of education, the little red schoolhouse, with its one room-one teacher providing a variety of subjects for a heterogeneous student body, has given way to the consolidated school district. State universities, many in the 30,000 student category, are overwhelming the small, inefficient but proud and independent private colleges. In turn, these superuniversities are merged into state systems controlled by 10 to 15-man boards of higher education. These multiversities certainly can be considered academic conglomerates.

Religious institutions, proliferating since the Reformation into all shapes and shades of cults and schisms, are now compromising their once-absolute dogmas and are melding the assumed incompatibles into a Christian confederation. Ecumenism is just a fancy word for church conglomeration.

The reasons for confederation, alliance, consolidation, and other expressions of union in government, education, agriculture, religion and other sectors of society are many and varied. If a single cause were to be selected, it is the almost universal belief that a world whose population is exploding at a startling 2 to 3% annual rate must have improved technology. This means not only bigger and better mechanisms but also bigger aggregates of capital and more efficient organizations.

In industry growth and success are synonymous. A corporation which grows at the same rate as population or GNP is rarely viewed as an attractive investment. The mass of investors equate a firm's performance potential with commensurate price-earnings ratios. This P/E indexing is probably the single best yardstick of a corporation's future ability to contribute to our society. A high P/E ratio indicates that the investors consider this a growth company which will prosper and get bigger. Conversely, the investors assign a low P/E ratio to any firm with poor prospects of getting bigger at a better-than-average rate.

Considered from a different point of view, large-scale enterprise is invariably associated with managerial excellence. In nearly every survey of outstanding management, the best run companies are among the biggest companies. There are, of course, some exceptions, but it is safe to assume that Standard Oil (New Jersey), General Motors, Ford Motor, General Electric, IBM, Du Pont, and other giants will invariably qualify for the outstanding and excellent rankings. In simple terms: name a good company and you name a big company.

These paeans for big business follow from the recognition that scale of enterprise seems to be closely correlated with both economic and social progress. However, the argument is not one sided. Bigness does lead to bureaucracy with its standardization and orderliness but also with its stultification and squelching of initiative. Presumably, big business, bureaucracy, and Big Brother go hand-in-hand. If they do and if conglomeration means an acceleration toward bigger business, more bureaucracy, and an even Bigger Brother, then continued conglomeration can mean the end of individualism and democracy.

THE PENDULUM PHENOMENON

Some economic fatalists shrug away the centralization-decentralization dilemma as a manifestation of the pendulum phenomenon. Just as the pendulum, once in motion, inexorably swings from one side to the other, so also do groups of people in their adherence to institutions and beliefs. This can be expressed simply as in Figure 21-1.

In Figure 21-1 the degree of organization can run the gamut from anarchy to automation. Actually, anarchy represents a complete lack of organization, whereas automation is organization in the superlative de-

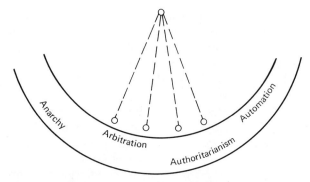

Figure 21-1   *Source:* Stanley Vance, Industrial Administration,
McGraw-Hill Book Company, New York, 1959, p. 106.

gree. In practice modern organizations keep well within these extremes
and swing back and forth between degrees of arbitration and authoritarianism.

There are differences of opinion as to which direction the organizational pendulum is now swinging. As was stressed in the previous chapters, the neoentrepreneurs, the first generation conglomerators, are
invariably "chips off the old block," modern replicas of the old-style entrepreneurs. In this context it would seem that the pendulum is swinging
sharply toward authoritarianism. Also, the loss of autonomy and of identity in perhaps 30,000 corporations in the decade of the 1960's seems to
be incontestable proof of more centralization and resurgent authoritarianism.

The phrase, resurgent authoritarianism, is used to emphasize the current uncertainty. Since World War II there appeared to be a tremen-
dously increased interest in democracy in industry. This was the era of
multiple management, "bottom up" management (sometimes referred to
disparagingly as "bottoms-up" management), collegiality, group-think,
and committee mania. This conviction was manifested in many ways
such as in the tremendous expansion of business administration schools
and the introduction of management development programs. Here we
have a democratic movement whereby the sons of workers, the American proletariate, could enter the very top strata of our society. Previously,
the typical second- and third-generation executives formed very exclusive Ivy League alumni clubs.

Together with this seeming pendulum swing away from elitism and
authoritarianism, there were other equally strong manifestations. Labor
mobility, and particularly executive mobility, once an anathema, be-

came an accepted fact of managerial life. One-man mandates gave way
to collective counseling and, so it seemed, to group decision making.
Ownership of industry likewise underwent democratization with one
American in six an owner-in-fee of voting shares in American industry
and with virtually every citizen at least an indirect owner of common
stock. Concurrently, there was a tremendous interest in the behavioral
science aspects of business administration. It was assumed that industry
must get to know what makes the individual worker tick. Stress on inter-
personal relations—the getting of individuals to perform more effectively
as a team—seemed to show that the organization pendulum was swinging very sharply toward arbitration, and perhaps even close to anarchy.
This swing seemed self-evident until the mid-1960's. Perhaps the wild
wave of the 1960-decade mergers is an economic reaction or even revul-
sion to the groupistic and collectivistic momentums of the 1950's.

From an organization theory point of view, if the pendulum is reversing its swing, then we must make a decision. Should we let the physical
forces propelling the pendulum be permitted to work "naturally?" This
might be termed the countervailing catharsis which cleanses, rejuven-
ates, and puts drive into a new and frequently reverse course of action.

There are obviously other possibilities. Interposing a powerful field of
resistance in the presumed path of the pendulum can slow down its reversed swing or setting up an immovable road-block can even stop the
pendulum. The feasibility of interference has been mentioned in several
of the previous chapters, particularly in the section on Merger Constraints. Likewise, the desirability of imposing restraints on mergers of
all kinds, even to the point of making them unlawful, has been
broached. Uncertainty as to what would follow, a Twenty-First Century
Golden Era, or a return of the Dark Ages, reduces analysis to conjecture.

THE CONGLOMERATE DILEMMA

Much of this conjecture follows from the relative recentness of the
conglomerate phenomenon, the diversity in conglomeration techniques,
and the extreme variety of conglomerate neoentrepreneurs. Numerous
references have been made in the previous chapters to the dissonance
among conglomerators. A number of prominent leaders among the conglomerators have even argued in favor of quite restrictive legislation.
Mr. Ling's proposal to tax mergers was previously stressed. Rupert C.
Thompson, Jr., chairman of Textron, "welcomes a government inquiry.
'It's not a threat,' says he. 'It's fact finding, and we're glad to have them

do it. The practices that have raised questions are ones that we have never employed, yet we get cast in with the go-go fellows.' " [1]

Similarly, "Henry E. Singleton, chairman of Teledyne, with 20 mergers and acquisitions in 1968, says, 'Speculation and wild deals have been going on too long, and have gotten out of hand. We're on their (the critics) side. We want the speculative takeovers to taper off.' " [2]

Much of this sort of sentiment might follow from a "who? me?" innocence. On the other hand, it does emphasize that confusion, uncertainty, heterogeneity, and even irreconcilable differences plague the phenomenon. From a management theory and practice point of view, the really crucial but quite confused issue concerns the optimizing of organizational endeavor through the integration of many diverse and unrelated components. How can you mix meat processing and steel fabrication and moviemaking and insurance selling together with a dozen other unrelated activities without getting some sort of conglomerate hash? How can you get men with widely varying technical and functional interests to work as a team for a single conglomerated goal? This goal must be viewable and attainable or the unrelated corporate components will see only what each wants to see and the hoped-for commonalty will become chaos.

As previously stressed many of the neoentrepreneurs give ample evidence of rigid authoritarianism. There is little question about Harold Geneen's boss-role at ITT. Similarly, there is very little doubt as to who holds the top spot at any of our newer conglomerates. Yet there is periodic lip-service to the concept of autonomy, presumed to be integral in so many conglomerates. For example, when R. R. Wright was named director of operations of G. W. Murphy Industries in February 1968, this was hailed by company spokesmen "as evidence refuting one criticism that had dogged the blunt, colorful Mr. Murphy since he took control. This was the contention that he insisted on running a one-man show, keeping tight control over even relatively minor administrative decisions." [3] Six months later Mr. Wright resigned in a disagreement with Mr. Murphy, the conglomerate's initiator, chairman, president, chief executive officer, and largest stockholder. The relationship "foundered on the issue of which man was to be primarily responsible for day-to-day administrative decisions. After citing the policy differences, Mr. Wright added: 'George has to learn to delegate authority and responsibility.' " [4]

[1] *Business Week*, 28 (March 8, 1969).
[2] *Ibid.*
[3] *The Wall Street Journal* (August 23, 1968).
[4] *Ibid.*

There have been equally heavy crackdowns in other "autonomy-prone" conglomerates when key executives attempted to assert themselves. Harry Figgie's instantaneous and drastic housecleaning of "Automatic" Sprinkler's divisional presidents has been described in detail. The list of authoritarian edicts by ensconced conglomerate heads continues to grow. At Bemis Company, the bagmaker turned conglomerate, F. Gregg Bemis, Jr., a supposed eventual shoo-in as top man, left the company over a policy disagreement. Bemis, Jr., "was a staunch defender of the decentralized 'let the guy run the ball' school of management." [5] He felt that his uncle, who was company president, subscribed to this concept in theory but that in practice he did not hesitate to intrude on his executives' supposed autonomy. "They can talk about synergism, but I disagree. I think they are using synergism as a hook to put a lot of these operations under tighter control—control they don't need. If people want to cooperate, they will. If they don't want to they won't—despite the structure you superimpose on them." [6] Leaving the big burlap bag maker (plus other products) his family had founded, F. Gregg Bemis, Jr., facetiously stated, " 'I was fired' thus becoming the first member of the Bemis family to get the sack." [7]

While there seems to be ample evidence that virtually all conglomerators keep a very tight hold on the corporate reins, most top-level conglomerate spokesmen seemingly subscribe to almost an extreme in decentralization and divisional autonomy. In addition to the cases cited in preceding chapters, Paul L. Davies, the guiding force in FMC Corporation (one of the earliest conglomerates), stated, "Our division heads are practically heads of their own business." [8] At LTV headquarters there are only 180 staff members including just 18 corporate officers who oversee a conglomerate generating nearly $3.5 billion in sales. This would imply considerable division autonomy.

Textron, in a double-page advertisement in *The Wall Street Journal*, focused on the ideal of the new corporate structure. "Total conformity is out. Individuality is in." [9] The advertisement stressed that "the old authoritarian kind of company, where everyone looks the same and thinks the same and somebody up there makes all the decisions, is getting to be a thing of the past." [10] At Textron each of the 30-plus Divisions is supposed to function as an individualist, doing what each is best qualified

[5] *Business Week*, 114 (September 7, 1968).
[6] *Ibid.*
[7] *Ibid.*
[8] *Time*, 82 (September 21, 1962).
[9] *The Wall Street Journal*, 20–21 (April 7, 1970).
[10] *Ibid.*

to do. But, and this presumably is the essence of the new way, the parent ties it all together. Textron provides its many components with the advantages of centralized corporate planning, large-scale financing, and most other benefits of large-scale enterprise. At the same time local autonomy is emphasized. In this instance, the company signed the advertisement: Textron. The Individualists.

Signal Companies' president and chief executive officer, Forrest N. Shumway, has succinctly stated:

The philosophy we adopted was to get into some good areas and leave them alone, and I think that's a pretty damned good philosophy. . . . I think there are very few companies that operate the way we do, with the degree of freedom in day-to-day operations that we allow our acquisitions. Most conglomerates that I'm familiar with have an over-all group running the whole show. We take the opposite approach. Mack and Garrett, for example, have their own board of directors, even with some outsiders.[11]

As a means for effective control, Signal's board includes representation from its more important subsidiaries (Mack, Garrett, Signal Oil, Signal Investments, Signal Properties). In addition, the seven-man executive committee which meets weekly consists exclusively of major division representatives. The objective of the company is to get a maximum interchange of ideas, yet to keep the headquarter's staff small (only 31 persons including secretaries) and to minimize centralization.

Every Wednesday afternoon at 4:30, for example, the company's 22 operating vice presidents sit down with the Signal board of directors, in what is basically a 'chew-the-fat' session. Later the same group adjourns to Signal's plush executive lounge, where they mix with as many as fifty department heads. . . . The idea is to get away from the phones and communicate directly with each other in a relaxed atmosphere.[12]

COMMUNICATIONS: THE VITAL LINK

Maintaining effective communications is probably the single biggest obstacle to large-scale conglomeration and to the corporate confederate states' concept. This certainly is not a problem peculiar to late twentieth century business organization. The fall of every empire, in antiquity and in the recent yesterday, was preceded by communication's chaos. Hammurabi, founder of a powerful eighteenth century B.C. Babylonian empire and author of the oldest code for the management of nations, is

---

[11] *Dun's Review*, "Signal: The Careful Conglomerate," 38–42 (March, 1969).
[12] *Ibid.*, p. 42.

also credited with building the biblical tower of Babel. Here, Noah's descendants who spoke the same language, because of their perverse ambition to build a tower into the heavens, suddenly found themselves in a linguistics jungle. Soon thereafter Babylon began to crumble.

For a short time Alexander the Great, with his military genius and his invincible phalanxes, ruled the known world. After his death at the age of 33, his generals, troops, Greek citizens, and assorted vassals ceased communicating, and Greece went into oblivion. Hannibal with his pachydermic war machines humiliated Rome, the mightiest empire of all time, but was himself decisively defeated due to Carthage's jammed lines of communications. The epic list includes nearly every conqueror: Attila the Scourge of God was probably less persuaded to lay off Rome by Pope Leo I's eloquence than by the Hun horde's realization that their lines of communication and supply were much overextended. Napoleon's historic Russian retreat and rout, Hitler's blitzed blitzkrieg, and even the British lion's humiliating retreat to its island den illustrate the inevitability of imperial disintegration when communications become ineffective and control dissipates.

On the American industrial scene there are still far too few examples to prove this point. However, keep in mind that history is measured not in years or decades but in centuries, millenniums, and eons. What appears, in the flashing brilliance of the present to be so significant and successful too often, with the passage of time, turns out to be inconsequential. The modern American corporation still has quite a few years to go before it reaches its first century birthday. Yet even now a number of well-known corporate names have faded from the scene. Certainly not all these corporate deaths or demotions can be attributed solely to insufficient or ineffective communication's channels. But, as a challenge to the informed reader, what would you rank higher as a corporate desiccator?

The need for fast and effective communications is recognized by most modern corporations. The conglomerates, however, have a special problem since, as previously stated, they stress decision making at the local level. Consider the magnitude of the communications dilemma at a conglomerate such as Litton Industries which makes 10,000 products through 120 operating divisions, divided into nine groups and 225 profit centers. It is difficult enough in a hierarchical-type organization or even in a planned economy with its totalitarian setup to move messages expeditiously and with minimal garbling and leakage. But in a confederation such as Litton Industries it would seem to be even more of an impossible chore. Yet, in a confederacy, the partners need even better and faster interchange of information and ideas. Lacking such, the confederates will inevitably lose their zeal, go their separate ways, and the confederacy becomes just a token union inviting takeover.

Most corporate confederates recognize the vital need for effective communication. In a recent *Business Week* article,[13] Litton's new management information system (MIS) was enthusiastically described as a communication's expediter which cut the conventional 45-day interval between performance and performance evaluation to a new low of only 8 days. This significant cut in reporting time was made possible by feeding monthly data from each of the 225 profit centers via Teletype to the headquarter's computer. Almost immediate analysis follows the data feeding. The 20 best performers are singled out for emulation and the 20 worst performers are scrutinized to find out what caused the lags.

Although this MIS approach at Litton Industries is not entirely new, it does offer some hope that the compounded communications problems of the corporate confederates might get a measure of relief. If this is the case, then perhaps the conglomerates because of their loosely knit structures are not necessarily doomed to early extinction in a communications chaos.

CORPORATE PARTNERSHIP

To date most conglomerate firms subscribing to the concept of maximum autonomy for the major subsidiaries rely on the profit-center notion for ultimate performance evaluation. (As stated, Litton Industries has 225 such profit centers.) As long as the predetermined rate of return is met or exceeded, all is well and headquarters tends not to meddle in profit center affairs. However, inability to meet the prescribed norms invariably precipitates a corporate crackdown on the laggard. This leads to the fairly obvious inference that the conglomerates' subsidiaries must have competent and dedicated managers. What constitutes managerial and executive competency in the dynamic conglomerate is almost certainly very different from the managerial and executive abilities adequate in smaller scale, limited-product-line, regionally-oriented firms. People-resistance to corporate integration can be disastrous to the company. In some instances, the very threat of noncooperation by key personnel has been sufficient to end merger maneuvers. On three separate occasions Arthur G. McKee and Company, a $150 million sales volume Cleveland engineering and construction company, has repulsed acquisitive suitors. McKee president, Merrill Cox, has emphasized the point

---

[13] *Business Week,* "Litton's Electronic Information Machine," 158–162 (March 28, 1970).

that the company's main asset is its pool of technical talent. If these high caliber technicians were to be acquired by an unwanted suitor, they would quit and leave a corporate shell. This threat, to be stuck with a backlog of contracts but with no staff, has served to keep the firm free. Early in January 1969 Charles Bluhdorn, chairman of Gulf and Western, capitulated in his bid by selling his 193,000-share holdings back to McKee.

What seems to be absolutely essential for conglomerate success is an enthusiastic pooling of the many subsidiaries' resources: financial, production, marketing, and managerial. Integrating financial and physical units presents one set of problems, but melding managers into a more effective unit can be an impossible chore. This leads to the inference that in the manpower sphere conglomeration should be replaced with confederation. (A confederate is a person or entity in league with others for mutual support or joint action.) Confederates are allies, equals seeking a common goal. In dramatic contrast, acquisition implies a superior-inferior relationship where even managers and executives acquired in the merger are viewed as chattel, lacking freedom and dignity.

In a half-page *The Wall Street Journal* advertisement, Alco Standard, a Valley Forge, Pennsylvania, based firm proudly proclaims, "Alco Standard has 135 men who call each other 'partner.' Once these men owned and managed their own successful companies. But they were frustrated by increasing complex administrative details and the difficulty in obtaining investment capital. So they merged their companies into Alco Standard's 'Corporate Partnership' to gain the financial leverage of a $30.5 million corporation." [14]

The advertisement goes further to emphasize that the 135 partners have relinquished only the secondary administrative and technical activities and thus are free to concentrate on what they do best—producing and selling their goods and services at a profit. Also, each partner is highly motivated through large holdings in Alco stock.

According to the company, Alco's partners or confederates have done a splendid job with a 33% compounded annual growth rate in earnings per share for the past five years. Earnings per share have gone from 38 cents to $1.55 during the same period.

U. S. Industries Inc. is another excellent partnership-confederation example. Started in 1899 by "Diamond Jim" Brady as a manufacturer of freight cars, the firm was propelled into diversification after 65 years of cyclical existence by I. John Billera, who became president in 1965. In a five-year span the company doubled its sales to more than a $1.1 billion

[14] *The Wall Street Journal* (March 11, 1970).

volume. Much of this was accomplished by the merging of 110 medium-sized companies into USI. Confederation presumably is the tie that binds, since virtually all the 110 merged components continue to be run by the men who built and previously controlled these firms. One of the conditions for merging into USI was that the old management stay on for at least five years. Another condition was that only part of the gener-ous purchase price be paid at merging; the rest was to be paid in five years and only if the merged unit continues to grow by 15 per cent an-nually and returns a gross profit of 20 per cent on assets.

As a consequence the managers of these merged companies own more than 40 per cent of USI outstanding stock. Another consequence is the feeling of partnership or confederation. USI endeavors to let each com-ponent run itself, just as it did before merger. However, the performance of every president is matched against that of his peers. The presidents, divided into related groups, meet quarterly for mutual criticism. USI headquarters, staffed by fewer than 100 persons, including secretaries, exerts a scarcely felt control over the 110 confederates.

Although USI, Alco Standard, Textron, Signal Companies, and sev-eral score of the more progressive conglomerates presumably stress the partnership and confederation concepts, it should be kept in mind that there are significant semantic nuances associated with these supposedly advanced management practices. The test of time, and particularly the acid test of adversity, must be applied before these examples of confed-eration can be accepted as working models.

CONSOLIDATION OR CONFEDERATION

Most recent conglomerates, despite public pronouncements to the contrary, are not confederations; they are consolidations resulting in the complete absorption of the acquired firm. Even when the identity of the acquired firm is maintained, or where two peers presumably merge, in-herent hierarchical tendencies too frequently lead to domination by one force. Organization control in such cases is singular and authoritarian. It is virtually identical with the "no-questions-asked" type of control exer-cised by most of yesterday's rugged entrepreneurs.

If conglomeration is to continue as a viable force, it seems imperative that it takes the confederation rather than the consolidation route (Fig-ure 21-2). The "high road" of confederation means a high degree of local autonomy, individual responsibility, individual initiative, individualized rewards and penalties, group consensus, and collegiality. By contrast the "low road" of consolidation relegates many of the divisional heads to the level of high-paid "hired-hands."

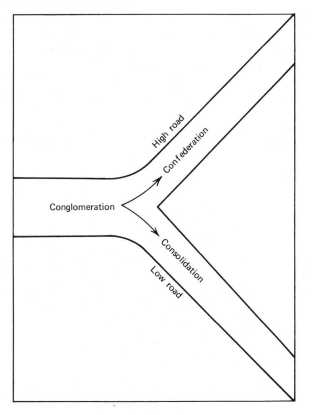

Figure 21-2

But even if we accept the superiority of confederation, such a union of peers does not come about either from dreams or by Draconic edicts. A willing and preferably an enthusiastic participation in confederation is essential for success. The failure of lofty Utopian visions, even such as the League of Nations and the United Nations, is proof of what happens when confederation lacks conviction. How can we motivate all components of the confederacy to work with high and equal zeal? How can we prevent the many divisions, subsidiaries, and product groups merged in conglomerate fashion from drifting into narrow provincialism or, even worse, into seditions or schismatic fragmentation? The vital force in historically successful confederation has always been faith in the common purposes. Whenever such faith flickered and faded, that confederation fell apart.

Our classic confederation, The Confederate States of America, fought a desperate losing battle against insurmountable odds. Despite the massive might of the Northern forces, the outmanned and outgunned confederates manifested a fighting zeal and courage unmatched in history. However, when the Confederacy's fighting manpower was decimated and its economic resources were destroyed, when its women, children, old folks, and Rhett Butlers became hungry and restless, then its will to confederate and to fight evaporated.

The parallel between the Confederate States of America and the Conglomerated Corporate Confederates might be worth further comparison. Both hit the scene with tremendous zeal and initial success. Both engendered super loyalty in their partisans. Both were serious threats to the existing establishments. The parallelisms could be extended. As of the last· opportunity (August 1970) to update this text, a large number of our conglomerates were experiencing battle fatigue and seemed to be headed for the unconditional surrender of an Appomattox.

As was philosophically pointed out in the very first few pages of this study, everybody loves a winner and most conglomerates, as of the first half of 1970, appeared to be sure losers. On the average, the bigger conglomerates had shrunk to one-fourth their 1969 heyday size. Defection, desertion, and outright hostility toward conglomerates and their architects were the order of the day. Yet it is precisely at such a time of seeming defeat and imminent disaster that common sense should tell us that we probably are overreacting. If the merger and conglomeration phenomenon is strictly a fast-buck gimmick, then may it speed into oblivion. However, if it is something bigger and more significant, if it is a real attempt at corporate confederation, then it has new and vital organizational, managerial, social and productivity implications and we must not abandon the ideal in panic.

What then can be done to revive this faltering but necessary faith in conglomerates as corporate confederates? In the past confederations have been successful when they

(1) had a common bond;
(2) imbued a religious zeal in the confederates;
(3) accepted each confederate as an equal;
(4) encouraged free discussion but also set reasonable time limits for debate.
(5) gave each confederate a proportionate if not equal voice in decision making;
(6) fairly judged each member's contribution;
(7) rewarded each member according to his contribution;
(8) meted out swift and severe sanctions upon recalcitrants;

(9) periodically convened the confederates to reappraise goals and to set new courses of action;

(10) continued to believe that confederation, even with its many constraints, was better than fragmentation.

If conglomerators are sincere in their preachments of local autonomy, partnership, individualism, and divisional quasi-sovereignty; if they subscribe to these and all other postulates of corporate confederation, then the challenge is simple—Show me! If the architects of the neo- and supercorporation have collegiality as the big objective, now is the time to implement their ideals. If, however, conglomeration is just a sleezy pseudo-legal and sub-ethical ruse to bilk the public, then these are simply second generation "raiders," descendants of the late nineteenth century robber barons and should be treated as such.

CONCLUSION

Our generation has been privileged to witness a phenomenon which could be a renaissance of business enterprise. "Just as the publicly-owned corporation superceded the privately owned corporation which in turn replaced the joint ventures which took over from partnerships and from individual enterprise, so too the multi-industry corporation, called a conglomerate or by any other name, presumably is here to stay." [15] You and I have seen the birth of the megocorporation. We have alternatingly viewed with awe and suspicion the genius and daring of several hundred most imaginative, competent, and courageous entrepreneurs who seem to have revitalized our enterprise system. We must now develop a new breed of managers, the macromanagers, who have the competency and the zeal to optimize and not simply to "satisfice" the new superorganizations' potential.

[15] Stanley Vance, "The Management of Multi-Industry Corporations," *Academy of Management Proceedings*, 42 (August 1969).

SUBJECT INDEX

INDEX OF PEOPLE

INDEX OF COMPANIES AND UNIONS

277

278